A New Introduction to Theology

A New Introduction to Theology

Embodiment, Experience

and Encounter

**Richard Bourne and
Imogen Adkins**

t&tclark

LONDON • NEW YORK • OXFORD • NEW DELHI • SYDNEY

T&T CLARK
Bloomsbury Publishing Plc
50 Bedford Square, London, WC1B 3DP, UK
1385 Broadway, New York, NY 10018, USA

BLOOMSBURY, T&T CLARK and the T&T Clark logo
are trademarks of Bloomsbury Publishing Plc

First published in Great Britain 2020

Cover design: Nick Evans.
Cover image: *The Prodigal Son*, oil on canvas, Fundación Pedro Cano (Spain)
© José Luis Montero.

A catalogue record for this book is available from the British Library.

Library of Congress Control Number: 2020932384

ISBN: HB: 978-0-5676-6668-0
        PB: 978-0-5676-6667-3
        ePDF: 978-0-5676-6669-7
        eBook: 978-0-5676-6670-3

Typeset by Integra Software Services Pvt. Ltd.
Printed and bound in India

To find out more about our authors and books visit www.bloomsbury.com
and sign up for our newsletters.

RB: For Josiah and Ella, whose delight in the very best of human embodiment, experience and encounter underlies this book.
IA: For Charlie, for learning with me how to embody Christ in the world, and for making me laugh.

Contents

Acknowledgements

This book began life in conversation between two friends reflecting on our experiences as teachers, friends and church members – particularly our experiences of those polite, and sometimes less than polite, facial expressions of intellectual strain, puzzlement or worse, confusion, we had encountered as we sought to introduce others to the enterprise of making sense of Christian theology. Moments of intellectual challenge are a natural and exciting part of any learning process. But we have found that the experience for both teacher and student is made all the more interesting and enjoyable by establishing practical and reflective ways into complex topics. Our thanks, then, to all those students and friends at the University of Cambridge, the University of Cumbria, Leeds Trinity University and York St John University who in various forms and ways have encountered our approach to introducing others to the delight of Christian theology.

Our thanks, too, to Anna Turton and her colleagues at T&T Clark for their support, understanding and commitment to our project. Anna has been patient through the many and various embodied contingencies of our lives that have extended the preparation of the book.

We are grateful for permission to reproduce here extracts from:

Augustine: *The City of God against the Pagans*, edited by R. W. Dyson. Cambridge: Cambridge University Press, 1998.
The Independent, 'Payday Lenders? The Church Should Keep to Matters Spiritual', 26 July 2013.
Williams, Rowan, 'The Body's Grace'. In *Theology and Sexuality: Classic and Contemporary Readings*, edited by Eugene F. Rogers, 309–21. Oxford: Blackwell, 2002.
Unless specified otherwise, all Scripture quotations are from New Revised Standard Version Bible, copyright © 1989 National Council of the Churches of Christ in the United States of America. Used by permission. All rights reserved worldwide.

Finally, our greatest thanks to our families – to Kristen, Josiah and Ella Bourne and to Charlie Adkins – for their patience with our distractions, delays, deviations and discussions. This book is dedicated to them.

Just as the book began in friendly conversation between us, we hope that readers will find it a stimulus for their own conversations and theological friendships.

Introduction: Theology as full-bodied thought

This book contains surprises. We don't know what they will be for you, but we are pretty sure there will be some. No one quite knows what they are getting into when they start exploring theology – that is, when they become theologians. You will be engaging some of the largest questions human beings face, as they are elaborated and pursued within Christian thought and practice. Encountering theology for the first time is exciting, but it can also be daunting. In many years of teaching we have observed that students initially struggle to connect with doctrinal discussion they perceive to be abstract or abstruse. Others find it dizzying to engage the scope and interconnection of theological topics. In order to sustain this excitement and address these difficulties we offer a new type of introduction to theology, which takes you through a range of accessible, practical, experiential and interactive encounters with the major elements of academic Christian theology.

The book's guiding motif is the claim that theology is full-bodied thought. The wordplay in the phrase 'full-bodied' shows both the richness of theology and its nature as a thoroughly embodied discourse regarding God and God's ways with the world. While there is nothing inherently wrong with intense abstract conceptual thinking about theological matters, too often the rigours of theological thinking take place at a remove from the practices of Christians and their embodiment of their faith. None of us, whether we would describe ourselves as Christians or not, engage in thought without our sensory experiences shaping the way we think. We suggest here that this is as true for intangible objects of knowledge as it is for tangible ones. I know a chair or a table through my sensory explorations of its properties – its size, shape, texture, hardness, weight and so on. But I also imagine God, love, the soul, in ways that are deeply shaped by my sensory experience. Thought is never disembodied, never apart from the ways our bodily experiences and encounters enable us to think.

The first letter of John in the New Testament begins to describe the revelation of eternal truth made known through a range of sensory experience: 'We declare to you what was from the beginning, what we have heard, what we have seen with our eyes, what we have looked at and touched with our hands, concerning the word of life' (1 Jn 1:1). To know God is to know the world aright. Indeed, for one of the most influential figures in Western Christian thought, St Augustine, coming to know God enlivens a knowledge of the world dulled by the anaesthetic of sin and self-love. He writes:

Late have I loved you,
Beauty so old and so new:
Late have I loved you.

And see, you were within
And I was within the external world
And sought you there,
And in my unlovely state
I plunged into those lovely created things
which you made
The lovely things kept me far from you
Though if they did not have their existence in you
They had no existence at all.

You called and cried out loud
And shattered my deafness
You were radiant and resplendent,
You put to flight my blindness.
You were fragrant,
And I drew in my breath and now pant after you.
I tasted you,
And I feel but hunger and thirst for you.
You touched me,
And I am set on fire to attain the peace which is yours.
(Augustine, *Confessions* X.xxvii, 2009: 38)

This book will not provide you with many answers, but it may help you to ask slightly more interesting questions. It is an introduction to theology but it isn't a conventional textbook. It doesn't provide you with a comprehensive grounding in every area of Christian doctrine; it does not survey all of the immense diversity of contemporary Christian belief; nor does it work through in any detail the history of the development and disputation of Christian thought. There are many fine theological textbooks that do such things. It is best to regard this as a companion to such literature. When you are introduced to a new friend, say at a party, you begin to get to know them not by a lengthy narration of their life story, but by shared encounters and experiences. This book offers an initial range of encounters with theological thinking – each focused around a sensory experience (sight, hearing, touch, taste and smell) and then two forms of necessary human experience (loving and resting). It draws upon a range of innovative and interdisciplinary elements of the contemporary theological scene, including theology through the arts, sexuality and the body, the nature of the church's everyday life, mystical theology and spirituality, political action and ecology. Each chapter provides a range of activities, guided discussions and reflections on key theological texts, authors and issues. The book is adaptable for individual reflection, classroom work, or flexible and distributed learning. We imagine that the majority of our readers are encountering theology for the first time and are doing so in an academic setting – perhaps a university, college or seminary. However, many of the explorations would work just as well for those who are outside a formal academic setting, but who nonetheless have a budding interest in theology.

We have found that reflecting on sensory experience works as an important conceptual 'bridge' into matters of theology. It is important not to see these reflections as a convenient set of sensory metaphors, which transport one to a cerebral plane where such sensory experience can then be discarded in favour of pure disembodied thought. Rather, in theology, as in so much else, we think through our senses. Our knowing is structured by our seeing, tasting, smelling, hearing and touching.

This would not be a theological book without some caveats being listed. First, one of the most obvious ways in which our own embodied experience shapes our understanding of theology is in the simple use of gendered pronouns for a God who has no genitals, no chromosomes, no hormones and thus no sex at all. God is neither male nor female. Words matter; for good or ill they create meaning and also constrain our thinking. And so a word about divine pronouns. We have avoided pronouns for God wherever possible, as long as doing so does not lead to convoluted prose. Where pronouns are necessary we have utilized the male pronoun not because we believe God is male, or that males enjoy a special status in God's ways with the world, but merely for some broad consonance with traditional language. We have placed pronouns in scare quotes – 'he', 'him' and 'his' – as a constant reminder of the caveated nature not just of gendered language of God but of all language used to describe God, and in recognition of the fact that many theologians, in different ways, mount a strong biblical argument for applying feminine or neutral pronouns to God. Where quotes utilize gendered pronouns for God, we have retained those used by the author.

A second caveat. Given that this book began life as a conversation, we wanted to keep a sense of our own 'voices' in the writing process. We have therefore written chapters separately and edited each one together. We hope that the inevitable stylistic differences will not be disruptive to the reader, but will instead be seen to embody the very theological plurality that we have endeavoured to present.

Finally, depending on your reason for using this book you may be a Christian, but equally you may not. In church or seminary settings it is likely that more readers will be Christian – but perhaps not all. In university settings the majority of readers may not be Christian. We do not presume a Christian readership but do believe that there is both skill and virtue in the rigorous, empathetic understanding of the depths of a theological position. Our hope is that this textbook provides some initial resources for you to develop such a sense, no matter your personal faith commitments or absence thereof. Irrespective of how you identify your religious and spiritual views, there will undoubtedly be some theological claims explored in this book that you will not agree with. There is still value to be gained from understanding those views, where they come from, and how they shape belief and behaviour. Throughout this book we have outlined diverse and sometimes conflicting views. We have not highlighted our own particular views or commitments, which differ between the two authors let alone among our varied readers. But nor do we pretend to be neutral in our own views. There is no neutral stance from which to undertake theological work – that is part of what makes it so interesting, so involving and so human.

1

Seeing: Reading and being read by the Bible

Seeing is believing

It all begins with sight. 'God said, "Let there be light"; and there was light' (Gen. 1:3). The same is true in our daily experience. Every morning our days begin, after some semi-conscious fumblings with an insistent alarm clock, when we open our eyes. From that moment our eyes provide our minds with a constant array of stimuli – many mundane, some delightful, some upsetting. Perhaps more than any other time in history, in twenty-first century Western societies images play before our eyes in such giddy saturation that we may sometimes lack the capacity to truly focus. We live in what the French philosopher Guy Debord famously named 'the society of spectacle' (Debord, 1994). Perhaps no wonder then that to find sabbatical rest from this incessant parade, to truly focus, many close their eyes in prayer or meditation. In seeing the light and in the enveloping darkness, vision defines our experience of God, the world and ourselves.

Sight is perhaps the defining sense of the modern world. For many of us knowledge itself is intimately connected with sight. Colloquially, 'I see' means not just that I have the capacity to process optical stimuli, but that I understand. Sight is perhaps the controlling sensory metaphor of much theology – flowing right back to the shared founding narratives of the variety of Jewish and Christian traditions, the invisible God upon whom no one can look (Exod. 33), who creates humanity in 'his' image (Gen. 1–3), who becomes visible in Jesus (Heb. 11), but paradoxically remains, for now, only visible in a darkened blur (1 Cor. 13:12). This chapter will explore much of that potent metaphorical use of sight, but seeing is more than a guiding metaphor. It is central to the way in which theology is constructed, and the way in which it conceives its limits. In this chapter we will attend to actual practices of seeing – in particular watching films, reading fiction and encountering the Bible – to show something of the sensory richness of theological method.

John Ruskin, writing in his reflections on painting, reflects on 'the truth of space' as 'dependent on the power of the eye'. 'The greatest thing a human soul ever does in this world is to *see* something, and tell what it saw in a plain way. Hundreds of people can talk for one who can think, but thousands can think for one who can see. To see clearly is poetry, prophecy, and religion – all in one' (Cook and Wedderburn, 1903–12, 16.333). To genuinely 'see', with clarity of vision and focus, is not just to cut to the heart of an area of knowledge, but to attain the capacity to move from theory to action. As Zoe Bennett puts it, commenting on Ruskin's account of seeing clearly, 'upon good seeing depends our capacity to make judgments, to communicate anything worthwhile or to have any material fit for reflection. Seeing does not only furnish us with imagination; good seeing makes possible evaluation and discernment. In other words, it makes possible not only knowledge, but also wisdom' (Bennett, 2013: 81). Theological truth, as both wisdom and knowledge, is well understood as a practice of seeing.

The Christian faith speaks of a God who acts. This God creates, sustains, guides, delivers, rescues, punishes, lapses into silence, is moved by compassion, becomes incarnate, restores creation, redeems 'his' beloved creatures and rests. In each of these events God makes 'himself' known. This chapter is about the method of theology – in particular about its sources, and about how use of these sources brings theological matters into focus. It is, then, about how we see:

- The Bible
- God
- Truth
- Jesus
- Our actions
- Ourselves

Reflection – The experience of seeing

Despite the constant flow of images we are presented with every day, some experiences of seeing have a special quality. Think to yourself of your most memorable experience of seeing. It could be something peculiarly intense: a spectacular landscape, a traumatic discovery, a striking moment of beauty or ugliness, the wide-eyed glance of infatuation or the first sight of a newborn child. Memory of the actual details is likely to be imprecise, as we don't always remember visual stimuli well.

- What kinds of experiences of seeing spring to mind?
- We sometimes describe a striking view as 'awe-inspiring'. Medieval theologians often spoke of God as not just beautiful, but as beauty itself. Do you think memorable beautiful views tell us anything about God?

- Some people are more comfortable with this kind of approach to knowledge of God than others. For some it begins with the most profound of religious experiences, open to any and all. At the other extreme, some worry this general approach produces platitudes of twee piety; more befitting a poster or meme on social media than the commencement of a rigorous theological journey. Where would you place yourself on that continuum, and why?

The grandeur of a great vista can evoke in us an echo of God's own declaration at the culmination of the initial creation of the Universe; 'And God saw everything that he had made, and indeed, it was very good' (Gen. 1:31). All of creation is said to display the glory and beauty of God (Ps. 19:1), such that all can know of the power of God (Rom. 1:20). This is still somewhat incomplete. That more anonymous knowledge of God might later be seen in the light of more expansive and detailed theological understanding (Acts 17:22ff). Such knowledge of God is sometimes known as natural theology or general revelation. The term 'general' here refers to knowledge of God available to any person through observation and experience of the created order itself, through some kind of universally available human experience. It is distinguished therefore from the specific but all-encompassing claims about God, humanity and the cosmos made on the basis of God's self-revealing action in history, especially in Jesus Christ. Theologians differ considerably on the extent to which this general knowledge of God is possible. They have diverse views on the extent to which the obscuring visual interference of sin compromises such knowledge. For Catholic, Orthodox and many Protestant views, the partial knowledge of God, specifically 'his' existence and attributes (all-powerful, all-loving, all-knowing, immortal, etc.), may be discerned through the divine gift of human reason. For Thomas Aquinas (1225–74), the great medieval theologian and prime influence on Catholic thought, such knowledge is always in need of perfecting and completing through the special revelation of God in Christ. A number of contemporary theologians find in the notion of general revelation a way of affirming the partial truth accessible to those of other faiths, some while seeking to maintain the fuller truth of their own tradition. This theology becomes imbalanced if general revelation becomes a source of knowledge of God that stands alone or even competes with the self-disclosure of God in Christ, as attested in Scripture (i.e. special, as distinct from general, revelation). General revelation is open to all, but cannot thereby be merely a basis for a generic theism. Christianity is resolute in claiming that God created through Christ (Jn 1:3, 1 Cor. 8:6, Col. 1:16, Heb. 1:2) such that there can be no absolute separation of creation from Christ, or general from special revelation.

Such a caution is particularly strong in Reformed and other forms of Protestant theology, where the sovereign decision of God to reveal 'himself' in Christ is the only means of bringing to unclouded focus the wider self-revelation of God found in sin-obscured general experience. Where more optimistic accounts of general revelation may view special revelation as a completion of the knowledge derived therein, for John Calvin (1509–64) the foggy outlines of knowledge of God through general revelation all too often lead to misrecognition, confusion and idolatrous error. Special revelation does not merely complete but corrects this knowledge, it is 'another and better help'.

> For as the aged, or those whose sight is defective, when any books however fair, is set before them, though they perceive that there is something written are scarcely able to make out two consecutive words, but, when aided by glasses, begin to read distinctly, so Scripture, gathering together the impressions of Deity, which, till then, lay confused in our minds, dissipates the darkness, and shows us the true God clearly. (Calvin, Institutes 1.6.1)

For the great twentieth-century Reformed theologian Karl Barth (1886–1968), the divine initiative in revelation admits no possibility of a natural theology separate from this divine decision to make God-self known. There is not an innate human capacity to know God by our own wit, or subject to our own agenda. God's choice to reveal 'himself' is the only foundation for knowledge of 'him'. Barth memorably asserts that the form of this may be anything God so chooses – 'God may speak to us through Russian Communism, a flute concerto, a blossoming shrub, or a dead dog' (Barth, 2004, CD I/1:55). Critics have found an excessively passive account of human ability and action in this emphasis on the exclusive initiative of the self-revealing God. However, Barth does give some due to the human role, which is to actively receive and reflect this divine reality, enabled and empowered by the Holy Spirit (Barth, 2004, CD I/2: 203–79).

Theological textbooks often identify four sources available to the theological task:

- Scripture: the Bible is understood in some way as being, containing or becoming the word of God.
- Reason: which merely refers to rigorous thought. This is not necessarily the individualistic 'autonomous reason' which some critics in the Modern period have polemically contrasted with 'irrational' faith. Rather, with Aquinas, reason is a God-given gift bestowed upon humanity, which furnishes some initial insights to be shaped, developed, corrected and completed through special revelation.
- Tradition: a shorthand term for the complex, dynamic and occasionally meandering conversation through which the church has sought to elaborate, understand and practise the truth about God, humanity and the cosmos. That the previous sentence contains clusters of three adjectives, three verbs and three nouns may indicate something of the fullness and breadth of the notion of tradition.

- Experience: understood either in a restricted sense of the intensity of particular religious/mystical experience or increasingly is broadened to encompass a wider variety of experiences of the human condition itself – from sexual desire to artistic or cultural production.

These four are not to be understood as separate or even competing resources or forms of theologizing. We can never read the Bible in a way that suspends our own reason, forgets the backstory of tradition or separates our thinking from our experience. No matter whether this is the first time you've read a book on theology, or you are an experienced doctrinal thinker, the ordinary lived and embodied experience of encountering theology occurs in the complex and even messy combination of these four sources. Thus the remainder of this chapter continues our exploration of the four sources of theology, guided through the formative and foundational experience of reading Scripture. A separation of these four sources can lead to a competitive privileging of one over another. When held fully distinct, they may also become an idol in themselves, rather than pointers to God. The use of reason may become an arid and restrictive rationalism in which the mystery and wonder of God are denied or concealed; dynamic tradition becomes either a petrified traditionalism working against the ongoing work of the Spirit or a petulant anti-traditionalism in love with novelty more than truth; the vibrancy of experience drifts to becoming an uncritical baptism of our current human sinfulness as if it were already sanctified and redeemed; and even the spectacles of Scripture may fail in their function – if the Bible itself takes on semi-divine status, Scripture shifts from being something looked through to something idolatrously looked at.

Key points

- Visual metaphors convey the limits and forms of theological knowledge.
- The four sources of theology are not distinct and competitive, but mutually implicated.

Reason in its most exalted mood: The Bible and the imagination

'Reason' has become a rather politicized and polemical term. In popular presentations of the relationship between 'Science' and 'Religion', reason is equated purely with experimental method, of testing hypotheses through repeatable empirical testing.

Reason is contrasted with 'faith', which is then taken to be belief that flies in the face of evidence, as essentially irrational. This view is a rather simplistic outflow of Enlightenment rationalism – the view that truth is accessible to human reason unaided and unencumbered by authoritative institutions, traditions, superstitions or conventions. The picture of the reasoning person is of a solitary individual sitting down and thinking very hard, or conducting a range of experiments, and thereby seeing truth. Certainly both of these are good methods for accessing certain types of truth. When evaluating an abstract philosophical argument, giving myself the space to sit and ruminate is both a necessity and a delight. However, when I take medication I want to know not that the scientists who developed it sat stroking their chins and deliberating, but that the medication has been subject to rigorous tests for its effectiveness and its safety. However, these are only some of the many kinds of truth, just part of the breadth of knowledge we need to navigate our way through the world. Laboratory experimentation can say very little about the truth of claims about goodness, value or beauty.

We have defined reason above in a much broader way – as the practice of rigorous thought. The picture of the exercise of reason that we suggest is diverse, communal and imaginative. Its image may better be the clamorous, free-flowing but unfalteringly honest conversation of the (ideal) family dinner table. It is diverse because it needs to be deployed to a variety of types of truth claim – claims of science, history, morality, creativity, of who God is and who we are as a result. Those who engage in theological reasoning are in some way shaped and enabled by participation in the long and often-heated history of Christians living and worshipping together, as a community, and in so doing making sense of themselves and their God. In that sense reasoning is tradition-ed, inevitably and inescapably shaped by previous generations of argumentative Christian discussion.

Imagination is central to what it is to think – without it creative connections cannot be drawn, new ideas cannot be thought, older views cannot be brought to life. Without your imagination, these words on this page would not do their work – they would remain mere ink marks without meaning or significance. All of our senses are more or less constantly bombarded with an extraordinary flow of stimuli – the brain may collect these images, connect them, developing ever more complex associations between them. This fundamental pattern of sense and cognition is often referred to as an 'imaginary'. Psychoanalysts like Jacques Lacan and Cornelius Castoriadis show that this unconscious imaginary is the very foundation of all thought. Importantly for the claims of this book, this means that our sensing, our desires and emotions are not as radically distinguishable from 'reason' as many might first suppose. Our capacity to imagine is what allows us to generate an understanding not only of the physical world around us, but of society and culture – which exist in our affective connections with others, in what we think life is for, what gives it meaning. Imagination is how we make sense of ourselves – it works through the stories we tell about ourselves and our world.

Reasoning is a highly visual process – not least because writing has proven necessary to capture the fleeting effervescence of oral accounts. Reading and writing are central practices of thought in most cultures. The American author Joan Didion captures this when she writes 'I write entirely to find out what I'm thinking, what I'm looking at, what I see and what it means. What I want and what I fear' (Didion, 1976). The very earliest writings we have, going back to Sumerian pictographs pressed into clay, served to capture the important details needed for life, probably financial, military and trade accounts; but these were quickly followed by narratives. Creation myths, floods, battles, quests and romances are not mere relics of ancient entertainment, they capture and create a culture's sense of identity – who they are, and why they do what they do.

The Christian narrative, by which the early Christians began to make sense of what they held to be world-changing events, flowed through both oral tradition and writing. It is often said that the oral culture dominated, with the need to write only coming to the fore as historical memory faded. There is some truth in this when it comes to the writing of the gospels, beginning somewhere around the year 70 CE. However, the production, circulation and communal reading of texts, perhaps most famously letters, gave even the earliest missionary expansion of Christianity a distinctly bookish and literary character (Hurtado, 2016). That bookishness continues to be the modus operandi of theological reason. Christian theologians scatter parenthetical bits of code throughout all their writing – some more fully than others, some with more persuasive power than others, but all will back up their claims with quotes and allusions to the Bible. The second sentence of this chapter did so, ending with '(Gen. 1:3)'. It is not that Scripture and reason are two different sources – one we read, the other we think for ourselves; rather we think through reading and writing. The Bible is the indispensable means by which theologians reason.

This emphasis fits well with the view of the Romantic movement, which sought to reconnect creativity and reason, after a rather dry and formal rationalism had forcibly separated the two. Famously, William Wordsworth shows the connection between imagination and reason not as two different faculties, but the former as the pinnacle of the latter. Importantly though, this is a reason not devoid of desire or love. It is possible only in theological frame, in which our own desires and loves are completed in the awed and elevated love of praise of God.

> This spiritual Love acts not nor can exist
> Without Imagination, which, in truth,
> Is but another name for absolute power
> And clearest insight, amplitude of mind,
> And Reason in her most exalted mood.

(Wordsworth, 1850, Book 14, 361)

In a similar vein, Samuel Taylor Coleridge reflects on the power of symbols, particularly in biblical literature, for the exercise of rigorous thought. Our reason, our understanding and our sense images are unified by the imagination to produce a symbol, or in our terms a narrative or story. Focusing on the Bible, Coleridge describes these symbols as 'the living educts of imagination' which are characterized, in striking continuation of visual metaphors, by 'a translucence of the Eternal through and in the Temporal' (Coleridge, 1832: 38–40).

Key points

- For Christian theology reason and faith are not incompatible.
- Theological thinking requires imagination.

Reason and the experience of seeing

There is a certain elitism to the way Coleridge viewed this translucence – a rather patrician division of high culture from low culture. But need that be so? To carry forward the image of translucence further we suggest that it should include the more everyday experience of reading a novel or watching a film (where the literal translucence of 70mm film run through a projector was the technological medium of the image). That said, these visual practices may often be rather passive and insignificant. Slumping down in front of the television to watch, almost mindlessly, some formulaic reality television show or procedural drama is hardly likely to leave much of a lasting impression, let alone provide a formative experience. Similarly, much use of the Bible, both in everyday life and in theological reflection, seems to merely reach for a small collection of well-worn phrases and tropes. However, at their best there is nothing passive or inconsequential about our practices of seeing. Viewing film or reading a novel is active when it engages the imagination, when it shapes the way we see ourselves and our world, and when it moves us to action (whether mental or physical).

But, you may ask, why focus on fiction if theology is a quest for truth? We should question the assumption of that contrast, that fiction is 'untrue', because it doesn't clearly denote actual events, people or places. What film and literature bring alive for us is the deep and complex texture of our lives and our place in the world. Stories place us. In seeing other characters from outside, and from the insight of other character's internal monologues, we understand others better. Just as in a religious epiphany, there can be a dramatic moment of self-realization, reading a novel or watching a film can provide a moment of clear-sighted realization. Indeed some are frank in identifying the power of film as a means of deepening devotional life and spirituality. Film, says Gareth Higgins, 'should be treated with the same respect as church or poison, for it can change your life' (Higgins, 2004: xix). He focuses on the capacity of the audience to identify with anti-heroic figures, in a kind of religious catharsis. Recounting a scene in the 1999 film, based on Chuck Palaniak's novel *Fight Club* in which the main character, Tyler Durden, describes himself as one of the 'middle children of history'. Durden explains that the middle children did not experience the Great War or the Great Depression; instead, their great war is a spiritual one, and their lives *are* their great depression. Higgins response is to identify imaginatively with that character – 'when I watch it, I want to shout "Amen!" That's us, people' (Higgins, 2004: 79, as discussed in Johnston, 2006: 71).

Reflection – Thinking about seeing

Many films and novels deal explicitly with theological themes. Some with profound power and insight, others, regrettably, produce little more than a clumsy pastiche, reinforcing unquestioned assumptions rather than exposing them to the light of reflection. Upon its release Mel Gibson's *The Passion of the Christ* (2004) divided opinion in this way. On the one hand it was greeted by many Christians as a profound meditation on the true extent of the suffering endured on the cross. It was therefore used as both a proselytising tool and a kind of modern-day means by which to fulfil the injunction of spiritual writers across the history of Christianity, to contemplate paschal suffering as a means to attain spiritual perfection. For others though, the film does not so much elevate us to empathize with Christ, as it reduces Christ down to the level of a simple horror film. There are two key theological objections to the film: first that it undoes divine transcendence in seeking to manipulate the audience's perceptions and responses, which is both bad theology and bad film-making; second that the theology informing such strategies is deeply flawed – it is accused of anti-Semitism and, in its relentless and sadistic violence, of trading on an understanding of the death of Christ in which the nature of salvation is tied clearly to the level of agony endured. (For more on this issue, see the discussion of atonement in Chapter 6).

Reflect

- If you have seen the film, what kind of reaction did you have to it?
- Thinking of other novels and films, what are of some of the best and worst of your reading and viewing experiences?
- Do your judgements of 'best' and 'worst' entail any theological commitments?

There are a great many 'Jesus films', each with their own take on the Gospel narratives. Some are criticized for importing into the story anachronisms that don't fit well. It is important to note, though, that historical accuracy may not be the most important concern. Both Jeffrey Hunter (in the film *King of Kings*, 1961) and Robert Powell (in the TV series *Jesus of Nazareth*, 1977) are white with striking blue eyes, a far cry from the typical first-century Galilean features of the historical Jesus. Nonetheless, in the symbolic evocations of cinematography blue eyes bespeak 'the heavenly origins of Christ; blue being the colour of the divine, of truth, of purity' (Kozlovic, 2004). Filmmakers dealing with theological themes are never simply representing a gospel – even Pier Paolo Pasolini's *The Gospel According to St Matthew* (1964) which claims to take the Gospel itself as its script (in fact there are omissions and errors) is very clearly an interpretation of the Gospel. Indeed, as much as the script was taken from the Gospel, Pasolini had recognized that film audiences come with many preconceptions: 'I did not want to reconstruct the life of Christ as it really was … I wanted to do the story of Christ plus two thousand years of Christian translation' (Telford, 1997: 126). That process of interpretation is unavoidable. Indeed, it is precisely what theologians have been doing for centuries. The complex decisions required of writers and directors, as well as actors, are all acts of interpretation. They have to balance clarity, accuracy and fidelity to the original story (whether a gospel or a novel or a bespoke script) with the desire to make their own point, to entertain and to challenge.

In that sense, just as with the theologian's use of the Bible, the reading of a novel or the viewing of a film is a creative act that draws upon reason, tradition and experience. In theologians' uses of the Bible, interpretation is inescapable; but that does not mean that every interpretation is as good as any other. A response to the filmic presentation of Jesus as a blue-eyed Caucasian man that claimed this to be historically and physiologically accurate would be a poor account, but to recognize those blue eyes as an established symbol of divinity is not (though it has its limits). One of those interpretations is thus better than the other.

One should beware of the theologian who naively boasts, 'You may have your interpretation, but I prefer to believe what the text clearly says'. Behind this lurks the claim that this one theologian, denomination or school of thought have some privileged access to the meaning of the text that has been hidden or kept secret, waiting for their singular insight. Ironically, it does not place authority in the Bible, or in the word of God that is encountered there, but instead in that individual's powers of insight. This is not to say that the text does not speak clearly, just that it does not always do so, and when it does that clarity (real or apparent) is a function of interpretation, not an escape from it. This is no real limitation on us, for meaning does not reside behind the text, but in its reading, in our seeing and speaking it.

This is key to the complex texture of theological truth that we are exploring here. The limited sight of brute literalism is ridiculed in John's Gospel, when Nicodemus hears Jesus pronounce 'no one can see the kingdom of God unless they are born again' and objects 'How can someone be born when they are old? Surely they cannot enter a second time into their mother's womb to be born' (Jn 3:3-4). For those familiar with the theological imagery of the day, it would have been clear that the phrase 'born again' also meant, in Greek, 'born from above'. Indeed, some translations like the NRSV render it this way – which may be clearer in some respects, but makes Nicodemus's misunderstanding somewhat incongruous. Beyond its surface meaning, an imagination shaped by that tradition would see deeper layers of significance. This notion of spiritual seeing as discerning deeper levels of truth and meaning has always been key to theological sensory imagination. Here it is a powerful contrast between Jesus and those who oppose him. Thus later in the fourth Gospel Jesus heals a blind man with the stark statement 'for judgment I came into this world, that those who do not see may see, and that those who see may become blind' (Jn 9:39). In contrast with the attempt at interpretation-free understanding, true sight is found in the use of the imagination to detect the trajectory of God's active restoration project in history.

Thus the emphasis we are placing on imagination should not be read along the lines of those who argue that Christianity, or any religious claim, are merely constructs of human imagination, the projection of longings for immortality or significance. Instead, the gift of the poet, the artist, or the prophet, is to present the world to us afresh, to help us see more fully than we have before. If imagination is so central to seeing, then seeing is not passive. Reading is no distraction or escapism from life, but a mode of reflective engagement with it. As the philosopher Pierre Hadot notes regarding reading the classical philosophers, or reading the Bible for early Christians, their first readers were not engaged in abstraction, but in a kind of training in the art of living – 'spiritual exercises'.

Key points

- We make sense of our world and ourselves through imaginative seeing.
- The experience of reading a novel or seeing a film can bring us to fuller understanding.
- Interpretation is unavoidable; some interpretations are more persuasive than others.

Tradition: The messiness of seeing together

Have you ever watched a film, read a book or viewed a television programme, and been struck by the sense of knowing how it will all turn out? Sometimes that prediction is frustrating – a formulaic and unimaginative episode, just like many others you have seen. Other times, the author or director plays with our expectations, and twists the narrative to surprise us. But even then surprise requires a certain degree of familiarity with the usual pattern of narratives. When we watch a film or read a book, we encounter them through our already established interpretive and imaginative framework. We are sufficiently used to the structures of stories that in viewing and reading we will know something of where we are headed. We pick up the hints of the genre, language and characterization. We have our expectations shaped by the language and pace of a text or a film. In particular, we are keyed into the expectation of happy endings (the comedy), we savour the melancholy delights of tragedy, which provoke reflection, lament, or for some, appreciation of God's blessings. Those narrative shapes have been influenced by the kind of story told throughout the Bible. We don't just mean here that biblical themes characters and stories are familiar and have shaped Western fiction, though surely they have. Rather the moment of tragedy and the overall structure of a comedy arise in part from Christian views of historical movement and the promise of its culmination (which we shall explore further in Chapter 7 – there is a 'happy ending' though it may not be what you think).

But it is not just that our encounters with stories are shaped by Christian theology. The same is true the other way around. In theological engagement with the Bible, we are shaped both by what the text itself says, as words on a page, by our own social and historical context, and by the great weight of diverse interpretations and communal discernment of Christian history of reading. This history of reading and acting is 'tradition'. Tradition is not so much a constrained and defined framework for viewing the truths of Scripture, but more dynamically, the well-worn, heavily annotated and perhaps slightly dog-eared map by which theologians begin to navigate the consequences of a Christian commitment to the truth of Scripture. While it serves to delineate safe from unsafe territory, orthodoxy from heresy, within these at times rather loose bounds it can still allow diverse wanderings, direct routes, missteps and moments of disorientation. For Christians these all add to the adventure of living with, and as we shall see it, living within, the Scriptural narrative.

We have been making much of the commonalities between reading fiction or viewing film on the one hand, and the use of Scripture on the other. But like all metaphorical connections, this can mislead if taken to be too direct an equivalence. The sources of theology are unlike most books and films in two respects, both of which are pertinent to the complementary authority of Scripture and tradition we are now exploring.

First, unlike the vast majority of books and films, the Bible is not a straightforward single narrative. It does not have one narrator, one perspective or one audience in mind. The Bible is a collection of vastly different ancient literatures serving a wide variety of purposes and agendas. In gathering these together, and declaring the collection as a whole, to be authoritative, the church has committed itself to identifying an overarching story – reaching from creation, then fall, then through the formations, dissolutions and reformations of Israel, into the denouement of Christ, and on to the story of the church itself, culminating in visions of the restoration and rest of creation. But we may miss a great deal, and cause ourselves problems, if we try to eradicate the messiness when we seek to tell that story. The church is a community of those committed to the imaginative and rigorous enterprise of connecting the diverse literatures of Scripture in such a way that they make sense as a big story. The closest parallel to that in literature might be something like Robert Grudin's *Book: A Novel* (1992), a text made up of letters, an interview, encyclopaedia entries and other texts, as well as usual prose style of a novel. It is a murder mystery and a love story, a campus novel and satire – but for it all, remains a coherent story. Likewise in the great fiction of Dostoevsky, according to the Russian literary theorist Mikhail Bakhtin, we encounter a genuine 'plurality of independent and unnoticed voices and consciousnesses, a genuine polyphony of fully valid voices'. It is not in the voice of any one character, but in their interactions that meaning emerges (Bakhtin cited in Lamb, 2013: 129).

Activity – Same story, different perspectives

There are unavoidable differences in the claims, for example, of Samuel and Kings, on the one hand, and Chronicles on the other – they simply have different 'histories', and different agendas. Famously, Chronicles presents both David and Solomon as morally and spiritually ideal rulers, and thus excises from the story the inconvenient embarrassments and moral failings of both – such as David's adulterous machinations in pursuit of Bathsheba.

- Read and compare 1 Kings 1–2 and 1 Chronicles 28–29 on the transition of power from David to Solomon.
- Do these texts seem to say the same thing to you?
- Where they appear to disagree, what does that disagreement mean for the kind of authority the texts can be claimed to have?
- Are we supposed to choose one story over the other, or live with the differences?

Like any conversation, the dialogue of Scripture, carried on in tradition, brings together different views, different theologies and different accounts of the past, the present and the hope of the future. The complex practice of interpretation, what biblical scholars and theologians call 'hermeneutics', cannot seek to cut out that difference. Imagine how little of the cut and thrust of a debate would remain if we redacted it to show only the points of clear agreement. There are ample differences and tensions between the four canonical Gospel accounts too. Indeed, the canons of the Hebrew Bible and the New Testament were compiled deliberately to include obvious and significant diversity. Indeed, there isn't just one Christian canon – there have been and remain significant differences across the globe. Perhaps the most famous effort to harmonize the four Gospels was Tatian's *Diatessaron* written somewhere between 165 and 170. This was an attempt to bring together the stories of all Gospels into a single narrative – but it ended up with a narrative sequence that does not fit any Gospel accurately, excluding some sections of each Gospel. While the text received widespread use in some churches, it never replaced the diversity of canonical texts (indeed, it is not clear that Tatian ever intended it to). This should be a warning about forcing biblical diversity into too neat a story – one cannot respect the authority of scriptural texts by treating them all as timeless pronouncements of disembodied theological truths.

The second way in which sources of theology differ from films and novels is that the latter have an end; we can close the book, the lights come back on in the cinema as the credits roll. Tradition is, in a sense, simply the ongoing conversation of interpreting and elaborating Scripture – albeit a conversation where some voices have accumulated their own authority through repeated citation, influence and eminence. Tradition, from the Latin *tradere,* to hand on, is simply the ongoing conversation of the church making sense of what God has done and is doing in Christ, and how God remains fully active in the world through and as the Holy Spirit.

The relationship between tradition and Scripture is much debated, with a typically Protestant emphasis on the primacy of Scripture downplaying the authority of tradition, and Catholic and Orthodox views, in different ways, asserting the impossibility of reading Scripture well except through the accumulated wisdom of the dominant history of interpretation and practices of worship. Protestant denominations insist on Scripture alone as the determinate source of theology, *sola scriptura.* The Catholic Council of Trent conceived of Scripture and tradition as two distinct but connected sources. Protestants often rejected beliefs and practices that were not found in scripture but emerge later in tradition. By contrast, the Council of Trent regarded these as legitimate. Going further than the magisterial reformers, some on the radical wing of the Reformation rejected, or significantly downgraded, even central creedal claims, on the basis that these could not be fully established within the pages of Scripture itself.

Quests to reconstruct an original and pure Christianity free from later mystifying additions of tradition, or conversely to reject Christianity itself as the out of date remnants of the past, must reckon with the basic human need to construct meaning through narrative. This, at root, is the function of tradition, and it is almost inescapable. At most, the attempt to live free from the constraints of tradition means that one invents and lives within a paradoxical tradition of anti-traditionalism. This runs the risk of a peculiarly deliberate amnesia. That is not to say, though, that one cannot reject elements of that tradition – that can be pivotal. Indeed, rejecting, modifying or re-emphasizing elements of tradition are equally inescapable. Many ways of doing this develop, rather than discard, tradition as a whole.

We have seen that the sources of theology are distinct neither from each other nor from our use of them. A closed book or a conversation lapsing into silence are not sources – something becomes a source, and thus gains some form of authority, only in its use. In that sense, paradoxical as it may at first sound, Scripture and tradition are not objects but connected practices of reasoning together. More specifically, we can understand them as a skilful practice of seeing. Therein lies one more similarity with literature and film – in those forms of seeing (reading and watching) we develop skills of discernment. A badly written character lacks the complexity of motivation and ambiguity of action that 'ring true'. If theology is, as we here affirm it to be, a full-bodied form of knowledge, then just as spiritual seeing allows us to see in depth, beyond the surface, so too fiction allows us to see beyond the surface of ourselves, our lives and our world. That is certainly true of Scripture as the source of truth. Our contention is that the Bible is true not because it serves as a repository of spiritual aphorisms or religious 'facts'. Its truth, and thus its authority, is not merely in the information it conveys. Indeed, it is hard to think what it would mean for the Bible as a whole to be true in this sense of truth as accurately conveying information. There is too much poetry, wise aphorism, song, lament, wild adventure and turgid legal minutiae, all mixed together for that to be an adequate account of Scriptural truth.

That richness of reading comes not in haste, but with the close, perhaps slow, attentiveness of imaginatively entering into the story. Undistracted, the eye picks up the rhythm of prose, imagination brings the reader into the atmosphere of the plot. Careless reading insulates Christians against the work of the Spirit to shape, surprise and delight; that is, to serve all the purposes of Scripture attested by the New Testament itself – teaching, reproof, correction, and training in righteousness (2 Tim. 3:16-17).

Like every other area of theology, understandings of tradition are diverse. All place some emphasis on the consistency of tradition, which allows some alignment with a continuous stream flowing from the apostles to the present. However, if we characterize the flow of tradition along the lines of Vincent of Lérin's (d.450) famous dictum that the church, as the custodian of tradition, preserves 'that which has been believed everywhere, always and by all people' we may gain an impression of a static but comfortable consensus untouched by fractious heretics at the margins. That does little justice to the drama, political and personal intrigue, and the ebb and flow of ideas that comprise the history of Christian theological discussion. Tradition is more dynamic than that. Indeed, as the philosopher Alasdair MacIntyre insists, all reasoning takes place within a tradition, and that tradition, if it is functioning well, is 'always partially constituted by an argument about the goods the pursuit of which gives to that tradition its particular point and purpose'. It is not so much about valuing stability over conflict, rather tradition 'embodies continuities of conflict' (MacIntyre, 1985: 221).

We might say then that tradition is not 'outdated', it resides in the present, made active there through the continuing work of the Holy Spirit to reveal God. It is, we have suggested, messier than some influential theologies allow – it is not a neat continuous unfolding of understanding, guarded by custodians of correct interpretation; nor is it an unchanging edifice. Indeed it continues the power and the delight of the experience of reading. In reading the Bible, as in fiction, film or art, our imagination allows us, in a partial way, to become somewhat dislocated from our own perspective on life, to engage empathetically with the lives, pains, hopes and fears of others. Judith Butler has suggested this is the virtue of all education in the humanities – that in such an experience of reading, when we return to our own perspective we find it expanded, more gracious, more patient, more critical than before (Butler, 2013). The stream of tradition is wide and deep; if theologians engaged the Bible from their own situation, but refused to engage the history of disputation that has shaped the assumptions that influence their reading, they would deprive themselves of the resources for this expanded imagination.

Discussion – Seeing the authority of tradition

God's activity within the history of tradition might be detected in different ways. Does the weight of historical practice trump new realities or understandings of the human condition (one thinks of issues of gender and sexuality here, to which we shall return in Chapter 3), or might the dissenting traditions of the outsiders, radicals and reformers be a clearer strand of divine grace in historical action? David Brown poses the tension well when he says:

'To locate divine activity only within the tradition would be to ignore what is sometimes an indispensable contribution from a wider cultural context. Equally, though, to leave the final say with the present would also seem a mistake, since tradition gains its power not only through its capacity for change but also sometimes from its past returning to haunt it, requiring a return to earlier views. In other words, God defies our desire for tidy categories, and so in trying to tell the revelatory story we need to recognise a God at work everywhere in his world in helping to shape our comprehension of his purposes' (Brown, 1999: 374).

- How might Christians understand the ongoing authority of tradition?
- Are innovation and novelty appropriate in theology?
- Do you regard truth as timeless, the same always and everywhere?
- What advantages and dangers can you see in the close connection here asserted between the authority of the Bible and the interpretive function of the Christian community?

Indeed, it would be a mistake to assume that Scripture is prior to and distinct from tradition. Rather, tradition runs throughout Scripture itself. We have already seen that this is not simply a case of internal repetition – Chronicles and Kings differ radically in their presentation, but there is little doubt that the Chronicler is responding to Kings, or some earlier version of it. Paul urges his readers and hearers to remain faithful to the teachings 'handed on to them', that is literally their tradition (2 Thess. 2:15). The New Testament writers think with and through their own Scriptures – Luke gains his understanding of Jesus through the lens of Isaiah (Lk. 4:17-2, drawing on Is. 58:6 and 61:1, 2). The book of Hebrews is one extended and complex meditation on Christ through the lens of the Hebrew Bible. The New Testament is a text written by readers, those skilled in seeing the world around them through the lens of their own transformed and transformative texts. In Richard Hays's memorable notion, the New Testament writers framed their understanding of the definitive event of Christ's life, death and resurrection by a practice of 'reading backwards' their own Scriptures – the Hebrew Bible.

Activity – Theology as a practice of intertextual imagination

On a computer, tablet or paper copy read Hebrews 1 and highlight where the text takes from the following:

Psalm 2:7
2 Samuel 7:14 (or 1 Chronicles 17:13)
Deuteronomy 32:43
Psalm 104:4
Psalm 45:6-8
Psalm 102:26-28
Psalm 110:1

What contrasts is the author of Hebrews making?
What argument is being put forward through these contrasts?

Sometimes our imagination leaps in ways that may surprise us.

1. Read Genesis 16:1-16 and 21:9-21 (skim)
2. Read (more closely) Galatians 4:21–5:1
3. Discuss:

(a) What do you think is the original intention of the writer of Genesis in including these stories? What did they want to say about God, Abraham and the people of Israel?
(b) Paul's interpretation of the story is 'allegorical'. What do you understand by that term?

(c) What do you think is Paul's argument in this passage of Galatians?

(d) How much does Paul reshape the original meaning of the story to bolster his own overall argument?

(e) Is Paul's interpretation of the text 'correct'? Is there such a thing as *the* right interpretation?

(f) What does the way he uses this story tell you about Paul's approach to the Hebrew Bible?

(g) Do you think allegorical reading is a proper way of reading an ancient authoritative text?

Your answers to some of the above questions carry with them a set of assumptions about the authority of theological sources. The term 'authority' has been used extensively in this discussion, but it is worth pausing to reflect on what it actually means. For many 'authority' smacks of bossiness, hierarchy – authoritarianism. The term *auctoritas* in Latin does not merely mean the exercise coercive forms of power, it also indicates an origin (our word 'author' also comes from this term). The associated verb in Latin, *auctorare,* means to bind together. So authority can be a determinative standard – a binding legal decision, perhaps imposed against our will, but it can mean simply the definitive foundation or reliable source – less the vision of a harsh legal judgement and more the testimony of an expert witness.

Indeed, we suggest that the authority of Scripture, as it is made real to Christians through reason, tradition and experience, can be understood best through two different but related visual metaphors: one legal and one theatrical. We come on to the theatrical metaphor shortly. The legal metaphor is of 'witnessing'. Witnessing is a particular kind of active seeing – a testifying to the truth as it has been perceived. Major theologians like the Catholic Hans Urs Von Balthasar (1905–88) and the Reformed Karl Barth describe the Bible as a witness in this sense – the 'real witness is not identical with that to which it witnesses, but it sets it before us' (CD 1/2:463). To extend this image further, we might suggest that Scripture is the collection of witness statements, and tradition the accumulated practices of discernment and judgement – the case law that sets the precedents for our own theological judgements. For this metaphor, the Bible is only 'derivatively and indirectly' the word of God, but witnesses to the event of revelation. This event of revelation, most particularly culminating in the revelation of God in Christ, *is* the Word of God (CD 1/1:117). Indeed, the 'Word of God' with a capital W is personified, not just an utterance. Think of the beginning of the Gospel of John – 'In the beginning was the Word, and the Word was with God, and the Word was God' (Jn 1:1). This is not, however, to demean the authority or centrality of Scripture. The Holy Spirit continues to act on hearers and readers of the text in such a way that makes the Bible the Word of God. In that sense, key to the Christian view of the authority of Scripture is the commitment to the trinitarian action of God – the Holy Spirit is envisaged as accompanying, guiding and enabling human readers. Both in the current empowering work of the Spirit and in the great weight of previous readings known as tradition (whether one agrees with them or not), an individual reading Scripture is never really doing so alone. Reading the Bible, like reading any text, is an event, a moment of immense power and potential; but it is in God's active choice to make 'himself' known through it that it becomes authoritative – Scripture is an event of encounter.

If one stops to think about the way that witnesses are reputed to 'see' the same event, but recollect it in a variety of different ways, we can see again how the inescapable interpretive nature of perception itself must shape the way theology is done. Walter Brueggemann describes the canon of the Hebrew Bible as less a single account of the nature of God, or of God's dealings with 'his' creation, and more as a series of fragmentary and partial testimonies and counter-testimonies, each from historically and culturally shaped perspectives. The authority of Scripture flows not then from its consensus on God, or from its escaping the interpretive practices the rest of us are bound to; but rather this interplay of testimony and counter-testimony yields a complex embodied testimony which can disclose something of the reality of God (Brueggemann, 1997: 121). Tradition is a set of imaginative interpretive precedents and discussions about God in the light of these various testimonies.

This is to fully value the humanity of the biblical authors. It is a view that contrasts strongly with those mostly fairly recent forms of Christianity that see God as the direct author of the Bible. Often this more recent approach conceives of God writing through various forms of dictation or intervention by the Holy Spirit which annulled the humanity of the human biblical authors. There may be a striking impatience with the human condition itself in such attempts to accord authority to the biblical text in itself as distinct from the ongoing revealing action of the Holy Spirit. St Augustine (354–430) asserts as much in the preface to his *On Christian Teaching*, where he argues that the truths revealed in the pages of Scripture 'could certainly have been given through an angel, but the human condition would be wretched indeed if God appeared unwilling to minister his word to human beings through human agency' (1997: 5). Barth himself is even more acerbic – to seek to escape or downplay the humanity of the Biblical texts is to let one's view of the Bible be severely compromised by a 'foolish conception of its divinity' (CD 1/2: 518).

Indeed, any desire for certainty escaping the fallibility of any human text runs in significant tension against two central Christian doctrines: the Trinity – where God in Godself is eternal communicative relationship, which God chooses to pour out into creation and history; and the incarnation, where God becoming human is the 'unshakable foundation and pinnacle of God's en-formed self-communication to creation' (Dickens, 2006: 204). Both of these doctrines challenge one of the most persistent errors we encounter in doing theology – what we will call the zero-sum assumption, that divinity and humanity are incompatible categories. I.e., if human beings were active in the construction of biblical texts, then God cannot also have been so.

Key points

- There is an irreducible complexity and diversity to Christian Scriptures. It takes developed crafts of literary sensitivity and close reading to interpret it well.
- Skills of reading Scripture are shaped by tradition – itself ongoing and complex.
- Both Scripture and tradition are polyphonic (they speak with diverse voices).

Seeing ourselves: Experience, perception and performance

If Christian scriptural reasoning is an enterprise of imagination and interpretation, as we have argued so far, then we must also ask – Why do Christian thinkers do it? For what purpose? One short answer might be 'in order to see themselves well and to act accordingly'. One way of understanding the nature of theological truth is to say, without any naive suggestion of infallibility, that doctrine enables Christians to see themselves correctly as creatures of the triune God. Christians read Scripture through the lens of tradition, reasoning together to make sense of themselves and their place in the world, that is their 'experience', in the light of what they believe about God, and God's purposes with creation. Human beings are fundamentally imaginative and storied creatures – we make sense of ourselves and our place in the world through narrative. In particular we articulate the value of our lives and our world in ways that identify a particular purpose, goal or hope – what is technically known as 'teleology'. Alasdair MacIntyre argues that traditions embody such teleologies. If we set up society in a way that ignores this (perhaps in seeking to avoid unduly privileging one particular teleology), then, MacIntyre thinks, we run the risk of depriving ourselves of the means of making sense of our lives. That would be analogous he thinks, to depriving children (or adults come to that) of stories. 'Deprive children of stories and you leave them unscripted, anxious stutterers in their actions as in their words' (MacIntyre, 1985: 216).

Christian doctrine is not an abstract enterprise yielding an interesting but essentially inert output – like academic textbooks! While we have been exploring the interpretation of Scripture, and the use of tradition, reason and experience, through visual processes and metaphors, it is important to understand that sight, like all of the senses, is part of a complex integrated bodily interpretation that shapes both individual lives and the life together of the Christian community – the church.

Theology is both an academic discipline and an ecclesial one – that is a discipline for the church. The relationship between these two arenas is complex. On the one hand we do not here expect all academic engagement with theology to be undertaken in a context of belief, or by those who identify as believers, but nor can academic study ignore the ways that doctrine shapes and enlivens religious practice. One can read Shakespeare, undertake detailed scholarly investigations of the text and its diverse interpretations, but one misses out if one doesn't at least view a performance.

Theatrical performance is a second visual metaphor that is often used to capture something of this. Studying doctrine is like watching a theatrical performance. Indeed, for theologians across denominational divides (Balthasar, Vanhoozer, Wright, Young) the story told by Christianity is likened to a play – a complex interweaving of strands in epic scale, fitting also with the structure of a comedy. That is, it is not just that it is funny (though parts certainly are), but that it is a story still moving towards a happy ending – the vindication of God's love in the coming of 'his' Kingdom at the end of history. First, Creation and the arrival of sin; second, God's electing of 'his' people Israel for the purpose of restoring creation; third, the denouement of that effort in the life, death and resurrection of Jesus; fourth, the story of the church; and finally, the arrival of the time when God is all in all (1 Cor. 15:28) – classically expressed in imagery of the restoration of Eden, the perfection of Jerusalem, and the gathering of rebellious humanity around their loving creator. If the Christian view of God's purposes with the world is structured in this way – as N.T. Wright puts it, like a five-act Shakespearean play – then we find ourselves in the midst of the fourth act. That is a surprising twist in the visual metaphor – but we've insisted here that seeing is not passive. Our eyes draw us to act – for good or for ill (Mt. 5:29, 8:9). The church is a kind of interactive play – the stage is not separate from the audience (not unlike the Globe theatre of Shakespeare's Elizabethan performances – replicated now on the shores of the Thames in London). Actor and former theatrical director Mark Rylance describes the lesson he learned in staging plays with the audience and performers intermingled in the same area, without darkened spaces and glaring lights, where actors could see and engage the audience:

> It was about thinking of the audience as other actors, and not just when you were projecting on them the role of the helpful crowd, like Henry's army or the citizens of Venice at the trial in The Merchant of Venice. It was more about the fact that anything they did was like another player on the stage doing something, so they were always there and when you were alone, they were your conscience or your soul. (Rylance, 2008: 107)

An implied or actual dialogue with the audience, the deconstruction of the 'fourth' wall separating audience from cast, makes the performance more engaging and varied. Rylance observes that the more experimental form of performance was unsettling to directors, many of whom were reticent to lose the control they would normally have to shape their own vision of a play. It was unsettling too for the audience, who, just like the actors and directors, were learning how to be in that space – how to be an audience (Rylance, 2008: 115). Life in the middle of the fourth act calls all believers to participate, but to do so in ways that cohere with the previous acts. They are oriented to the final act, but enjoy the freedom to play with their role in the present. For that reason, the sources of theology, Scripture most of all, do not so much provide the script for Christians to recite. A script speaks with a single voice, and we have already seen the polyphonic nature of Scripture. It also contains prescriptions of the words and actions of all players – but that kind of stage direction isn't established in Scripture, or indeed in tradition. Thus, Kevin Vanhoozer rightly mixes the metaphor. Scripture is not really a dramatic script, though it does provide the plot development and the backstory for the current act, but it is also, he says, more like 'the lights that illuminate the stage and allow us to see what is going on' (Vanhoozer, 2014: 23). In that sense the Christian life is more like a form of improvisation – not just making things up as they go along, but creatively continuing the story (Wells, 2004).

Thus tradition and experience may work together – tradition providing an interpretive history beyond our subjective preferences (thus serving as a 'rule of faith'); experience inevitably integrating the believer into that broad and diverse tradition. Christians engage the Bible not just in academic reflection but in personal devotion, in communal worship and in preaching. Think of the increasingly popular practice of prayerful or meditative reading of the Bible known as *lectio divina* – 'divine reading' in Latin. It is an originally monastic devotional engagement with Scripture intended to encounter God through God's living word. Through a cycle of reading, meditation, prayer and further contemplation, the intention of this reading practice is to open oneself to God's active speaking in and through the text, to set aside presuppositions and agendas, and to thereby encounter God's word as alive, enriching and perhaps surprising. There is a complementarity, but also a potential tension, between such devotional reading of the text and the academic enterprises of historical critical investigation of biblical texts. Both academic reading and the open devotional approach should be open to surprise. Not least because encountering the strangeness of the Bible, when we realize it doesn't quite say what we had expected, gives us an opportunity to see some of our own assumptions. This is why 'experience' should not be understood so much as a separate 'source' for theology, but as an inescapable part of the theological process. Indeed, theologians of various stripes have been cautious to avoid saying that some form of experience can produce a knowledge of God distinct from that attested in the Bible. In the trinitarian reality of reading, the Spirit 'inspires' our reading in that the text comes alive, takes on new significance, surprises us with the depth of its meaning. There are no secrets of divine knowledge in tension with the Bible, or indeed any covert extra meanings locked within its pages that only a privileged few super-spiritual types might get to unlock.

Activity – Surprising sight

Even the most experienced academic reader brings with them a variety of assumptions. Try this simple exercise: before reading the text write down the events and characters of Genesis 3 – that is the story of Adam and Eve in the Garden of Eden. Then write down what you think it means and how it relates to wider Christian beliefs.

Now read the text. This is a highly influential text – you'll have seen pictures, cartoons, movies, even advertising campaigns, making use of the famous imagery. Each of these forms part of the pre-history of your reading – they shape your assumptions. We develop habits of imagination from our experience of culture, our exposure to political agendas and our engagement with social media. Those habits of imagination influence what we see and don't see in a text.

- Where in the text is the Serpent named Satan, or equated with the devil?
- Is there any suggestion in this text that after Adam's disobedience every human being will be born into a state of inherited guilt and an ingrained inability to avoid sin?

It may surprise you that neither of these assumptions can be fully supported from the text itself. The equation of the Serpent with Satan occurs only later in Christian tradition. The doctrine of Original Sin is not present here but finds some support in the New Testament (Rom. 5:12-21 – hardly an unambiguous text), and comes to full development much later – around the fifth century. None of that is to say that these wider understandings are wrong – though both are subject to disagreement and controversy. Rather it is simply to note that our reading always goes beyond 'what the text actually says', because our experience is inescapable.

The storied nature of our lives shows one way in which the enterprise of theology is central to the Christian life as a life in its fullness. We are perhaps used to thinking of orthodoxy as restrictive, and heresy as vibrant, exciting, countercultural and radical. Heresies are often heard in our own time in light of the dominant narrative of the glamorous rebel, the rogue hero who operates outside of the constraints of staid tradition – but heresies in the early church are often rejected not because they are too dramatic, but because they are not anything like dramatic enough. The arch heresy of much Christian theologizing – Gnosticism – tends to want to sanitize the Gospel by excluding the complexity and messiness of a God become human, and in so doing settles for an account that diminishes the radicality of the Christian claims about reality. Some contemporary theologians suggest, then, that orthodoxy is vibrant colour, heresy all too beige. Orthodoxy a groundbreaking narrative, heresy is tedious and derivative schlock. Both the resurgent radicality of orthodoxy and the romanticized rebellion of the heretic can be overplayed, especially if orthodoxy is defined in narrow or ungenerous terms that bar new insight from experience, rigorous scholarship or developments in our understanding of the world.

However, the diversity of biblical materials, the breadth of tradition and the delightful but dizzying range of experiences people bring to their theology inevitably mean that Christianity is a story capable of being performed in diverse ways. Diversity of performance may well be a good thing, but it can also lead to a performance that misses out central elements of the story, misconstrues the intentions of the author or culminates in a rather disappointingly thin ending. In that sense the tasks of Christian doctrine are less like the audience of a film or theatrical performance, and more like the role of a director. At their best a director does not set every element of the content, but guides the performance so that the story isn't overwhelmed by other agendas, performers' egos or confused dialogue.

This requires careful discernment. We began by describing the way in which imagination allows us to see – an imaginary is a particular construction of cultural symbols, institutions, rules, values, thought patterns and habits of interpretation. They filter what we see. All too easily Scripture and tradition can function as an echo-chamber, repeating back to us our own preferences – but this time in a more authoritative voice. We will tend to find in theological sources what we are looking for – whether moral instruction, spiritual guidance, history, a political programme or a self-help guide. The same is true for simplistic critics of religion for whom the all-too-evident brutality, exclusion and sexual violence found in the Bible bespeak a primitive worldview to be discarded in the face of modern scientific understanding. It is likely that our national identity, our sexuality, our gender, our socio-economic class, our educational background and multiple other factors shape our imaginary.

The fact that our experience, broadly understood, shapes our theology is not to say that we cannot change. To avoid such a theological cultural determinism we can engage in fuller reading, facing up to the diversity of Scripture, wrestling with the uncomfortable elements of tradition, drawing in the perspectives and experiences of other readers, allowing the Bible to 'read us' and critique our agendas and experience. Nor does this inescapable influence of experience mean that all theologies are equally right (or equally wrong). We have seen that there are better and worse interpretations of a biblical text; more broadly there are also better and worse theological imaginaries – though to make such a judgement one would need to carefully articulate the purpose and calling of theology. In the rest of this book, we'll explore just some elements of the full-bodied experience of theological thought. We might suggest this is why encountering theology is both unsettling and exciting – it is an adventure in self-discovery and in seeing the world in all its truth, goodness and beauty.

Key points

- The metaphors of witnessing and theatre convey the active calling of seeing theologically.
- 'Experience' is not a separate competing source of theology but an inevitable part of the process of interpretation of Scripture.
- The four sources identified in this and other textbooks place upon the theologian a demand for careful, rigorous, self-critical forms of seeing. That is the adventure of theology.

Extended task – Theological ground rules

Write your own ground rules for how theological sources – scripture, reason, tradition and experience – should and should not be used in theological thinking. You can do this individually or as a group.

Follow-up task for later – once you reach the end of this book, or the end of your course or module, revisit these ground rules. Did you stick to these rules? What revisions would you now make?

Chapter summary

- The sources of theology are complex, polyphonic and diverse.
- The use of these sources is always selective and open to challenge.
- Christian thinking is a form of imaginative seeing through these sources.

Recommended reading

Brown, David (1999), *Tradition and Imagination: Revelation and Change*, Oxford: Oxford University Press.

Lamb, William (2013), *Scripture: A Guide for the Perplexed*, London: T&T Clark.

Vanhoozer, Kevin, J. (2014), *Faith Speaking Understanding: Performing the Drama of Doctrine*, Louisville, KY: Westminster John Knox Press.

2

Hearing: The life of doctrine

In this chapter we suggest that your experiences of music can take you a long way into understanding Christian doctrine. Some of you might be immediately concerned that you can barely remember recorder lessons from school or are unable to sing in tune. In which case, please be reassured: we will simply be reflecting on some of music's special qualities and how we encounter music in everyday life. To give you a taste of how music can assist theological thinking, we will pair up Christology (the doctrine of Christ) with musical performance, the Trinity with our perceptual experience of hearing a triad (a kind of three-tone chord) and creation with acoustical resonance. At various points you will be asked to listen to music that is freely available from the internet or carry out practical tasks, but you will not need any musical skill to be able to participate. Along the way we will touch on important debates within church history, but we deliberately keep this information to a minimum. In-depth explanation and analysis are provided by the books that we recommend as follow-up reading. Our primary goal is to give you musical pathways into important doctrinal topics. The discussions will also get you thinking about how different types of imagination shape doctrine.

We start by eliciting your experience of hearing music and any involvement you might have had with musical performance, no matter how little, or long ago. These thoughts will feed our engagement with Christology.

Introductory reflections

1. Have you ever been to a live gig or concert, or seen a live recording of one? What makes for a successful performance? What is the relationship between the performer and audience like?
2. Do you think cover bands relate to the music differently compared to the original performers?

Christology

In this section we suggest that musical performance can help you to understand:

- Christology (Jesus Christ 'performs' God)
- The development of Christology (the church 'performs' Christ)
- Our involvement in Christology (Christians can 'perform' Christ themselves)

Christology addresses the mystery of the incarnation. This word comes from the Latin verb *incarnare*, meaning 'to make flesh'. It is not in the Bible, but it conveys what Christians believe to be scriptural truth: the Son of God (also known as the Word of God) assumed human form in Jesus of Nazareth, such that Jesus Christ is fully divine and fully human. This is an extraordinary statement. As Karl Barth wrote, 'Christ is the infinitely wondrous event which compels a person to be necessarily, profoundly, wholly and irrevocably astonished' (1963: 68). Some people find the incarnation so astonishing that they feel compelled to dismiss it instantly. Some theologians try to soften its challenge, by either abandoning aspects of Christ's divinity or over-expanding Christ's humanity such that it can 'contain' the fullness of God. Either way the incarnation is denied rather than explained. Reflecting on musical performance gives us a coherent way to start thinking about the person of Jesus Christ, while still acknowledging the mystery of his person.

In thinking about what makes performances successful and engaging, you might have written something about music 'flowing' freely through an artist or the artist 'becoming one' with the music. (Just think of the difference between Queen's legendary performance at Live Aid and utterly painful school concerts, for example.) Perhaps you also considered a paradox: excellent performances can both lift you out of your present moment and drive you more deeply into the world. Or perhaps you listed the way that superb artists can communicate great emotional range and intensity – sometimes to the point of creating a sense of quasi-religious, other-worldly transcendence. Related to this, you may have mentioned that a fine performance succeeds in drawing listeners into the experience. If you are a bit of a classical music buff, you might appreciate subtleties in interpretation or value how accurately a performance matches the intentions of the composer. Several of these responses are in play in Rowan Williams's (b.1950) metaphorical description of Jesus being 'shot through' with God's life, rather like a musician is 'shot through' with the music's 'life' (2003: 6). He writes:

> When you see a great performer … at work realizing a piece of music, you are looking at one human being at the limit of their skill and concentration. All their strength, their freedom, and you could even say their love is focused on bringing to life the work and vision of another person. … The vision and imagination of … the composer, has to come through – not displacing the human particularity of the

performer but 'saturating' that performer's being for the time of the performance. ... these performers are not becoming less human, less distinctive. In the fullness of their skill and joy, another is made present. So with Jesus; this is a human life and a human will whose power and joy is the performance of who God is and what God wants, the performance of the Word of God. (2007: 74)

In other words, Jesus is so caught up in the stream of God's life that God is heard, without distortion, through Jesus's humanity – a humanity which is freely given over to rendering the ineffable Word of God for the world. This is such a flawless performance that we cannot say that what Christ does as man and what he does as God are two different actions. Further, if Jesus 'is understood ... to do the work of God, he cannot finally be separated in thought and being from God' (Gunton, 1997a: 8–9). The purity of Jesus's translation of the Word is such that we can confidently know, as the Scottish theologian Thomas. F. Torrance (1913–2007) put it, that 'God is eternally in himself what he is in Jesus Christ, and, therefore, that there is no dark unknown God behind the back of Jesus Christ, but only he who is made known to us in Jesus Christ' (1997: 135). Theologically, the 'oneness' between the activity and being of God and Jesus Christ (the incarnate Son) is expressed by the term *homoousion* ('*homos*' – same, '*ousia*' – essence). This term 'establish[ed]' a new ontological principle: that there can be a sharing in being' (Gunton, 1997a: 9).

A metaphor describes one thing in terms of something else entirely (e.g. Jesus's description of himself as the bread of life – Jn 6:35). For this to work, we need to stay alert to the differences within the metaphor.
In what ways could the performance metaphor for Christology become theologically misleading? How could it be pushed too far?

A weakness of this metaphor is that both a performer and a piece of music are squarely within the realm of the creaturely. Even so, Williams's metaphor can help us avoid what Jeremy Begbie calls a 'critical danger' – namely the assumption that 'deity and humanity are ontologically comparable categories, instances of the same genus jostling for the same space – in this case, the ... physical space of Jesus of Nazareth' (2013: 151). Audibly thinking of the way in which the 'particularity' of Jesus Christ is 'saturated' with the Word, so that the Word is 'performed' in him, tells us that Christ's person is a place of hospitable co-presence and generous mutuality, not competitiveness. And remarkably, Jesus holds open the *homoousion*, this sharing in divine being, to humanity. This invitation is heard most clearly in – quite literally – the performance of his life: his cross and resurrection. Herbert McCabe expresses it like this:

[Jesus] wanted that [all people] should be as possessed by love as he was, he wanted that they should be divine, and this could only come as a gift. Crucifixion and resurrection, the prayer of Christ and the response of the Father are the archetype and source of all our prayer. It is this we share in sacramentally in the eucharist, it is this we share in all our prayer. But the crucifixion, the total self-abandonment of Jesus to the Father is not just a prayer that Jesus offered, a thing he happened to do. What the church came to realise is that he was a revelation of who Jesus *is*. When Jesus is 'lifted up' – and for John this means the whole loving exchange of the lifting up on the cross and the lifting up which is the resurrection – when Jesus is lifted up, he appears for what he is. It is revealed the deepest reality of Jesus is simply to be *of* the Father. (McCabe, 2005: 219)

An early and influential challenge to the church's teaching about Jesus came from an Alexandrian Presbyter called Arius (c.270–366). He laid out his views in a partly extant work entitled 'Thalia' (c.320s):

'God himself in himself remains mysterious. He alone has no equal, none like him, none of equal glory. We call him unoriginated in contrast to him who is originated by nature ... we praise him as without beginning in contrast to him who has a beginning, we worship him as eternal in contrast to him who came into existence at times. He who was without beginning made the Son a beginning of all things which are produced, ... and he is not equal ... far less is he consubstantial to God. ... Certainly there is a Trinity ... [but] their individual realities do not mix with each other, and they possess glories of different levels. The sole glory is of the Sole, infinitely more splendid in his glories. The Father is in his substance alien from the Son because he remains without beginning.' Quoted by Athanasius, *De Synodis* 15. Extract (reproduced in Ford and Higton, 2002: 86–7).

1. What are Arius's key points about Jesus?
2. In what ways does his language sound like Christian teaching?

An Alexandrian Bishop, Athanasius (c.300–73), relentlessly pursued Arius and eventually defeated his ideas. Alister McGrath identifies two arguments that formed the backbone of Athanasius's critique (2007: 146–7). First, Athanasius argued that only God had the power to save, and yet Jesus was praised as Saviour in the New Testament and in Christian worship. While Arius accepted Jesus as Redeemer, he understood this only in terms of emulation (action) and naming (honour), rather than in terms of Jesus sharing in the being of God. For Athanasius, this meant that Arius's view of salvation was just a kind of radical self-improvement, sealed with the honorary title of 'son'. Second, Athanasius pointed out that Christians had always prayed to Jesus. Arius also worshipped Jesus, but refused to accept the logic that, from his own perspective, this was idolatry. Arius's teaching was denounced at the Council of Nicea (325CE) and the line 'begotten, not made' was added to the Nicene Creed in order to ward off future confusion: the Son shared in the being of God and was not a creature.

Some might say that this is a fine example of Christians arguing over words instead of getting on with the task in hand – feeding the poor, helping the oppressed and so on. However, it is important to appreciate – as Athanasius did so perceptively – that words can derail, as well as deepen, our understanding of the divine Word taking on human flesh. Our vocabulary then dictates our actions. Take, for instance, the kind of diluted Arianism that crops up in the common view that Jesus is just a great moral teacher. This puts enormous pressure on people to replicate Christ's goodness by their own efforts – only, in the end, for them to have no secure salvation. For an Arian-style Christ cannot have perfect knowledge of God, cannot genuinely reveal God and cannot quite reach the transcendent divine being. Only a union of action and being – only the *homoousion* – can bring humanity into life-giving communion with God. Compared to Arianism, Nicene orthodoxy offers a far more profound picture of humanity's predicament (i.e. humans cannot save themselves), and a far more radical divine solution to it. Far from existing in untouchable isolation, the God of christological orthodoxy is self-giving to the core – and is so, as we shall see in the next section, only because of the full divinity of both Son and Spirit.

'One of the outcomes of the Arian controversy was the recognition of the futility, even theological illegitimacy, of biblical "proof-texting" – the simplistic practice of believing that a theological debate can be settled by quoting a few passages from the Bible' (McGrath, 2009: 143).

What is the alternative to proof-texting? (If you are not reading this book in sequence, Chapter 1 will help you here.)

The early church dealt with myriad other ways of unbalancing Christology. If Sophia, the social humanoid robot developed by Hanson Robotics, were to start piano lessons, this would take our performance metaphor in a different direction – that of Docetism (from the Greek word *dokein*, meaning 'appear to be'). Docetists claimed that Jesus only 'seemed' to be human. The Apostle John combated a very early version of this teaching (1 Jn 1:1-3, 2:22, 4:2-3, 2 Jn. 7); Irenaeus of Lyons (*c*.115–*c*.202) countered a more sophisticated version.

Extract – Irenaeus's 'Against Heresies' (Book 1, Chapter 9, Paragraph 3)

'For according to them, the Word did not originally become flesh. For they maintain that the Word assumed an animal body, formed in accordance with a special dispensation by an unspeakable providence, so as to become visible

> and palpable. But flesh is that which was of old formed for Adam by God out of the dust, and it is this that John has declared the Word of God became' (2018: 33).
>
> Here, Irenaeus is disputing the view of Valentinians (followers of Valentinus, a gnostic), who conceived of Christ's humanity in a docetic way: it was 'animal' but not material. Gnosticism and docetism can therefore be linked.

Docetism was rejected by the Council of Nicea (325) because it failed to do justice to Jesus's humanity. Docetism then provoked a reaction that over-emphasized Jesus's humanity. Some Christians called adoptionists said that Jesus had been 'adopted' as the Son of God at a certain point in his life; as if a performer had practised badly for a long time and then suddenly the piece just 'clicked' and flowed perfectly. This teaching was also rejected by the Council of Nicea – this time on the grounds that Jesus's divinity was undermined. In a later swing of opinion, that also misread Jesus's translation of the Word, Nestorius, the Archbishop of Constantinople, was accused of separating Christ's two natures. This teaching was thrown out by the First Council of Ephesus (431). One of his most vehement opponents at this council was Eutyches, a Presbyter at Constantinople, who argued that Christ was a *fusion* of divine and human elements – a view discarded at the Council of Chalcedon in 451.

Chalcedon was something of a watershed moment in Christian history. Convened by the Roman Emperor Marcian, it affirmed the creeds of Nicea (325) and Constantinople (381) and added a definition. It simply marks out the boundaries of what must be upheld regarding Christ's divinity and humanity. Part of it reads:

Extract from the Council of Chalcedon's Definition of Faith

'Following the holy Fathers we teach with one voice that the Son and our Lord Jesus Christ is to be confessed as one and the same, that he is perfect in Godhead and perfect in manhood, very God and very man, of a reasonable soul and body consisting, consubstantial with the Father as touching his Godhead and consubstantial with us as touching his manhood; made in all things like unto us sin only excepted; begotten of his Father before the worlds according to his Godhead but in these last days for us men and for our salvation born of the Virgin Mary the Mother of God according to his manhood. This one and the same Jesus Christ the only begotten Son must be confessed to be in two natures, unconfusedly, immutably, indivisibly, distinctly, in separably, and that without the distinction of natures being taken away by such union, but rather the peculiar property of each nature being preserved and being united in one person and subsistence, not separated or divided into two persons, but one and the same Son and only-begotten, God the Word, our Lord Jesus Christ, as the prophets of old time have spoken concerning him, and as the Lord Jesus Christ, hath taught us, and as the Creed of the Fathers hath delivered to us' (reproduced in Higton and Ford, 2002: 100–1).

Like the creeds, which were agreed by the Church Councils to help preserve the fundamentals of Christian faith, this definition has an enduring capacity to speak to us. Negatively, it warns that heresy is always possible, and so hard-won lessons need to be understood, claimed and given fresh expression by every generation of believers. Positively, the fact that it came about after lengthy theological disputation witnesses to the lively dynamism of Christian tradition and ecclesiastical willingness to debate truth claims.

Discussion task

1. Which elements of the Chalcedonian Definition and Nicene Creed are designed to protect against the early christological heresies?
2. Can you think of old heresies which are circulating in new forms right now? If so, what theological issues/problems are created?
3. Do you think Christians find the creeds restrictive or reassuring? (You could look back to the discussion of tradition in Chapter 1.)

The early Christians therefore wrestled painfully and protractedly with points of christological doctrine, and this journey of faith is ongoing. It may feel altogether safer (and perhaps more faithful) to imagine that truth is passed down through time, untouched by historical processes. Yet on closer examination, this is an expression of the zero-sum problem – i.e. 'the more active God is in the world, the less active we can be' (Begbie, 2000: 3, n.2) – and it creates extreme options. Either God completely bypasses human input (such that doctrine is pure revelation) or else humans cut God out (such that doctrine is purely invented). The experience of musical performance helps us to appreciate how church history offers us more than this binary choice. If, for the sake of argument, we look to the Western classical tradition, a musician will learn to play a piece of music by reading a score of some kind and repeatedly playing it until it is firmly in her mental and physical memory. She might well engage with previous performances by other artists, or – if it is an ensemble piece – discuss interpretive ideas with fellow performers. One of the joys of music is that the same piece is endlessly repeatable in non-identical (but not necessarily good) ways by different performers. As performers give themselves over to interact with the music, this brings new things out of the music for the enjoyment and participation of others. Even the multiple contingencies – distractions, acoustics, accidents, etc. – involved in each performance become part of the piece's performance history. These combined characteristics of discipline and freedom, selflessness and enrichment, and individuality and incorporation make for an engaging performance.

As with musicians playing a piece, Christian engagement with God-in-Christ is deepened by surrendering to him, responding to a particular context and working together to ask questions about our encounter with him. Doctrine is therefore both discerned and constructed by the church community (McGrath, 2007: 28). Men like Arius, Nestorius and Eutyches were fervent Christian believers who were seeking new ways of understanding Jesus's 'performance' of God, and it took time for the church to assess whether these teachings were going against the grain of apostolic inheritance or developing it more fully. Were they performing non-identical versions of the same Christ, or different Christs entirely? These ideas had to be tested before the church could produce authorized statements of faith. For the musical view of doctrine we are presenting here, orthodoxy does not predate heresy; it emerges through its fires, by the grace of God.

Music can also help us to grasp that Christology tells a hopeful story. Think back to the answers that you gave to the opening questions. You may well have thought that good performances demonstrate an energetic reciprocity between those on stage and those in the audience. The performer must be well-rehearsed, but people must also be invested in joining in. Likewise, God invites people, through the presence and direction of the Holy Spirit, to be incorporated into, and actively participate in, the performance history of the church. Indeed, this was how doctrine evolved. Theological ideas born out of the church's encounter with God-in-Christ, through the Spirit, interacted with the intense christological debates of the first few centuries of the Christian era. Through worship, prayer and reflection, early Christians discovered that God was shaping them, their communities, their practices and their beliefs (and eventually creeds). They found themselves led by the Spirit on an ever-deepening journey: to share in, and understand, Jesus's form of life and Jesus's relationship to God the Father, and so be brought into the presence of God in newly intimate and thought-provoking ways (McIntosh, 1998, 2008). A musical emphasis on performance gestures towards this awareness that Christianity is a way of being and thinking (a way of 'joining in') made possible by the Spirit, who directs Christians to the Father, through Jesus Christ. Doctrine and the creeds protect this narrative of life, which God gives to be performed for the world.

Christology, then, has a performative dimension: it aims to gather up individual lives into ongoing, transformative performances of Christ, in the Spirit. The connections with music here are striking and challenging. As Philip Stoltzfus poetically puts it, 'Music is about a performance taking place, and about each of us playing our part in the performance. And theology, too, is about a performance taking place, and about each of us finding our voice in the cooperative movement of keeping the song alive' (2006: x).

Key points

- Jesus Christ (one person, two natures) uniquely and perfectly 'performs' God the Son, responding in love to God the Father, in the power of God the Spirit.
- God entrusts Jesus to human history and, through the Spirit, ongoing performances of his life – in the church as a body and in lives of individuals – such that Christology is a lived reality and witness.
- The rulings of Church Councils show the dynamic nature of doctrine and tradition.

Questions for discussion

1 Does the church perform Christ as if he is a musical score, or does the church improvise with his life? Or both?
2 Is the church's performance of Christ the same as its performance of the Bible (discussed in Chapter 1)?

Extract – Gregory of Nazianzus's Epistle to Cledonius, 'Against Apollinarius'

'For that which [Jesus] has not assumed he has not healed; but that which is united to his Godhead is also saved. If only half Adam fell, then that which Christ assumes and saves may be half also; but if the whole of his nature fell, it must be united to the whole nature of him that was begotten, and so be saved as a whole. Let them not, then, begrudge us our complete salvation, or clothe the Saviour only with bones and nerves and portraiture of humanity. ... But, he asserts, he could not contain two perfect natures. Not if you only look at him in a bodily fashion. For a bushel measure will not hold two bushels, nor will the space of one body hold two or more bodies. But if you will look at what is mental and incorporeal, remember that I in my one personality can contain soul and reason and mind and Holy Spirit; ... For such is the nature of intellectual existences, that they can mingle with one another and with bodies, incorporeally and invisibly. For many sounds are comprehended by one ear and the eyes of many are occupied by the same visible objects, and the smell by odours; nor are the senses narrowed by each other, or crowded out, nor are the objects of sense diminished by the multitude of the perceptions.' (Reproduced in Ford and Higton, 2002: 92)

- What heresy is Gregory writing against here?
- Pick out one sentence that summarizes a ground rule of orthodox Christology.
- How does Gregory understand different types of perception to affect Christology?
- How does Gregory learn from the senses?

The Trinity

Task – What do you hear?

Think of songs or pieces of music that have layers of vocal harmonies. For example, Handel's 'Hallelujah Chorus', Abba's 'Waterloo', Lady Gaga/Bradley Cooper's 'Shallow (A Star Is Born)'. How would you describe what you hear to someone who is deaf?

When the church understood that the incarnate Son, Jesus Christ, shared the same substance as God, and that he indwells believers in the Holy Spirit, the monotheism inherited from Judaism had to undergo development. The gradual unfurling of truth became known as the doctrine of the Trinity. It affirms that there is only one God, who is a unity of co-equal divine persons (Father, Son and Holy Spirit). Christians believe that Scripture anticipates this doctrine, which was also shaped by the church's experiences in prayer and worship, and in response to those who denied the divinity of Christ and the Holy Spirit. (As already mentioned, the deity of Christ was confirmed at the Council of Nicea [325]. The deity of the Holy Spirit was confirmed at the Council of Constantinople [381].)

Understanding God to be the Trinity opens the door to immense spiritual riches of great practical consequence. Sadly, though, this doctrine is a stumbling block for many. It can be undervalued, or dismissed outright, for a number of reasons: its subtle complexities are misunderstood, it is badly communicated as an unappealing 'lifeless tension' (Begbie, 2013: 154), or it is (wrongly) believed to have been fabricated and enforced by some power-hungry members of the ecclesiastical elite. Perhaps you can relate to one or more of these trends. Or perhaps you see the Trinity as a bizarre conceptual puzzle that has little to do with a journey of faith.

The doctrine of the Trinity can be dismissed, for instance, because mathematical logic is inappropriately applied to the nature of God. Just as $1+1+1 = 3$, so – it is reasoned – three beings form three distinct gods, not one. More sophisticated arguments suggest that each divine person possesses part of the one divine essence, and therefore each has a different essence. These are examples of tritheism, which the church discounts as trinitarian heresy due to its inconsistency with Scripture. Some versions of social trinitarianism (which interpret the Trinity along the lines of human social relationships) sail very close to tritheism. Cornelius Plantinga, for example, has been accused of projecting a modern, individualist sense of 'person' into the Godhead, resulting in God's 'three-ness' being valued more than his 'one-ness'.

Scripture was (and is) vital to understanding the nature of the God revealed in Jesus and the work of redemption, but it may surprise you to know that the word 'Trinity' does not appear in Scripture. It was coined by Tertullian (b.155–160) and there are only two New Testament verses that could be read in an explicitly trinitarian way: Matthew 28:19 and 2 Corinthians 13:13. Nevertheless, Scripture 'bears witness to a God who demands to be understood in a trinitarian manner' (McGrath, 2007: 247). McGrath uncovers the connections, as follows. The Hebrew Scriptures contain three personifications of God which reveal God as immanent and transcendent, to be present and active in creation: Wisdom (Prov. 1:20-23, Job 28; Eccl. 2:12-17), Word of God (Ps. 119:89, Is. 55:10-11) and Spirit of God (Is. 42:1-3, Ezek. 36:26, 37:1-14); the New Testament is shot through with consistently close connections between the Father, Son and Holy Spirit: (1 Cor. 12:4-6, 2 Cor. 1:21-22, Gal. 4:6, Eph. 2:20-22, Thess. 2:13-14, Titus 3:4-6, 1 Peter 1:2) (McGrath, 2007).

Musical perception can give us a way to start thinking about these divine relationships. Recall your descriptions of what it is like to hear vocal harmonies. You may have come up with something along these lines: the voices do not compete (adding more vocals to the mix does not exclude or push out others), they are not confused (simultaneously sounding harmonies do not merge, creating something new) and they are not separated (simultaneous voices cannot be heard apart from one another). The music theorist Victor Zuckerkandl says something similar when describing a triad (a type of three-note chord):

> The first tone, as it sounds, spreads through all space. Joining the first, the second tone [finds that] all available space is occupied by the first. The second tone has to spread out in the same space in which the first has previously spread. Nevertheless, it is not covered by the first: the first turns out to be, as it were, transparent for it. The second tone is and remains audible through the first. The same is true of the third tone: the tones connected in the triad sound through one another. Or let us say that they interpenetrate one another. (1956: 299)

Zuckerkandl is pointing out that when we hear a triad, we hear unity and difference at the same time. This experience makes its own kind of sense. After all, whatever kind of music you like, we are guessing that you would agree with the theologian

David Cunningham, who says, 'We do not consider the simultaneous sounding of notes to be contradictory, meaningless, or against reason. Nor do we believe that this has somehow violated a principle of music (or of reason); … In music, such simultaneous multiplicity seems not only to be allowed, but to be encouraged and rewarded' (2002: 127).

> ### Tip
> Visit http://trainer.thetamusic.com/en/content/triads and use the demo app on the homepage to hear a triad. Similar clips are readily available elsewhere online.

Jeremy Begbie has explored the analogous connections between the co-presence of tones and the person of Jesus Christ (2000: 23–6) and, in a wonderful phrase, he also speaks of the Trinity 'as a three-note chord, a resonance of life' (2008: 293). The Father, Son and Holy Spirit 'sound through' one another (2008), they 'indwell' one another or 'co-inhere'. In theology, these ideas are expressed by the word *perichoresis*, a Greek word which was accepted into general use in the sixth century. It means something like 'mutual interpenetration' and it conveys how God's life is one of radical equality, where the divine persons are 'always about the business of giving themselves to one another' (Cunningham, 2002: 294). They hold nothing back from each other, for all is given, surrendered and exchanged in love. Rather like tones sounding through one another in our perception, the divine persons are an inseparable unity without collapsing into uniformity. (Over the course of any future theological studies you will explore trinitarian vocabulary in far greater depth. For ease of understanding here, and following Tertullian, 'substance' unites the Trinity whereas 'person' signifies internal distinctions.) Begbie has also suggested (2001: 150) that a three-part musical form, like a fugue, might better express the 'particularity of the persons' and the joyous life of giving and receiving that is the Trinity (2001). Likewise, with good reason, Hans Urs von Balthasar (1905–88) expresses God's trinitarian being as 'symphonic' (1987: 12). A chord sufficiently intimates, however, that the Trinity is not illogical per se.

> We have used Zukerkandl's description of a triad, and the evidence of our own musical experiences, to point towards the Trinity. In the process, a vocabulary has arisen which resonates with the Chalcedonian Definition. What does this suggest about the connection between Christ and the Trinity?

Yet as we saw with tritheism, the 'simultaneous multiplicity' of trinitarian doctrine can easily slip out of balance. Another major departure from orthodoxy is that of modalism, whereby God is thought to be an undifferentiated being who appears in different 'modes'. This belief is thought to have originated in Asia Minor in the late second century, and it developed into two types. In chronological modalism, God acts like a 'shape-shifter', moving from 'Father' mode, to 'Son' mode, then 'Spirit' mode for the sake of revelation. You might have encountered this thinking in the metaphor of 'water': God comes in three different forms (ice, water and steam). As water cannot be in all forms at the same time, this image undermines Jesus's revelation that Trinity is who God is. In functional modalism, each divine person is thought to have a designated activity; for example, Creator (Father), Saviour (Son) and Sanctifier (Spirit). This is also inadequate, as Scripture narrates a drama of three divine persons, not just three distinct actions, and each person works appropriately, but not exclusively, in distinctive ways (e.g. the incarnate Son died on the cross, not the Father, but the whole Trinity is at work in salvation). It is also important to remember that a divine 'person' is not understood to be an 'individual' or 'distinct site of consciousness'.

> In his work 'Against Praxeas', Tertullian (160–220), disputes the modalism of Praxeas. Tertullian wrote: 'He maintains that there is one only Lord, the Almighty Creator of the world… He says that the Father Himself came down into the Virgin, was Himself born of her, Himself suffered, indeed was Himself Jesus Christ' (1994: 597). Tertullian saw that this was incoherent: 'Either, then, the Son suffered, being "forsaken" by the Father, and the Father consequently suffered nothing, inasmuch as He forsook the Son; or else, if it was the Father who suffered, then to what was it that He addressed His cry?' (1994: 626)
>
> Research task: Do an internet search for 'patripassianism' and find out how it connects to Praxeas' ideas. This will give you a feel for how the interconnectedness of theology can work against Christian belief as well as for it.

Modalism is still around in different forms today. The United Pentecostal Church International (UPCI) in the United States holds to a form of modalist belief, attractively re-packaged as a doctrine of 'Oneness'. Believers are baptized in the name of Jesus – rather than in the name of God the Father, God the Son and God the Holy Spirit (as traditional) – in the belief that the Father and Holy Spirit are Jesus in another form. The language of divine persons is also rejected in favour of divine 'manifestations'. Modalism can equally show up in what is *not* said. For example, some churches focus so heavily on a believer's personal relationship with Jesus that the other divine persons are eclipsed. Modalist preferences can also be detected in some forms of natural theology, where all eyes are on the Father as Creator, to the detriment of the

Word and Spirit, or in political theologies that separate the radical actions of Jesus from the Father. The latter tends to create a static, anti-materialism view of creation, and a soteriology which echoes Arius's version of the ethical imitation of Christ.

What is needed is a better appreciation of how the Father, Son and Spirit relate to one another. Extending our example of a triad can be useful here. When you hear a chord you are not just hearing simultaneous co-existence, the like of which happens if you detect two different smells in the same room. You are hearing tones encountering each other in mutual relations of likeness and attraction (Begbie, 2000: 23). In the West, these relationships are created by a compositional system called diatonic tonality. This organizational structure is hundreds of years old and supports most (if not all) popular music today. The tonal centre (Tone I) is the first tone in a stepwise motion of tones called a 'scale', and it configures how all the tones relate to one another in an orderly way. There are three tones within the scale which create a very strong sense of musical coherency: Tone I (the tonic), Tone IV (the subdominant) and Tone V (the dominant). Both the dominant and the sub-dominant point to the tonic, but the sub-dominant does so less strongly.

> ### Tip
>
> Search for 'MMMBop' by Hanson on YouTube. One of the reasons why the chorus is so strong is that it has the chord progression I, IV, I, V. If you listen a few times you will recognize the 'home' sensation of chord I, and the 'homing' quality of chord V. Once you have identified this structure, you will be able to hear it in many other popular songs.

This bit of theory can give us an experiential bridge to another crucial aspect of trinitarian doctrine: the divine persons are only distinguishable by the different relationships that they have with one another. It can also demonstrate an important difference between (most) Eastern and Western theologians on this matter.

If we were to focus on how, when we hear a triad, we hear one sound that is made up of three tones, we would be analogically close to Eastern trinitarian theology. The main thinkers here are the three Greek Fathers (also called the Cappadocian Fathers): Basil of Caesarea (330–79), Gregory of Nyssa (332–95) and Gregory of Nazianzus (329–89). They argued that one divine substance is common to all three divine persons. Yet even though all the persons are divine, the Father is the fountainhead of all things – including the Son and Spirit, who derive their divinity from the Father in equal, but different, ways: the Father begets the Son and breathes out the Spirit. (This is a little like how, in a triad, we hear that the first tone – the 'home' tone – gives different weightings to the third and fifth tones.) The begotten/ breathed delineation is not pernickety: it prevents the theological difficulties that would follow from God having two Sons.

If, on the other hand, we were to concentrate on how three tones in a diatonic triad are related to one another, we would be analogically close to Western trinitarian theology. Augustine (354–430) is the Latin giant here. He gave attention to how the divine persons are defined by their relationships. In triadic terms, we could say that the Son (Tone V) is weighted and drawn towards the Father, his 'home' (Tone I) – for Christ's deepest desire is to respond positively to the Father, who has begotten him and sent him to estranged creation for the purposes of reconciliation. So far, so Eastern. However, Augustine also gave a distinctive role to the Holy Spirit and this set in motion a train of events that has deeply harmed church unity.

Imagine, for a moment, that you hear simultaneously two tones that are five tones apart (e.g. a C and a G). They interpenetrate in your hearing, but this is not enough to make you aware of the kinds of diatonic relationships are in play. It is only by inserting a tone in between them (in this case, an E) that a triad is formed, and you become perceptually grounded in musical connections. The middle tone is therefore essential if the relationship between the tones either side of it (the C and G) is to be clarified. It also means that, in a sense, the middle tone is equally related to the other tones. This perceptual experience can be an entry point into a key part of Augustinian trinitarianism: the Spirit (the middle tone, E) binds the Father (the 'home' tone, C) and Son (the 'homing' tone, G) together in love. This emphasis on relationality tied in with another of Augustine's arguments – that the Spirit proceeds from the Father and the Son (Jn 20:22 being one of his principal proof texts). This is called the 'double procession' of the Spirit, and by the ninth century this idea was so embedded in the worship of the Western church that the Nicene Creed was altered, without consultation with the Eastern church. The so-called 'filioque' clause, which stated the double procession of the Spirit by adding the phrase 'and from the Son', unfortunately still causes division today.

A criticism often levelled against Augustine's presentation of the Spirit as the 'bond of love' is that this de-personalizes the Spirit. Sarah Coakley, who views the Trinity as a simultaneous dynamic of divine persons, suggests that it is the Spirit who ensures the viability of the Trinity as a whole. She writes:

> The Spirit is the vibrant point of contact and entry into the flow of [God's] divine desire, the irreplaceable mode of invitation for the cracking open of the human heart. The Spirit is the constant overflow of the life of God into creation: alluring, delighting, inflaming, in its propulsion of divine desire. But the Spirit is no less also a means of distinguishing 'hiatus': both within God, and in God's relations to us. It is what makes God irreducibly three, simultaneously distinguishing and binding Father and Son, and so refusing also the mutual narcissism of even the most delighted of human

lovers; because its love presses not only outwards to include others, but also inwards (and protectively) sustains the 'difference' between two. (2013: 30)

Coakley thus understands the Spirit to displace 'mutual narcissism' within God by '[conjoining], and yet [keeping] distinct, the love between "Father" and "Son" within the Trinity' (in Shortt, 2005: 82). This action also ensures that God endlessly, ecstatically overflows into the world. (To refer back to our musical example: the presence of the middle tone, the Spirit, allows a whole system of diatonic relationships – not just the relationship between Father and Son – to spring into being and draw listeners in.) Working pneumatologically in this way, Coakley promotes a creative 'hiatus' in God which nevertheless never threatens the unity of God. In Chapter 4 we look at how Coakley begins trinitarian reflection with the person of the Spirit, through meditative prayer. Suffice to say here that, in addition to anchoring trinitarian reflection within the lived experience of Christians, Coakley's prayerful approach reminds us that God's relational life of self-giving love means that God is open to loving the world and that the Trinity is bound up with salvation history.

Karl Rahner (1904–84) is famous for contributing to our understanding of how God in 'his' internal being (the essential, ontological or immanent Trinity) relates to the whole way in which God works in the world to redeem and restore it (the economic Trinity). Their correspondence is summarized in what has become known as 'Rahner's Rule': 'The "economic" Trinity is the "immanent" Trinity, and the "immanent" Trinity is the "economic" Trinity.' This axiom allows Rahner to affirm that there is no other God 'behind' the economic Trinity, a God who might be completely at odds with the life manifested in Jesus. To take our triad in one last direction: if you were to hear a recording of a triad played on a piano, you would know that you are hearing a piano, and not, say, an electric guitar, because there is a direct correlation between tonal timbre (the characteristic sound of a tone) and the shape, size and construction of the instrument that produces it. In doctrinal terms, it is as if God's eternal life is like an unimaginable musical instrument, the size, shape and construction of which we know nothing about, who 'sounds' in the economic Trinity. This analogy is still inadequate (as all analogies are); for one thing we need to guard against any sense of 'two Trinities'. Nevertheless, it reassures believers that the economic Trinity reliably flows from the true character of God.

Key points

- The doctrine of the Trinity – that God is a relational life of giving and receiving – makes the best sense of biblical testimony and lived Christian experience.

- The Godhead is united in perichoretic unity.
- Eastern and Western trinitarianism differs.
- The essential Trinity is revealed in the economic Trinity.

Questions for discussion

1 If the word 'Trinity' is not included in the Bible, does this make the doctrine unscriptural?
2 Have you come across analogies for the Trinity before reading this book? Are they vulnerable to any of the trinitarian heresies outlined in this section? In comparison, are musical analogies more or less prone to misdirection?
3 What are the practical implications of the Trinity? For example, how might the trinitarian pattern of sacrificial love and non-exclusionary difference affect our ethics? Our understanding of power?

Melanchthon (1497–1560) – Theological manifesto

'We do better to adore the mysteries of Deity than to investigate them. What is more, these matters cannot be probed without great danger, and even holy men have often experienced this. The Lord God Almighty clothed his Son with flesh that he might draw us from contemplating his own majesty to a consideration of the flesh and especially our weakness. ... Therefore there is no reason why we should labour so much on those exalted topics such as "God", "The Unity and Trinity of God" ... What, I ask you, did the Scholastics accomplish during the many ages they were examining only these points? Have they not, as Paul says, become vain in their disputations, always trifling about universals, formalities, connotations, and various other foolish words? Their stupidity could be left unnoticed if those stupid discussions had not in the meantime covered up for us the gospel and the benefits of Christ. ... How often Paul states that he wishes for the faithful a rich knowledge of Christ! For he foresaw that when we had left the saving topics, we would turn our minds to disputations that are cold and foreign to Christ.' Extract (reproduced in Ford and Higton, 2002: 207).

1. Would Christians be better off not thinking about the Trinity?
2. Is the Trinity 'cold and foreign to Christ' – or separable from soteriology (i.e. the study of salvation brought through Christ, which includes redemption, atonement, sanctification and justification)?

Creation

> ### Task – Listening to the universe
>
> In 2017, NASA released recordings of the 'sounds' of our universe. Special instruments on board various spacecraft had captured the electromagnetic vibrations of stars and planets, and scientists converted these signals into sounds that we can hear. The results are eerily beautiful: soft pulses, harsh whooshes, snatches of melody.
>
> Listen to a few examples: https://www.nasa.gov/vision/universe/features/halloween_sounds.html

The above 'sounds' are reminiscent of an ancient idea called the 'music of the spheres', whereby the 'heavenly spheres were thought to compose through their movements and ratios a music unhearable by us' (Pickstock, 1999: 243). This idea is attributed to a Greek philosopher called Pythagoras, who lived around 500 BCE. The story goes that Pythagoras was walking past a blacksmiths and heard metal being beaten into shape. He noticed that the tones of the struck metal changed in proportion to the metal's weight and that some of the intervals – the octave, fourth and fifth – sounded nice together; their ratios were 'concordant'. Pythagoras had inadvertently discovered musical ratio. He then studied a stringed instrument called a lyre. He realized that halving the length (i.e. giving the ratio of 2:1) of a string produced a tone that was an octave higher, whereas a string that was two-thirds its original length (a ratio of 3:2) produced a tone five tones higher. From these humble beginnings, he created a mathematical cosmology that calculated distances between planets and peacefully regulated the universe's inhabitants. So began what is called the 'Great Tradition' of cosmic harmony, which stretches, in diverse ways, all the way into the Renaissance. Intriguingly, we now know that some of the planets in our solar system have orbital patterns that do indeed follow musical ratios – such as the octave (2:1), perfect fourth (4:3) and perfect fifth (3:2). (Take, for instance, two moons going around a planet. The moon closest to the planet may orbit it twice as fast as the outer moon, in which case their orbital ratio is 2:1.) It would seem as if we are 'pre-tuned' to enjoy the structure of our environment.

Augustine went daringly further and used musical ratio to measure the relationality of the Godhead (i.e. the state or condition which makes God, God – in the way that 'manhood' makes a man, a man). To Catherine Pickstocks's mind, this meant that Augustine '[created] the widest vision of attunement: the individual human body in its own musical ratios (*musica humana*) can be attuned to the suffering body of Jesus on the cross, which brings the whole universe into harmony (*musica mundana*) because it is attuned perfectly to the rhythms of the Trinity' (Fiddes, 2013: 374). Here is a musical hint that the doctrine of creation is tightly connected to Christology, soteriology and the Trinity.

No doubt you could provide countless other examples – perhaps from science, simple observation or personal experience – that demonstrate how our universe is intricately ordered. Yet the realities of dissonance and suffering should also immediately be acknowledged. Creation is not at present fully harmonizing with the life of God, but its ultimate status is anticipated in the scarred body of the risen Christ, who embodies the glorious hope of Second Creation – Romans 8:21. (We will return to some of these themes later in this chapter and again in Chapters 6 and 7.) Until that time, the world remains characterized by order, albeit one marred by suffering.

Creation and creativity

In the Hebrew Bible, God creates by bringing order to chaos – either artistically like a potter (Gen. 2:7, Is. 29:16, Jer. 18:1-6) or master builder (Ps. 127:1) or by subduing chaotic forces (Job 3:8, Ps. 74:13-15, Is. 27:1, Zech. 10:11). Crucially God creates all things, including the sun and moon (Gen. 1:1-5) which were worshipped by Israel's pagan neighbours. Creation is not therefore divine, but it is created by God who pronounces it 'very good' (Gen. 1:31).

One of Christianity's oldest nemeses – Gnosticism (from the Greek, *gnosis*, meaning 'knowledge') – disputed these last points. This is an umbrella term that covers great philosophical and historical complexity, but baldly speaking it posited an absolute division between God and the world. This dualism came out of a belief that a lesser god, the 'demiurge', created the physical world; God made the spiritual world and redeemed people out of materiality, which was construed as evil. Hints of this heresy are around today in the popular Christian teaching that the soul escapes the prison of the body through death and goes 'home' to heaven, whereupon it receives a purely spiritual body (the physical body having been scrapped). There is minimal support for such views in the Bible. Rather, material creation is highly valued by God, human beings are soul–body composites and believers wait for the 'redemption of [their] bodies' (Rom. 8:23). (We pick up on these themes later in this chapter and again in Chapters 6 and 7.)

Irenaeus and Theophilus (d.183–5) fought tenaciously against gnostic doctrine. For them, 'the claim that the ontological autonomy of matter marked a fundamental limit on God's sovereignty was inconsistent with Christian confidence in God's power to save, and they posited *creatio ex nihilo* [creation from nothing] as a means of affirming that no reality was ultimately capable of thwarting God's will' (McFarland, 2014: 19). Creation was not a naked act of power, however; it was the product of God's will and desire for something different to flourish in unity with the

Godhead, for its own good as much as God's glory. Creation is also partly given for the delight of humans, who are made in the 'image of God' (Gen. 1:27). As we will see in Chapter 7, this phrase has a long and complicated history, and its meaning is still up for debate. The traditional view is that humans are 'created as God's unique counterparts and hence God's representatives on earth, embodying, as creatures and alongside other creatures, the action and presence of God in and to the world' (Begbie, 2008: 202). One of the ways that humans do this is by themselves being creative. Human creativity is not of the same ilk as divine creativity, of course; for one thing, humans work with pre-existing materials whereas God creates *ex nihilo*. But the artistic work of 'making other' echoes God's act of making the world.

Reflective task – Divine and human making

Theologians down the centuries have found it helpful to think of creation as God's 'handiwork'. But do humans have a 'hand' in it somehow? Trevor Hart asks this question in his book *Making Good: Creation, Creativity and Artistry*:

'Having acknowledged and underlined the uniqueness and incomparability attaching properly to God's role as "Creator", we may nonetheless understand certain acts of human *poesis* [making] … as contributing directly to the fulfilment of this project, adding to the sum of things extant in the world in ways consonant with the pattern of God's own creative vision for it, drawing on an excess of value and meaning invested in it by God in the beginning, but deliberately left for creaturely discovery, unpacking and realization. … the world is not and cannot be "given" all at once; its inner reality "unfolds in time," shaped and reshaped by what Creator and creature together make of it, … Ultimately, … this dynamic of "making together" finds due fulfilment only in the flesh taking and self-substitution of God himself for us in Christ, … Acts of genuine human *poesis* must therefore be finally grounded and participant in the once-for-all priestly and *theopoetic* humanity of Christ and viewed from the perspectives afforded by the doctrines of Trinity and redemption' (2014: 8–9).

1. How does Hart think we should handle the presumed affinities between divine and human 'making'? How might the differences be interwoven?
2. Why does God generously resolve to include humanity's participation in the outworking of his creative vision for the world?
3. Should Christian artistry involve duplication or transformation? Or both?

The God–world relation

Reflection – The nature of music

Do you think music is more bodily than ethereal or vice versa? Or both? What is guiding your answer?

In response to the above questions, people will usually say several things. Some people stress that music is an embodied art form. In production, wood is scraped, metal is blown through and vocal cords are twanged; in reception, our brains and nervous systems are affected by music's sounds and rhythms; in society, music augments bonding. Other people may prefer to stress the 'spiritual' side of music. With its combination of wordlessness and expressive power it seems to give its hearers an intuition of, if not direct access to, a transcendent reality. Regardless of one's religious beliefs, it can induce feelings of being taken 'out' of ourselves and experiencing 'other-worldliness'. Yet others would want to stress that music is all of these things: it is a physical art form that can give us intimations of the divine. It is this last experience that most resonates with the doctrine of creation, which says that while the world is not itself God, it can bear witness to God in its own creaturely way (cf. Ps. 19:1-6, Ps. 69:34, Ps. 104:108). When God and the world are collapsed into one another, the world – as much as God – loses distinctiveness and therefore integrity (Rom. 1:25).

Some theologies, for instance, risk divinizing the world by bringing God too 'close' to creation. For example, pantheism – an eighteenth-century term for ancient beliefs – generally holds that God, often non-personally conceived, is in some way identical with, and goes no further than, the physical universe. Some forms of natural theology, which naively 'read off' divine characteristics from humanity or the natural world, also risk immanentism. (They would also, quite rightly, suffer the ire of critics like Stephen Fry, whose 2015 tirade against theodicy went viral.) To go to the opposite extreme, some theologies 'distance' God from the world. Deism, which began in the late years of the seventeenth century and thrived throughout the eighteenth and nineteenth centuries, argued that God created the world but is uninvolved with its ongoing existence.

Something of a middle course between pantheism and deism is detectable in process thought (founded by Alfred North Whitehead, 1861–1947). As the name suggests, reality is thought to be an organic process of growth. Building blocks, called 'entities', can influence one another only through persuasion. As God is an entity (albeit one that outlasts everyone and everything else) that can be influenced by creatures, 'he' evolves in partnership with creation. This approach ties in with evolutionary theory and produces a powerful theodicy (evil results from poor choices, not from God), but traditional theists argue that it bears little relation to the biblical witness that God is sovereign and ontologically distinct from creation, and that the latter is contingent upon the former. This means that the relationship between God and the world is asymmetrical, i.e. creation utterly depends upon God but not *vice versa*; if creation ceased to exist, God would remain God. On the one hand, this asymmetry could be taken to demonstrate a divine heartlessness which undercuts real relationship between God and the world. Alternatively, it serves as our guarantee that God has no agenda in making the world. As we learnt in the previous section, God is always already fulfilled as Trinity and so has no need to compensate for some lack or use the world for self-actualization. This divine freedom from ulterior motives means that God's love for the world is authentic and utterly trustworthy.

Creation as Christ-centred

> *Reflective task*
>
> Listen to 'Good Vibrations' by The Beach Boys (or if you prefer rap/hiphop, 'Good Vibrations' by Marky Mark and the Funky Bunch). Both songs are freely available on video-sharing sites like YouTube. Why do you think we instinctively connect vibrations with relationship and community? Are there traces in our use of language that support such a connection?

Pantheism, deism and process thought all reconfigure a central claim of classical Christian thought: God's transcendent freedom resources his immanence. In other words, it is because God is ontologically distinct from the world that 'he' is able to create, sustain and be present in all created reality, without change to 'himself'. Scripture testifies that in Jesus Christ God indwells his creation without being absorbed into it, and it is in Christ, and through the sanctifying power of the Spirit, that creation becomes alive in and through God's life – without becoming divine itself (Cor. 8:6, Heb. 1:3, Col. 1:15-20, Eph. 1:10). This pattern of 'unity in difference' flows from the trinitarian nature of God. As Jeremy Begbie expresses it:

> [Jesus] enacts who God is. He will be the clue as to *why* God created the world. Further, because he belongs to God 'on the inside', Christ is the central key to understanding *how* God relates to what he has made. God the Creator will act in a Christlike way and no other way. Further still, the declaration is that in this person God's purposes for all things have found their fulfilment. Christ is not only the instrument of God's plans

for creation, he embodies those plans. ... *The Spirit's role ... is to bring about in the world what has already been achieved in Christ and in so doing to anticipate the final re-creation of all things.* (2008: 189–90, emphasis in original)

We will explore these ideas by using two types of acoustical resonance. We explain and apply these terms in straightforward ways.

Activity – Conductive resonance

1. Strike a fork hard on a table top and listen to the sound.
2. Dampen the vibrations. Then strike the fork again and, while it is still vibrating, press the handle against the bone behind one of your ears.
3. How do the sounds compare?

With conductive resonance, a resonator (e.g. the bone behind your ears, the bridge of a guitar) starts vibrating because it is in physical contact with something else that is vibrating (e.g. a struck fork, a plucked guitar string). The resonator amplifies the sound, making the tone sound fuller than if the fork was struck, or the string plucked, in mid-air. Many patristic and medieval theologians, set within the Great Tradition, worked with this kind of acoustic imagery. They thought, for example, about the body of Jesus acting as a divine sounding-board, conducting the vibrant life of God in, through and to creation. Augustine – who agonized over whether music, as made and heard, was a spiritual help or hindrance – gave a figurative twist to the musical instruments mentioned in Psalm 57:8 ('Awake, my soul! Awake, O harp and lyre! I will awake the dawn'). Set as an Easter liturgical text, he hears the Father addressing the incarnate Son (the harp and lyre representing his divine and human natures, respectively) and celebrating his escape from the bonds of death (Fowler and Hill, 1992: 331). For the medieval polymath Hildegard (1098–79), our bodies are instruments and Christ is the 'Song of God' 'whose music restores harmony to divine-human relations' (Epstein, 1999: 99, 100). A wider incarnational aesthetic is found in *Protreptikos,* written by Clement of Alexandria (b.150, d.211–15):

A beautiful, breathing instrument of music the Lord made man, after his own image. And He Himself, surely, who is the supramundane Wisdom, the celestial Word, is the all-harmonious, melodious, holy instrument of God, what, then, does this instrument – the Word of God, the Lord, the New Song – desire? To open the eyes of the blind, and unstop the ears of the deaf, and to lead the lame and the erring to righteousness, to exhibit God to the foolish, to put a stop to corruption, to conquer death. (in Holsinger, 2001: 33)

Here, Christ as the 'holy instrument of God' brings eschatological healing, justice and wholeness by being the new song of creation, announcing redeemed relationship between God and all things 'by virtue of his embodied redemption of humanity' (Holsinger, 2001: 34). As a result, God's Kingdom on earth is amplified through him (Lk. 4:21). This is not to be thought of as a 'heroic' action on Jesus's part; it is possible because the Spirit enables Jesus to respond to God in full obedience, submission and love.

Thus far we have offered an account of: God as Creator (triune, lover of difference-in-unity), what kind of world God creates (an ordered, good one) and how God relates to it (through the incarnate Son and the Spirit). Another type of resonance can help us consider the destiny of all creation and the human role in this. (We attend to the intrinsic value of non-human creation in Chapter 7.)

Activity – Sympathetic resonance

Place your fingers on your larynx (commonly known as the 'voice box'), which is located at the front of your throat. Put your other hand either on the crown of your head or the back of your neck. Then sing a low note followed by a high note. You should feel different strengths of vibration.

What is happening is that the vibrations created by your vocal cords are travelling through the air inside your body up into different cavities in your throat and head. This causes them to vibrate and produce a sound.

Musical tones are more accurately called 'complex tones' because they are made up of many sound frequencies. We hear the lowest and strongest frequency – called the fundamental frequency – as tonal pitch (i.e. how high or low we perceive the tone to be). But in addition, there are other sound waves called overtones. They occur in a series (called the 'harmonic series'), and they get progressively weaker in strength. Overtones are usually too weak to be heard as pitch – although they can be produced deliberately (with great skill) and accidentally (just ask any parent whose child is learning the violin). Mostly they make their presence felt by contributing to the timbre, or tone-colour, of the tone. On a guitar, for example, a played string will cause an un-played string that is tuned an octave higher to vibrate sympathetically, because there is a strong acoustical resemblance: the latter is the first overtone of the former. The sympathetic response is weaker than the stimulus, but it still adds its own timbral characteristics to the sound of the first, initiating string.

The priest and metaphysical poet, George Herbert (1593–1633), picked up on this acoustical phenomenon in his hymn for Easter Day. He wrote, 'His stretchèd sinews taught all strings, what key is best to celebrate this most high day' (quoted in

Fiddes, 2013: 373). Paul Fiddes, who has written an account of wisdom based on the concept of attunement, notes that this line goes further than the imaging of Christ as an instrument: Herbert is suggesting that the 'vibrating strings of Christ's body can awaken vibrations in all other bodies' (Fiddes, 2013). In this way, human bodies and gifts can be tuned ('stretchèd') to the sound of Christ.

In terms of resonance, the incarnate and resurrected Son, Jesus Christ, resounds human nature as God intends it to be. As people respond sympathetically to Jesus, their individual timbres are 'set off' by the 'resonating agency of the Spirit', who enables them 'to live according to the liveliness intended ..., the specific form of [their] intended resonance of life with God' (Begbie, 2013: 166). The reverberations continue, as newly alive humans also help 'set off' the multi-timbral resonance of creation, energizing its own non-identical repetition of God's love. All these manifold differences are gathered into Christ's response to the Father, in anticipation of the ultimate re-creation of all things at the eschaton. We will return to this image of God being 'all in all' (1 Cor. 15:28) in Chapter 7.

Key points

- The one, triune God has created and sustains heaven and earth out of will and love; God is ontologically distinct from creation; creation is good but not divine.
- Creation is made through, redeemed by, and will be perfected in Christ. The Spirit anticipates the Second Creation.
- Theologians understand the God–world relation in different ways.

Question for discussion

1 Why might somebody find deism, pantheism or gnosticism attractive?

Extended task – Music as natural theology: Where to begin?

The extent to which music is disclosive (it reveals metaphysical reality) and affective (it gives a sense of direct connection to God) is an important topic in contemporary scholarship. Jeremy Begbie argues that hermeneutics must start with 'normative' theological criteria and then move out to musical engagement (2013: 214). Brown and Hopps consider this to be 'theological imperialism' (2018: 190); music must speak first. Debate the above question, drawing on the two texts below.

Text 1 – Jeremy Begbie, Music, Modernity and God

'Can music reveal the grace of the Creator directly? ... The answer ... is, of course, yes. But we can hardly avoid adding: no such claims can be made with any integrity, let alone be justified, without recourse at some stage to language and concepts – indeed, at some level, to language and conceptuality regarded as normative. ... This is not to deny for a moment the possibility of musical performance mediating the divine; it is only to point out that contending for this possibility will immediately press us to ask what shapes and grounds such a contention. Otherwise, the claim is vulnerable to being dismissed as vacuous' (2013: 216).

Text 2 – David Brown and Gavin Hopps, The Extravagance of Music

'What we wish to defend is the ability of music, for all its context-dependent character, to engender an awareness of something "other" (transcendent), which is at the same time incapable of complete description (ineffable). ... Begbie seems to assume that that hermeneutic priority is determined by sequence or order alone, as if beginning the act of interpretation with works of art rather than Christological criteria necessarily entails ceding authority to the former. Yet surely it is possible to engage in criticism from a Christian perspective without first of all seeking to fix the meaning of aesthetic forms in advance' (2018: 6, 192).

Chapter summary

In this chapter we have:

- Learnt that doctrine, rather like biblical hermeneutics, involves imaginative 'meaning-making'. It is grounded in, safeguards, and constructively responds to, divine revelation.
- Learnt that heresy compromises the divine and/or human life seen in, and offered to us through, Jesus.
- Used music-making and music-hearing to excite a passion for doctrine and encourage critical thinking about how doctrine can shape people's lives.
- Introduced three foundational Christian doctrines, their inter-connections and connections to further doctrines and wider issues.

Recommended reading

Begbie, Jeremy (2008), *Resounding Truth: Christian Wisdom in the World of Music*, London: SPCK.

Begbie, Jeremy, and Steven R. Guthrie, eds. (2011), *Resonant Witness: Conversations between Music and Theology*, Grand Rapids, MI: Eerdmans.

Begbie, Jeremy (2018), *Redeeming Transcendence in the Arts: Bearing Witness to the Triune God*, London: SCM Press.

3
Touching: Embodiment and the shaping of desire

Theology as full-bodied thought

In this chapter we reflect on the nature of touch and our embodied experience of the world. It goes without saying that we are all embodied, but theology's (sometimes necessary) tendency towards abstract thought can seem to downplay the importance of that embodiment. We deliberately say 'are embodied' rather than 'have bodies' because the latter phrase has unfortunate overtones of ownership and control. It may encourage us to distance the 'true us' from our bodies, and so forget the inevitability and inherent vulnerability of bodily life. We can detect this pattern in the way that Western cultural views of the body often use a term like 'soul' to designate a core-self that is distinguishable from the body. In fact, for much of the Christian tradition, it is precisely the *connection* between body and soul that is important.

This absolute distinction of soul and body, known as dualism, also contributes to the common misunderstanding – present both inside and outside the church – that theology is a purely cerebral exercise which renders one 'so heavenly minded as to be of no earthly use'. If you are reading the chapters in sequence, we hope you will recognize how misleading that perception can be. One of the contentions of this book is that in encountering theology we find our gaze drawn *toward* embodied life, not away from it. Drawing out this argument will involve addressing not just the falsely detached picture of theology, but a much broader and more forceful perception of Christianity as fundamentally anti-body. This is powerfully expressed by Simone de Beauvoir:

> The Christian is divided within himself, the separation of body and soul, of life and spirit, is complete; original sin makes of the body the enemy of the soul; all ties of the flesh seem evil .... And of course, since woman remains always the Other, it is not held that reciprocally male and female are both flesh: the flesh that is for the Christian the hostile Other is precisely woman ... the fact of having a body has been considered, in woman, an ignominy. (Simone de Beauvoir, 1984: 168)

Admittedly some strands of Christianity have negatively evaluated embodiment, as experienced in a fallen world, and the suggested reading at the end of this chapter will introduce you to the complexities involved in these discussions. Here, however, we will start the work of demonstrating that detaching Christianity from bodily life is unnecessary and moves against the grain of fundamental theological claims. We will do this by examining the nature of embodied life as an inescapable, God-given and God-inhabited context of theological insight. After all, all theology is contextual, and fuller reflection on the nature and influence of that bodily context is vital if our theologizing is to be honest about creaturely reality. While we all experience the world through our senses, that doesn't mean our experience is always the same. In practice we may vary in the extent of our sensory experiences – the acuity of our hearing, the precision of our sight – or may in fact be entirely without one sense (e.g. have no sense of smell, a topic to which we return in Chapter 5).

We begin with some reflection on the nature of touch itself. Then we will explore one of the most inescapable elements of our bodily condition – sex, and how it relates to gender. These issues are enormously controversial in contemporary debate, and we cannot hope to be comprehensive. To begin to explore the issues we'll discuss two broad approaches: a complementarity between the two sexes (a working together of two distinctly different types); and a questioning of the effect and theological basis of a rigid binary of male and female. In very different ways both these approaches seek to draw upon our experience of embodiment, desire and identity. They give a theological account of the human condition (theological anthropology). It is both important and difficult to do justice to the fleshly life of incarnation. This chapter provides the opportunity to reflect on a series of interesting, and sometimes provocative, images of the flesh of the crucified Christ. We then explore in more detail some ways in which Christian thought has connected the nature of embodied desire with divine love. Finally we draw some of these strands together by seeing how they connect with another embodied practice – prayer – as discussed by the Anglican theologian Sarah Coakley.

The importance of touch

A number of contemporary theologians have reflected on the need for renewed attentiveness to the body, and to the sense of touch in particular. James B. Nelson is an American theologian who argues that the doctrine of incarnation requires Christian theology and practice to place human bodiliness at the centre:

> Body theology is not primarily a theological description of the body. Nor is it principally an ethical prescription for how we ought to express ourselves physically. Rather, and most simply put, it is doing theology in such a way that we take our body experiences seriously as occasions of revelation.

An incarnational faith boldly proclaims that Christ is alive. In other words, God continues to become embodied in our common flesh in saving, healing, liberating, justice-making ways. (1992: 9–10)

Our everyday embodied experiences are therefore both a site and a source of theology. This is not surprising once we realize the importance of embodiment – particularly the intimacy and immediacy of touch – to Christ's public ministry. Lisa Isherwood and Elizabeth Stewart highlight this when they insist:

Christian Scriptures naturally have embodiment at their heart. From the moment when Mary agrees to give birth to a special child, bodies become sites of revelation and redemptive action. Jesus' mission is begun with touch, by water and by a dove. People are touched and healed, they are forgiven and healed. The dead are raised and a woman shows her love through her anointing and massaging of Jesus' feet. The life of Jesus as told by the evangelists is a very physical one; he was not a philosopher simply engaging the minds of people on his wanderings through the land. Here was a man who held people, threw things in anger, cursed things making them wither and cherished people back to life. Here was an incarnate/embodied being. (1998: 11)

A life of discipleship lived in imitation of the Jesus who touched the untouchable will inevitably involve Christians in the unspoken power and frightening ambiguity of touch. The priest and theologian Sam Wells speaks movingly of the power of touch for Christian ministry:

I'll never forget the moment when I was told my mother was about to die. I was 18 years old and three thousand miles away. Of course I was in pieces. A man I hardly knew started telling me mindless irrelevancies about when his grandmother had died, but none of that mattered because what he did was to cup my hands in his and to look at me and hold me. He touched me. And I was not so afraid. And ever since then when I've trained people for ministry and discipleship I'd said to them, 'maybe the most important thing in your ministry will not be what you say but the way you learn to hold people and to touch them when they are afraid'. (2011, xvii)

Exercise – The touch of Christ

Read some of the following accounts of touch in the New Testament:
    Four times in Matthew 8–9 (often with synoptic parallels), Jesus heals with touch. Notice that the woman in Matthew 9:20-23, Mark 5:21-43 and Luke 8:40–9:6 merely needs to touch the fringe of his cloak. Luke 4:40 perhaps demonstrates the commonality of this touch in showing Jesus touching many in the crowd. John's only touching miracle evokes the creation of Adam from the dust (Gen. 2:7, Jn 9:6-7). The practice of healing through touch is then found in the ministry of the disciples (Acts 6:6, 9:17-18, 28:8).

Touching may echo the priestly blessing of laying on of hands found throughout Leviticus (Lev. 1:4, 3:2, 4:15, 16:21). Thus Jesus lays his hand on children (Mt. 19:13-15, Mk 10:13-16, Lk. 18:15-17) and calms his disciples after their fearful reaction to his transfiguration (Mt. 17:7, but notably not in Mk 9:2-8 or Lk. 9:28-36). This calming touch is echoed in Revelation 1:17. Touch may also convey or confer authority (1 Tim. 4:14, Heb. 6:2), or a gift (Acts 8:17, 2 Tim. 1:6). For good or ill it binds together (1 Tim. 5:22). Touch informs and verifies; it places an object within our control, our grasp where in John 20:17 Mary Magdalene is enjoined from 'holding on' to Jesus, just a few verses later (24-29) Thomas is visceral in his touch of the risen Christ.

Some of the above texts may already be familiar. If so, had you noticed how central touching is to moments of revelation and redemption? Reflect on your own experiences of touching and being touched. It can be calming, inspire confidence, give recognition and communicate a range of complex emotions, or it can be an unwelcome encroachment on personal space and bodily integrity. Touch and the withdrawal of touch can also be instruments of power and control, manipulation or abuse. What might Jesus's own vulnerability to touch and his ministry of touching have to say about the nature and importance of our embodiment?

Key points

- Our embodiment provides both a site and a source for doing theology.
- Reflecting on Jesus's practices of touch can highlight important, and sometimes neglected, elements of his mission and ministry.
- Touch is powerful, but that power carries significant ambiguities and risks.

No generic body: Complementarianism and queer theologies

A gnostic dualism of body and soul, spirit and matter, is inimical to the foundational declaration in Genesis that God beholds 'his' creation as good. Moreover, as we shall see in our final chapter, the Christian vision of the Kingdom of God is properly understood as a renewal of creation. Everyday Christian life is a sacramental participation in that renewal. This means that worship and the sacraments are not, as spiritual exercises, non-bodily; they involve our entire being. As the third-century church father Tertullian (160–220) wrote, in opposition to gnostic denials of Christ's genuine human body, the greatest honour has been put on our 'flesh'.

> There is not a soul that can at all procure salvation, except it believe while it is in the flesh, so true is it that the flesh is the very condition on which salvation hinges. And since the soul is, in consequence of its salvation, chosen to the service of God, it is the flesh which actually renders it capable of such service. The flesh, indeed, is washed, in order that the soul may be cleansed; the flesh is anointed, that the soul may be consecrated; the flesh is signed (with the cross), that the soul too may be fortified; the flesh is shadowed with the imposition of hands, that the soul also maybe illuminated by the Spirit; the flesh feeds on the body and blood of Christ, that the soul likewise may fatten on *its* God. They cannot then be separated in their recompense, when they are united in their service. (1885, §8: 551)

With this final line Tertullian makes it clear that human bodiliness is not merely a vehicle for the salvation of the soul. It is the celebrated subject of redemption itself.

Likewise, contemporary theology emphasizes the embodied nature of our life and experience. The qualifier 'embodied' has become so frequent in contemporary writing that it may seem pointless. A theological emphasis on embodiment is useful for both what it affirms and what it denies. It affirms that we *are,* rather than simply *have,* bodies. It moves against trends that have been damaging to Christian thought and practice: abstraction, dualism, other-worldliness and cerebral rationality. A theological valuation of materiality must not succumb to simple dualism. Nor can it base itself on the reductive 'materialism' of New Atheism. If it is to escape banality, it needs to say something about the particular shape and texture of that embodiment. In other words, unpacking *how* we are embodied is as theologically important as affirming *that* we are embodied.

The problem of how to read nature

As God's beloved creation, our world retains something of the goodness, beauty and purpose of its original state. Theologians and Christian denominations differ significantly over the extent and severity of the marring of this condition after 'the fall'. Nonetheless, if the bodiliness of the human condition is integral to Christianity, we must ask the question, 'How do major facets of our experience of embodied life generate theological insight?' One feature of creaturely life that most occupies contemporary theological anthropology is that of our being sexed. The phrase 'being sexed' may strike you as strange or clumsy. How is this different to 'sex' (often male or female) or 'gender' (masculine and feminine)?

If you have never thought about it before, these terms may appear synonymous: males 'naturally' exhibit masculine features, and females, feminine characteristics. Yet our use of quotes on 'naturally' should give you pause. The term 'natural' functions not merely descriptively (establishing matters of incontestable fact) but normatively (articulating what *should* be the case). Once we invest a particular condition of creaturely life with the status of 'natural', it implies that this is something that is divinely intended: it is a permanent and positive element not only of our fallen world, but also of the world as God would have it be. When some theologians describe our gendered identity in ways that connect characteristics or behaviours to the maleness or femaleness of our bodies, and especially if they describe gender differences as 'natural' there are at least three moves being made, each of which needs unpacking:

1. A conflation or necessary connection between sex and gender.
2. An account of the current created order as in some way retaining and expressing the eternal will of God. That 'nature-as-we-have-it' remains to an important degree 'nature-as-it-should-be'.
3. On the basis of (1) and (2), a vision of maleness and femaleness of the human species as essential and good.

Sex and gender

It is increasingly common to draw a distinction between sex and gender. Sex names the biological given of our condition, commonly split into male or female. Gender is often seen as a cultural construct (i.e. the norms of masculinity and femininity change in different times and cultures). Thus Simone de Beauvoir famously claims, 'One is not born, but rather becomes, a woman' (1984: 18).

In recent debates theologians are just beginning to explore how a variety of 'intersex' conditions unsettle a simple correspondence between sex and gender. Moreover, approximately 1 person in every 2,500 is, in some way, intersex (around the same number as those born with cystic fibrosis). Some people have ambiguous or combined genitalia, others a 'mismatch' between internal and external genitalia. People with Androgen Insensitivity Syndrome (AIS) may qualify as male on the basis of XY chromosomes and the presence of testes, but may also have female genitalia, breasts and broad hips. The vast majority of people with AIS identify as women (Cornwall, 2013: 51–3).

However, as both Susannah Cornwall and Adrian Thatcher note, the pressure placed on intersex persons to identify as either male or female is often a cause for resentment and anxiety. Arguably this pressure would not be present in societies less strongly structured around a normative sexual binary (Cornwall, 2010; Thatcher, 2011: 13). Distinct from intersex experience, theology is really only beginning to take note of trans experience. Transgender and transsexual people may describe their experience as a pervasive sense of having been 'born into the wrong body', they may identify with a gender different from their assigned sex. Some will seek hormonal and surgical treatment to transition from one sex to another.

Church response to intersex and trans experience has been limited, not least because the nature of such experiences is hotly contested. Some seek to understand by speculating on causes, arguing that trans experience arises primarily through psychological conditions, or that there are physiological and hormonal differences, primarily in the brain, which predispose some to 'trans' identity. Some, like Oliver O'Donovan, have argued in the case of trans people that the genital sex should remain determinative. Sexual identity is so basic to the human condition that it is to be regarded as an unalterable natural given (O'Donovan, 1982). Others affirm trans identities, not least because both the church's sacramental practice (especially the eucharist) and its account of the unknowability of God destabilize and displace apparently settled 'gender scripts' (Isherwood and Althaus-Reid, 2009).

These embodied experiences press the question of how one can read theological meaning from 'nature-as-we-have-it'. If one identifies a simple binary of male and female as the created intention of God, then the unusual becomes the unnatural. Intersex and transsexual identities are problematized as deviant, in a way that other uncommon conditions, like left-handedness, are not (at least, not any longer). If 'the natural' is, to some extent, confused and broken by sin, how can human beings, as confused and broken sinners, gain access to, or know, what 'nature-as-it-should-be' is to look like?

'Then God said, "Let us make humankind [ädäm] in our image, according to our likeness; and let them have dominoion over the fish of the sea, and over the birds of the air, and over the cattle, and over all the wild animals of the earth, and over every creeping thing that creeps upon the earth."
So God created humankind [ädäm] in his image,
In the image of God he created them;
Male [zäkhär] and female [n'qëväh] he created them' (Gen. 1:26-27 NRSV).

'Then the Lord God formed man [ädäm] from the dust of the ground, and breathed into his nostrils the breath of life; and the man [ädäm] became a living being' (Gen. 2:7 NRSV).

'So the Lord God caused a deep sleep to fall upon the man [ädäm], and he slept; then he took one of his ribs and closed up its place with flesh. And the rib that the Lord God had taken from the man [ädäm] he made into a woman [ishäh] and brought her to the man [ädäm]. Then the man [ädäm] said,
'This at last is bone of my bones
and flesh of my flesh;
this one shall be called Woman [ishäh],
for out of Man ['iysh] this one was taken' (Gen. 2:21-23 NRSV).

How we read nature both informs and is informed by our understanding of key biblical texts. Take, for example, the two creation narratives of Genesis 1 and 2.

Many theologians have argued that here we find a divinely intended complementarity of male and female. The primary text here would be Genesis 1:27 where God is said to make humanity as male and female *from the very beginning*. However, there is a long and venerable tradition which draws more on the second creation story which treats our maleness or femaleness as secondary. God creates a sexless humanity [ädäm] first (Gen. 2:7) and then differentiates male ['iysh] and female [ishäh] (Gen. 2:21-23). Generic humanity comes first, only followed later by our sexed human nature.

It is possible of course, to read this in complementarian terms. However, in practice this led many in the early church, especially in the East, to posit that sex is a non-essential part of the human condition; a concession that will be undone in heaven. It is not just second in sequence, but secondary in importance. The fourth-century church father Gregory of Nyssa (334–94) famously read the 'garments of skin' of Genesis 3:21, in which God clothes Adam and Eve at their expulsion from Eden, not as a primitive loincloth, but as sexed bodies themselves. Thus sexual differentiation is not only a secondary phase to the creation of the human condition, but also a negative departure from the created intention, as much as is death (Brown, 1988: 294–295; but for the contrary, see Roberts, 2007: 24–28). It then becomes a matter of further speculation whether our gendered and sexed nature will be undone in the eschatological restoration of the body.

Then again, the complementarian position may read the ädäm at the start of Genesis 2:23 as an implicit male source and norm. The NRSV, quoted above, adopts two different translations for the term. In Genesis 1 it renders ädäm as the generic 'humankind', but in Genesis 2 it reflects a long-standing tendency to assimilate maleness and humanity, translating it with the word 'man'. Some other translations go even further, using the proper name 'Adam'. The woman, only later named Eve, is derived from and subject to her origin. This is the emphasis found in Paul (1 Cor. 11:12), and it provides a basis for the hierarchical reading of the second creation story, which describes the woman as 'helper' ('ezer kenegdo, Gen. 2:18, 20).

Yet not all complementarian accounts of a natural and stable binary of sex and gender will place men hierarchically above women (e.g. Pierce, Merrill Groothuis and Fee, 2005; Bird, 2014). Unlike the English word 'helper', the Hebrew 'ezer implies no hierarchy, so 'companion' may be a preferable translation. Indeed, of the twenty-one instances of 'ezer in the Hebrew Bible, sixteen apply the term to God as the helper of Israel. Moreover, the addition of kenegdo to 'ezer means 'in front of', 'in the presence of' or 'as a counterpart', and this suggests a co-equal status of the same essential nature.

Both views have an associated danger. Complementarianism tends towards what is sometimes called 'gender essentialism', which posits an unchangeable essence of maleness and femaleness. It has a tendency to naturalize particular social roles. For example, women are seen as emotional, nurturing, gentle or even submissive; men are seen as rational, strong, courageous or even dominant. Focusing on the primary androgyny of humanity provides a corrective, but it could overemphasize a generic humanity that is markedly different from our current sexed and gendered experience. It may thus inadvertently devalue our present bodily lives.

Queer bodies and the influence of culture

The choice to focus on Genesis 1 or Genesis 2 may be shaped by whether one believes there to be a strong biological foundation to gender difference, or whether one believes gender identity to be socially constructed. We have called the first view gender essentialism. The latter is often referred to as a constructivist view.

Some strong forms of constructivism argue that the very notion of a binary sexual identity is a social invention. In this sense gender is not something we *have* or *are*, it is something we *do*. In Judith Butler's famous phrase, gender is 'performed' (1990: 138). Other theorists suggest that culture inescapably *influences* our view of biology (a weaker form of constructivism), but does not deny the biological any reality outside of cultural *determination* (as Butler seems to do). All constructivist accounts share the idea that we come to our biology with a pair of interpretive spectacles given to us by our social context. Biology and culture are inseparable. Nor are we passive recipients of our social construction; there are subcultures, movements and individuals who bring our cultural construction to light. The most famous example given by Butler is drag:

> 'In imitating gender, drag implicitly reveals the imitative structure of gender itself – as well as its contingency'. Indeed, part of the pleasure of the performance lies in the recognition of a radical contingency in the relation between sex and gender, in the face of cultural configurations of causal unities that are regularly assumed to be natural and necessary. In the place of the law of heterosexual coherence, we see sex and gender denaturalised by means of a performance which avows their distinctness and dramatises the cultural mechanism of their fabricated unity. (1990: 137–38)

Constructivist viewpoints often coalesce around 'queer' theologies. This term includes not only LGBTQI theologies, but also many other theologies which reflect on how Christian practice can challenge and unsettle (i.e. 'queer' as a verb) social values and hierarchies. For example, if we consider dominant social constructions of masculinity, which can entail performances of strength, control, dominance, even violence: What would happen if we allowed Christian accounts of 'power made perfect in weakness' (2 Cor. 12:9), servanthood, peacefulness and gentleness to shape our vision of masculinity?

We know, for instance, that first-century society was founded on performances of gender that were structured around notions of honour and shame. Men were tasked with accumulating honour through great works and obtaining positions of stature; women gained honour through chastity, modesty and domestic talent (most prominently, childbearing). In this world, Paul's claim that Christian relationships are not to be rivalrous or driven by ambition (Rom. 12:10, 2 Cor. 12:20, Gal. 5:20, Phil. 1:17; 2:3) mirrors Jesus's injunction that his followers should not 'lord it over' one another (Mt. 20:25-28, Mk 10:42-45). Similarly, in Roman culture humility was for slaves, it was utterly dishonourable for free men; yet it is this vision of masculinity that most embodies the true humanity made possible in Jesus (Phil. 2:3-11, Eph. 4:2, Col. 3:12).

On a strongly constructivist reading of gender the declaration that 'there is neither male nor female, for all are one in Christ Jesus' (Gal. 3:28) implies a radical erasure of the supposedly 'natural' differences between men and women. It is the direct undoing of Genesis 1:27. There are, of course, other ways of reading the text. Critics object that this appeal to androgyny is an unnecessary conclusion, and the text simply means either that both male and female are equal (an egalitarian reading) or that these distinctions simply no longer matter (an 'adiaphoric' reading – 'adiaphora' meaning things that do not make a difference). However, at the time, these distinctions of sex and gender, ethnicity and social status were all held to be an ineradicable part of the natural structures that stabilized society. They were not to be questioned. Could there be, in Galatians 3:28, a sense of God making all things new in Christ? And if this remaking impacts upon the observable regularities and structures of the world as we see it, to what extent can we continue to assume that 'nature-as-we-have-it' displays something of 'nature-as-it-should-be'? At the very least, these questions are worth asking.

It is important to note, then, that the hierarchy of male over female does not necessarily flow solely from a complementarian biblicism of two permanently established and divinely willed sexes. Indeed, it may come from somewhere else entirely. Thomas Aquinas's (c.1225–74) highly influential account of natural law appears to include the notion that women are divinely intended to be inferior or at least subordinate to men. He draws on Aristotle's account of biology in which there is only one sex with various degrees of perfection – the male being perfect and the woman a failed or imperfect male (Aristotle, 1963, ii.3). This is a good example of the slippery way in which language of perfection and purpose, nature and divine intention, coalesce in theological arguments.

Activity – Biology and culture

Aquinas's claim is laid out in the first article of the q.92, in the first part of the *Summa Theologia*. It is therefore commonly cited as *ST* Ia. Q.92, a.1. Read and discuss his argument, it is available in various places online. Such texts lead the feminist theologian Rosemary Radford Ruether to note that, while we have largely discarded Aristotle's biology, the Thomistic natural law approach which adapts and develops it continues to exert significant influence (1983: 96). However, Aquinas's position is qualified in the third article of q.92. Here women are seen as part of the divinely intended plan from the start. One might read this as complementarian, but more complex or ambiguous on the status of women – while Aquinas accepts Aristotle as a biologist (explaining the nature of female anatomy) he modifies him as a social theorist.

We began this section by stating that a theology of embodiment must be attentive to the particularities of actual bodily existence. We have now seen that theologians read the nature of our bodily existence in a range of ways, and this diversity raises a number of questions for consideration.

Key points

- There has been a diversity of views of the naturalness of sex and gender in Christian thought.
- The creation narratives of Genesis have provided textual support for this range of views.
- The New Testament provides both an appeal to the divinely intended 'nature as it should be' and a vision of God's overturning of supposedly natural ranks and statuses.

Questions for discussion

1 Do you think there will be sex in heaven (both the status and the activity – cf. Mt. 22:30)?
2 Does complementarianism necessarily fall into gender essentialism?
3 Do the testimonies and experiences of intersex and transsexual people represent a decisive challenge to complementarianism?
4 Can Queer theology affirm that the divine intention for humanity is revealed in the world as we have it now?

Body image: Incarnate flesh in art

Artistic depictions of Christian figures (primarily, though not only, of the crucified Christ) can illuminate the promise and perils of a theology of embodiment. The unsettling power of art has to come with a warning. While some of the images we suggest below may be familiar to you (in which case, we hope you will see them afresh due to the previous discussions), some of the images you are going to look at may be uncomfortable. Others you may find very distasteful.

It is not our intention to shock or offend, and we certainly would not suggest that such reactions are necessarily inappropriate. The challenge of both a theology of embodiment and the art we are about to explore, however, is to bring to explicit reflection our own positive and negative instincts about our bodily condition, and to explore how we might make theological sense of those reactions. We hope you will share your reactions with others (if you are in a classroom or online discussion setting), though for some it may take time to identify and process what you think. All images are available via image search engines online.

1 Search the internet for two of the most famous and influential depictions of the visceral fleshliness of Christ: Michelangelo Merisi da Carvaggio's *The Incredulity of St Thomas* (*c.*1601–2), with the disciple's penetrating touch; and Matthias Grünewald's depiction of an agonized, pock-marked and emaciated crucified Christ in his *Isenheim altarpiece* (1512–16). Where are your eyes focusing when looking at the Caravaggio painting? To what extent does this cohere with your previous imaginings of the scene? In the Isenheim altarpiece we find something of the potency of combining the image of the crucifixion with the New Testament image of union with Christ. Grünewald's altarpiece was originally located in the chapel of the Hospital of Saint Anthony, where patients suffering from ergotism (commonly known as St Anthony's fire) would be cared for as they underwent hallucinations, skin infections and peeling, convulsions and nerve damage, and often death. There is huge theological potential in this image. We might, for example, take it as a challenge to pastoral presence, or reflect on the magnitude of the claim of the incarnation. Just as, in baptism, Christians are united with Christ's death and resurrection (Rom. 6), so they are caught up in Christ's identification with the vulgarities and mundane qualities of fleshly life. Hardly surprising, then, that after the horrors of the holocaust came to public consciousness, artists like Graham Sutherland (*Crucifixion* 1946) and Geoffrey Clarke (*Crucifixion* 1954) would take inspiration from the contorted figuration of Christ in Grünewald's altarpiece. Does Grünewald's image resonate with you? Is it relevant to your own thought and context?

2 Other depictions of Christ may question the way that much of Western Christian imagination renders Christ as a white male (like the blue-eyed

Hollywood icon Jeffrey Hunter in the 1961 film, *King of Kings*). Consider the following and try to articulate your immediate reactions.

   a Edwina Sandys's *Christa* (1975): one of the first sculptures depicting a female crucified figure.

   b *Crucified Woman* by Almuth Lutkenhaus-Lackey was displayed outside of the Bloor Street United Church in Toronto over Lent in 1979. It coincided with a Good Friday service on the theme of battered wives. The pastor said, 'When people were shocked that a woman was depicted as crucified and concluded that we were implying that Jesus was a woman, we realized that in our teaching of the incarnation we had implied that to become human was to become male' (Pastor Clifford Elliot quoted in Clague, 2005: 51).

   c *Christine on the Cross* by James Murphy was exhibited at the chapel of Union Theological Seminary in New York over Easter, 1984. By positioning the crucified figure in a spread-eagled way, does the sculpture highlight issues of sexual brutality and exploitation?

   d Perhaps tying in with our discussion of patristic androgynous or non-gendered visions of human identity, consider Colin Middleton's *Christ Androgyne* (1943).

   e The vulnerability of flesh is also figured in Mary. See Kiki Smith's *Virgin Mary* (1992) with its vivid lineaments of exposed muscle. Smith states that 'there are certain poses of the Virgin Mary, with her arms out to the sides, and if you actually stand that way, it opens you up and makes you vulnerable, maybe even compassionate' (Kimmelman, 1998: 73).

3 Moving to issues of race and ethnicity may elicit some interesting reactions.

   a What do you think of the Goan artist F. N. Souza's 1959 *Crucifixion*, which moves away from the classical tradition of depicting not just a white Christ, but a serene and passive, perhaps painless figure. Does the violence of the grotesque spectacle of crucifixion also give unsanitized expression to themes of divine wrath and vengeance?

   b Now consider Paul Fryer's *Blue Pieta* (2010) which focuses attention on the executed flesh of a criminal (notably a black male).

   c Fryer's *A Privilege of Dominion* (2009) seeks further challenge in displaying a crucified Ape. Obviously Fryer does not intend to represent the 'historical' event itself, but do you think it effectively unsettles the androcentric (focused on the male), eurocentric (focused on white Western people) and anthropocentric (focused on humans at the expense of non-human animals) construal of much of Christian thought?

4 Combining the 'profane' with the 'sacred' may strike some as inappropriate, even blasphemous. This raises the question of whether a focus on human flesh

can ever be excessive in Christian theology? For some, perhaps most famously in some Islamic critiques of Christianity, the very notion of incarnation produces this effect. The following two pieces are likely to arouse the strongest reactions. [optional]

a One highly provocative piece, by Chris Ofilli, combines issues of race and sexuality alongside the use of perhaps the most profane of substances – pornography and bodily excreta. Ofilli's *The Holy Virgin Mary* (1996) explores the representation of black women in contemporary culture through a highly sexualized and fertile Mary, whose nourishing and sexually exposed breast is constructed from a lump of elephant dung (covered in resin), and is surrounded by abstract angels (cut-outs of women's buttocks from pornographic magazines) contrasted against the gold background redolent of Eastern Orthodox iconography.

b Andres Serrano's *Piss Christ* (1987) displays significant deliberate ambiguity. The bare description of the photograph – a crucifix suspended in a tank of the artist's urine – might produce revulsion, but it may also enliven the sense of the humiliation of Christ, or a broader critique of the demise and disregard of religion.

Desiring bodies: Sexual desire and asceticism

We now turn to the intensity of bodily life, in particular to the excitement and promise of erotic touch and the power of sexual desire. Here, Christianity is popularly understood to hold two pictures in tension: contemporary conservative 'family values' and a strong valorization of celibacy. It is often taken for granted that the latter is borne of a hatred not only of sexual desire, but also of the body itself. This is, at best, a partial picture, as female celibacy was often a radical challenge to patriarchal structures that kept women in frequently fatal reproductive servitude. Christian teaching on celibacy is also complicated. For example, Jerome (347–420) suggests that marriage is to be praised only because it creates more virgins (1894, *To Eustochium* §20). He argued that, in the highly stratified ordering of gender roles with which he was familiar, women would struggle to develop a life of prayer and virtue amid the chaotic demands of 'prattling infants'. Yet to the extent that a woman attained godliness through sexual abstention, she ceases to live as a woman: 'Observe what the happiness of that state must be in which even the distinction of sex is lost. The virgin is no longer called a woman' (1894, *Against Helvidius, On the Perpetual Virginity of Mary*, §22 pp. 344–5).

Many church fathers exhort virginity as mirroring, or participating in, the purity of God. Gregory of Nyssa (d.385/386) even compares marriage with a tragic mistake which leads to betrayal and lust, greed, anger and hatred (1894, *On Virginity* §4). Yet the fact that Gregory wrote this treatise while married should give us pause for thought: there must be something more than simple rejection of sexual desire and matrimony going on here. In fact, for Gregory marriage is the pinnacle of our much wider relentless drive to escape death. Ironically, however, it is riven with the traumas of the deaths of spouses and children. The life of virginity is to be highly prized because it bypasses this anxiety and trauma. Thus Gregory's view does not focus on notions of impurity or the theological taintedness of sexual acts.

The same cannot be said for Augustine (354–430), who has a reputation for being the arch nemesis of contemporary theologies of the body. Perhaps most famously, he imagines, in Book XIV of the *City of God*, a condition of sexual reproduction before the fall, in which Adam's penis is fully under the control of his rational will. Only after the fall does lust take over, and the penis gains, in more modern parlance, 'a mind of its own'. Augustine's strong focus on disordered desire, an account of the image of God (*imago dei*) as found not in the flesh but in human rationality (*De Trinitate* §12.7.12), and a number of strikingly negative depictions of enslavement to lust and sexual desire (most famously in the *Confessions*) have led some to the view that Augustine has a deep hatred of all things bodily. A fuller and more accurate reading of Augustine, however, sees that it is the disordered heat of uncontrolled desire that Augustine regards as evil, not sexual organs or differentiation themselves. After Augustine the Christian tradition is then sometimes understood to move from negativity to ambivalence, as seen in the occasional, grudging acceptance of sexual pleasure as a modest good within marriage, as taught by Aquinas, Luther and Calvin. Here we can only scratch the surface of this long and complex history.

Divine and human love

It is not hard to see how the equation of desire with disorderliness, irrationality, lustfulness and the stain of sin represents a problematic inheritance for Christianity. Even so, many theologians have tried to distance God from erotic desire. This is seen most profoundly in the qualitative difference drawn between divine love and human love. The Lutheran theologian Anders Nygren (1890–1978) famously distinguishes between human love (*erōs*) and divine love (*agapē*). *Erōs* is driven by lack, it is conditional, acquisitive and moves upwards; *agapē* flows from gracious abundance, is radically self-giving and descends. Human beings only love insofar as we get something out of it, whereas God loves without regard for return. Our love is tainted with lust, whereas God's love is pure and holy. The Christian life is one that escapes or annuls *erōs*, and the unattainable ideal, which places the Christian in constant need of grace, is the calling to *agapē*. For Nygren, Luther empties the Christian account of love of any notion of desire. He evocatively claims:

> In relation to God and his neighbour, the Christian can be likened to a tube, which by faith is open upwards, and by love downwards. All that a Christian possesses he has received from God, from the Divine love; and all that he possesses he passes on in love to his neighbour. He has nothing of his own to give. He is merely the tube, the channel, through which God's love flows. (Nygren, 1953: 735)

However, other theologians have been cautious of this separation. Augustine himself seems to propose a synthesis of *agapē* and *erōs* in divine *caritas* (sometimes translated, somewhat unsatisfactorily, as 'charity'), and this trend continues in medieval theologies. More recently, theologians have either reshaped or rejected Nygren's stark separation. We will mention here two protestant theologians, the Reformed Karl Barth and the Lutheran Eberhard Jüngel, and one Catholic theologian, Pope Benedict XVI. Similar to Augustine's earlier synthesis, Karl Barth (1886–1968) accepted much of Nygren's contrast, but nonetheless argued that it is inevitable that 'as long as men love, even though they are Christians they will always live within the framework of *erōs*, and be disposed to effect a synthesis between [them]' (*CD* IV.2: 737). Barth still views this ultimately as a conquest of *erōs* by *agapē* (see *CD* IV.2: 751), and thus as a final diminishment of *erōs*. Moving further away from Nygren, Eberhard Jüngel (b.1933) claims that loving another person breaks down the separation between the two types of love, just as it breaks down the ungenerous possessive 'self-having' of an individual. He denies the view that the practice of *agapē* is devoid of legitimate concern for oneself, which he terms 'self-relatedness'. 'Love without some kind of self-relatedness would be, both in theory and in practice, an enormous abstraction and at the same time a falsification of the love from above' (1983: 319, n15). The mutuality of the event of love transforms the acquisitive grasping that often characterizes *erōs*, but does not diminish the role of *erōs* in the process. 'In love one I and another I encounter each other in such a way that they become for each other beloved Thous. I must always become a Thou to the other person if I am not to be had by the other I in such a way that I become an It' (1983: 320). Thus the mutuality of the erotic encounter of love is a form of mutual surrender which means that I only 'have myself' not as a possession but, we might say, as a gift. 'In the event of love the being of the lovers … [is] preserved by the beloved Thou and not by the loving I' (1983: 320).

Pope Benedict XVI's (b.1927) first papal encyclical *Deus Caritas Est* (*God Is Love*, 2005) argues against both Nygren's separation and the atheistic critique of Friedrich Nietzsche that Christianity has 'poisoned *erōs*'. Instead, Christianity rejects an intoxicated and undisciplined *eros* [which] is not an ascent in 'ecstasy' towards the Divine, but a fall, a degradation of man. Evidently, *eros* needs to be disciplined and purified if it is to provide not just fleeting pleasure, but a certain foretaste of the pinnacle of our existence, of that beatitude for which our whole being yearns. (*Deus Caritas Est* §4)

Thus, Pope Benedict XVI claimed, 'far from rejecting or "poisoning" *eros*, [Christian practices of purification, maturation and renunciation] heal it and restore its true grandeur' (§5). This is not so much a flight from the body as a proper unification of body and soul. In this way, not only is human *erōs* intertwined with the other-regarding movement of *agapē;* more justice can be done to the way in which God's love for humanity and creation is itself *erotic* – it is spoken of as passionate attachment, of spousal love (Benedict cites Hosea and Ezekiel), of bodily delight (Song of Songs) and even of sexual ecstasy (some mystical traditions). We must proceed with care here, as such claims can all too easily sanitize the oppressive or violent elements of these traditions – Hosea 2 and Ezekiel 16, for example, deploy spousal imagery not to show the conjugal beauty of mutual affection, but rather to image sexual violence (stripping as a precursor to, and metaphor for, rape) as an expression of divine wrath against an 'adulterous' (idolatrous) Jerusalem.

Learning to love

Of note in Benedict's theology is the motif of disciplining or educating desire. This is called asceticism, from the Greek word *askesis* which refers to a training programme. It is not equivalent to 'works righteousness' (Luther's famous phrase for any claim that human achievements earned salvation) and it is relevant to the married life as much as that of the celibate, as Gregory of Nyssa makes clear in his treatise *On Virginity*. Crucially, rather than downplaying or diminishing the erotic, Gregory's asceticism is an *intensification* of desire, as human desire is set aflame when it participates in God's inner trinitarian *erōs*.

The problem with sinful desire is not that it desires too much, but that its desire is misdirected and insipid. It is not that there is too much focus on the erotic, but that we are too easily satisfied with pale imitations of the genuinely desirable. In departing from the radiance of divine love, we become emaciated and shadowy figures whose stagnant desires reveal our nakedness only through a dysmorphic lens of shame. This issue, and therefore asceticism, is as relevant today as it was for Gregory. Margaret Miles has argued that a recovery of such practices can unsettle the ways we insulate ourselves from political crises, social injustices and our own individual wilful ignorance of the challenges of contemporary life.

Short fasts, fasts from the media, physical exercise, disciplined prayer and meditation, periods of celibacy, of solitude, or of silence: any of these practices – all as good for the body as for the soul – can overcome the habits and minor additions of everyday life and result in increased clarity of insight and what St Thomas Aquinas called 'the renewal of the senses'. (Miles, 2008: 18)

What do you think of Miles's suggestion? There are many ways of articulating the potential of asceticism:

1 One of the differences between the detox fasting in the secular world that follows upon seasonal excess, and the Christian practice of fasting, is that the latter aims at sanctification rather than merely counterbalancing excess. Post-festive detox, like the fabled Roman vomitorium (memorably reinstated in the decadence of the Capital city in the popular *Hunger Games* trilogy), merely gives licence to more consumption.

2 A media saturated with unattainable standards of beauty (malnutrition is really the only way for most women to achieve a 'thigh-gap') produces, especially in the young, a susceptibility to a sustained identity crisis, anxiety and an inability to see one's body as it truly is. In comparison, Christian asceticism may teach believers how to see, and therefore how to love, the bodies they have been given. Of course, this is to identify forms of asceticism which discipline, but don't destroy desire – which chasten, but don't loathe, the body. It is more about healthy balance than the kinds of religious practices – starving, flagellation, even self-castration – that also exist within the complex history of Christian ascetic practice.

3 It has become popular to see in contemporary life a kind of unruly stimulation of desire (from incessant war-making to the excesses of consumerism); ascetic discipline could be a way beyond the damage this does to our bodies and our communities.

4 It is possible to ground asceticism in a fulsome account of everyday, mundane bodily encounters. In an evocative essay, 'The Body's Grace', Rowan Williams argues that both celibacy and marriage are sacramental means of experiencing grace. Below is an extract:

> Grace, for the believer, is a transformation that depends in large part on knowing yourself to be seen in a certain way: as significant, as wanted.
>
> The whole story of creation, incarnation, and our incorporation into the fellowship of Christ's body tells us that God desires us, as if we were God, as if we were that unconditional response to God's giving that God's self makes

in the life of the Trinity. We are created so that we may be caught up in this, so that we may grow into the wholehearted love of God by learning that God loves us as God loves God.

The life of the Christian community has as its rationale – if not invariably its practical reality – the task of teaching us [that, to teach us] to so order our relations that human beings may see themselves as desired, as the occasion of joy (311–12).

... [T]he body's grace itself only makes human sense if we have a language of grace in the first place; this in turn depends on having a language of creation and redemption. To be formed in our humanity by the loving delight of another is an experience whose contours we can identify most clearly and hopefully if we have also learned, or are learning, about being the object of the causeless, loving delight of God, being the object of God's love for God through incorporation into the community of God's Spirit and the taking-on of the identify of God's child.

It is perhaps because of our need to keep that perspective clear before us that the community needs some who are called beyond or aside from the ordinary patterns of sexual relation to put their identities directly into the hands of God in the single life. This is not an alternative to the discovery of the body's grace? (317) (Williams, 2002: 309–21).

Key points

- Christian views of sexual desire are diverse.
- Christian accounts of sexual desire have historically contained strongly negative components, as well as positive insights.
- The disciplining and shaping of desire in asceticism can be an *intensification*, not a *negation*, of desire.

Questions for discussion

1 Has Christianity been too negative about sexual desire? Is this still the case?
2 Is it better to hold *agape* and *eros* distinct?
3 Do disciplines of asceticism imply a disparaging view of the body?
4 What aspects of modern life can work against asceticism?
5 What is the role of the church community in asceticism?

Sarah Coakley on the transformative embodiment of prayer

In this final part of the chapter we move from the ubiquitous experiences of touch, sex and desire to reflect on what may appear at first a more limited and rarefied experience – the embodied practices of Christian prayer, as explored in the innovative work of the Anglican theologian Sarah Coakley (b.1951). Her work opens up many of the themes that we consider in this book – Christian feminism, embodiment, asceticism, desire, sex and gender, the meaning and integration of faith, passion and reason, and how the mystical tradition of the 'spiritual senses' offers transformed ways of knowing and responding to God. Through it all, she highlights how many actions and ways of thinking are infused with gender assumptions and prejudices.

For Coakley, prayer is not distinct from theological knowing. Indeed it is in doing justice to this embodied religious practice that one can gain a sense of the theological transformation of human desire, sex and gender. This is seen most clearly in her book, *God, Self and Sexuality: An Essay 'On the Trinity'* (2013). In this book, the first part of a projected series entitled '*On Desiring God*', Coakley puts forward a 'vision of God's Trinitarian nature as both the source and goal of human desires' (6). In exploring the work of the Spirit in prayer, she reconceives the ultimate significance of sexual desire and gender in relation to the trinitarian God. For her – and, she argues, for significant stretches of Christian tradition – 'the questions of right contemplation of God, right speech about God, and right ordering of desire all hang together' (2).

The embodied discipline of prayer

It would be hard to underestimate the importance, for Coakley, of 'an explicitly prayer-based access to the workings of the divine' (6), and so it is good to be clear about what her approach does and does not involve.

Prayer is not:

- an isolated or final source of theological evidence. Prayer-based thinking is bound up with other ways of Christian 'knowing' – biblical exegesis, Christian tradition, reasoning and testing by the criterion of 'spiritual fruits' (25).
- reserved for a spiritual elite. Participating in the life of God through prayer is indispensable for any Christian who wants to be grafted into the body of Christ.
- self-centred. Prayer is the springboard which catapults Christians into building up the church, wider societies and world communities.

- disembodied. Prayer is not an abstract flight of the soul or mind from the body. It can be at its most profound and transformative when engaging the whole of the person – body and mind, conscious and unconscious – in silent contemplation.

Prayer is:

- theologically necessary. Coakley argues that 'particular graced bodily practices [can], over the long haul, afford certain distinctive ways of knowing' (19).
- Trinitarian and pneumatological. Through prayer, the Spirit 'incorporates' Christians into the life of God. (And as we saw briefly in the previous chapter, Coakley argues that such Spirit-led activity accounts for the equality and mutuality of three divine persons, and links the Trinity to its 'true matrix' [104] in worship).
- embodied. It is through the thoroughly embodied practices of contemplation and prayer – kneeling, breathing, maintaining silence and focus, for some the tactile handling of prayer beads, Catholic rosary or Orthodox *chotki* – that the encounter with God, and thus the transformation of our desires, takes place (43).

Coakley especially draws on, and thinks 'through', the silent waiting upon God in ecstatic or wordless prayer. This particularly deep kind of prayer focuses on surrendering to, and depending on, God. As a Christian feminist, Coakley is very aware that placing a high value on silence and vulnerability can be dangerous. When imperatives to 'surrender' or 'submit' are mapped onto contemporary fallen gender practices, it can and has encouraged the subjugation of women. She therefore qualifies her position carefully. She emphasizes that both men and women need to be transformed by a creaturely submission to God. Likewise, power is rejected in the sense of control or being controlled and understood as 'non-worldly' vulnerable freedom to allow oneself to be brought into relationship with God. With these provisos in place, contemplative prayer in the Spirit is, Coakley suggests, an excellent way to learn and practise submission to God and reap the rewards of participating in God's life.

Key to Coakley's vision is the claim that the radical exposure to God and 'graced vulnerability to the Spirit' (86–7) in prayer does not diminish our humanity. God does not somehow 'push' human beings out of themselves through prayer. Far from it; there is a gradual sense of 'the Spirit's … subtle reconstitution of human selfhood in God' (23). At the same time, a 'darkening' of the mind and 'disconcerting reorientation of the senses' (19) are a sign that the human capacity to think, feel and imagine is being transformed.

Gender, too, is reshaped by the Spirit in prayer. Commenting on Romans 8, Coakley argues that 'it is not I who autonomously prays, but God (the Holy Spirit) who prays in me, and so answers the eternal call of the "Father", drawing me by various painful degrees into the newly expanded life of "Sonship"' (55–56). 'It is', says Coakley, 'as if prayer in the Spirit both takes up and transforms the usual societal implications of gender, and renders them both labile and cosmic' (115). How then does Coakley understand the Spirit, prayer and desire to be connected? Rejecting Nygren's separation of *erōs* and *agapē* (30), she argues that as 'deep prayer in the Spirit … veritably magnetizes the soul towards God' it may also reasonably be understood as intrinsically 'erotic' in a 'primal sense' (13) – for the Spirit is 'that which propels the one who prays towards union with the divine, but whose tug is felt analogously also in every erotic propulsion towards union, even at the human level' (14).

The ordering of desire and the challenging of gender binaries

As advocated by Coakley, deep prayer therefore pushes Christians to recognize and celebrate how sexual desire and desire for God are 'entangled' (to use one of her favourite expressions). For Coakley, this conclusion is shaped by the thought-provoking witness of patristic writers – especially Gregory of Nyssa, Augustine and Dionysius the Areopagite – as much as by common contemplative experience. Both Gregory and Augustine relate their desire for God and their emerging trinitarian thinking with their 'concomitant views about men and women, gender roles and the nature of "erotic" desire' (2). Despite their differences on the nature and permanence of gender, they converge on a 'vision of God predicated … on the notion of incorporative, transformative, divine *desire*' (2). And for all three, in somewhat different ways, the mystery and transcendence of God yields a kind of 'ecstatic yearning' in which the human and divine meet in ways which cannot leave our current ordering and experience of gender untouched.

This vision powers one of Coakley's central aims: injecting new life into the tradition of Christian Platonism. For Plato, 'erotic' desire has a propulsion to the eternal form of 'beauty', and that one must therefore spend one's life in an attempt to climb back up the ladder of (progressively purified) desire to that divine realm where full '"revelation" of beauty may occur' (8). What is distinctive about the *Christian* Platonism of Gregory, which Coakley draws on in particular, is that the ascetic ascent towards God is not characterized by a growth in clarity and light, a culmination of the traditionally male virtue of rationality, but instead by a profound apophaticism – an ascent into 'dark womblike receptivity' of mystery and obscurity (286). We shall have much more to say about mysticism and apophaticism in chapter 5. For now we should note that there is a kind of double playfulness in Gregory's view: the eschatological and ascetic loss of sexual differentiation is intertwined with the complex mixing and transformation of forms of activity and knowledge that were, for many Platonists and others of Gregory's time, split along lines of gender – the 'male' intellect and *erōs,* and the 'female' affective (i.e. for want of a more precise term, emotional) response. Not only that, but the paragon of the male ascetical prowess for Gregory is always his beloved and adored sister Macrina, which elicits in Gregory himself the most womanish of responses – passion (281–3). In an earlier essay on the subject, drawing on the groundbreaking historical work of Verna Harrison, Coakley states:

> It is not that either 'body' or gender are disposed of in this progressive transformation to a neo-angelic status. Rather, as advances are made in the stages of virtue and contemplation, eros finds its truer meaning in God, and gender switches and reversals attend the stages of ascent: the increasingly close relation to Christ marks … a shift from active courting of Christ as 'Sophia' [wisdom or knowledge] to a passive reception of embraces of Christ as the bridegroom. (2002: 165)

Coakley's contribution turns, in large part, on the idea that the Holy Spirit progressively purifies human desires through bodily, ascetic practices of prayer. In prayer, the pray-er senses something of God's desire, God's 'active plenitude and longing love' (331) for creation. When theology starts in this place of longing, it is possible to detect some kind of analogical alignment between divine and human desire. It starts to make sense for 'sex [to be] really about God – the potent reminder woven into our earthly existence of the divine "unity," "alliance" and "commingling" that we seek' (316). This means that 'sexual desire is … the "precious clue" woven into our created being reminding us of our rootedness in God' (309). But it also means that 'the contemplative encounter with divine mystery will include the possibility of upsetting the "normal" vision of the sexes and gender altogether. It will also include an often painful submission to other demanding tests of ascetic transformation – through fidelity to divine desire, and thence through fidelity to those whom we love in this world' (310).

Divine desire is not distinct from, but itself undergirds and is translated into, human desire. This is no simple process, for 'no one', Coakley says, 'can move simply from earthly, physical love (tainted as it so often is by sin and misdirection of desire) to divine love – unless it is *via* Christological transformation' (316). God's grace is needed, if Christians are to make this move and share in the life of the Trinity. In practice, this means that the 'double pressure of the Spirit' (21) both builds up and breaks down Christian desires, such that a right desire for God is intensified (i.e. a Christ-like, non-grasping after God) and fallen desires are chastened and purged. For Coakley, therefore, the embodied experience of prayer is the ascetic practice in which wider human embodied experiences of desire, sex and gender are transformed through grace. It is not that a disembodied mind gains mastery over unruly flesh (though some of Augustine's language comes close to this picture), rather 'the contemplative task … is itself a refiner of human desire: in its naked longing for God, it lays out all its other desires – conscious and unconscious – and places them, over time, into the crucible of divine desire' (52).

Those seeking practical advice will be disappointed as Coakley does not expand on what transfigured gender might look like here and now. Nor does she explain what it might mean for humans to 'transgress' (57) maleness and femaleness while staying rooted in the created goodness of male and female bodies. That would be a massive task indeed, and perhaps too prescriptive for a work committed to the open-endedness of prayerful encounter with the divine. There is, of course, much more to be said on these issues. Coakley's work nonetheless brings to the fore the need for a theology of sex and gender to be attentive to the multisensory nature of both faith and religious practice. Her work is just one interesting way of doing justice to the full-bodied richness of theology; connecting the intensity of touch with the deepest elements of human identity and experience.

Key points

Coakley argues that Spirit-led contemplation:

- emphasizes the leading activity of the Spirit in human transformation
- brings to consciousness the 'messy entanglement' of sexual desire and desire for God
- reorders the passions to a fundamental passion for God
- recasts gender away from stereotypes

Questions for discussion

1 How might ascetic and prayerful practices become distorted, either by over-enthusiasm, evolution into hedonism, or association with a particular gender?
2 Coakley suggests that coming at the notion of desire *via* the divine provides an alternative to, and a deeper perspective than, entrenched liberal and conservative positions on sexuality. Do you agree?
3 Coakley offers little direction about what theologically transformed gender looks like. What do you think?

> **Extended task**
>
> How would you put into practice the theological stance you most sympathize with regarding gender and sexual identity? Write a set of pastoral or policy recommendations for a church, considering, for example:
>
> Sexual relationships / marriage
>
> Ordination / publicly recognized ministry
>
> Pastoral care – for example, of a trans or non-binary person encountering criticism, abuse or rejection from their family, friends or church.

Chapter summary

The experience of touch leads us into some of the most profound and difficult questions of human identity. We have seen that:

- Christianity affirms the God-given goodness of bodies, sex and gender.
- Theologians have differed significantly on how to understand the relationship between 'nature-as-we-have-it' and 'nature-as-it-should-be'.
- Christianity speaks in various ways of the education and transformation of human desire by God's grace.
- Many theologians look to traditions of asceticism as a critique of, and alternative to, the problematic formations of desire in late modern consumer capitalism.

Recommended reading

Coakley, Sarah (2013), *God, Sexuality, and the Self: An Essay 'On the Trinity'*, Cambridge: Cambridge University Press.

Cornwall, Susannah (2013), *SCM Core Text: Theology and Sexuality*, London: SCM Press.

Felker Jones, Beth (2007), *Marks of His Wounds: Gender Politics and Bodily Resurrection*, Oxford: Oxford University Press.

Loughlin, Gerard, ed. (2007), *Queer Theology: Rethinking the Western Body*, Oxford: Wiley-Blackwell.

Roberts, Christopher (2007), *Creation and Covenant: The Significance of Sexual Difference in the Moral Theology of Marriage*, London: T&T Clark.

Thatcher, Adrian (2011), *God, Sex, and Gender: An Introduction*, Oxford: Wiley-Blackwell.

4
Tasting: Savouring the sacraments

Intensification

By now you will have noted that this book intertwines two motifs: story – the narrative of Christian belief about God, the world and human history; and sensibility – the full embodied experience of the encounter with the God that story articulates. Indeed, these are not entirely separate motifs. Stories are not mere mental events, but sensory experiences that shape our everyday perceptions. The early church used two different Greek terms to categorize the truth of the Christian story: *kerygma* and *musterion*. *Kerygma* was the teaching proclaimed to all – a public message. In contrast *musterion* referred to the message that was a teaching for the community only – with connotations of secrecy and privacy. From *musterion* comes 'mystery' and 'mystical'. As we will see more in the next chapter, the mystical is a deepening of the knowledge of God available in the *kerygma*. It also issues a health warning against absolutizing that knowledge or turning God into an object that can be grasped by human knowing. It is instead a negation of the claim to know God fully. In the Bible God reveals the mystery: whether it is discerning the true meaning of a vision or a dream (Dan. 2:47), understanding the deeper meaning of a parable (Mk 4:11) or, paradigmatically, the dramatic unveiling of the divine in the transfiguration of Christ (Lk. 9:28-36). We may often use the term 'mystery' to refer to something puzzling or opaque. Its theological use is different: a mystery is something with a deeper reality and meaning beneath the surface. In the writings of Paul the term 'mystery' is often used to describe the providential plans of God for creation. God's plans are being revealed in the event of Christ and the empowering presence of the Holy Spirit (e.g. Rom. 16:25-27, 1 Cor. 2:6-9). That is the story of God's 'grace' – a term of enormous range in theology, but here meaning:

- the abundant generosity of a God who is goodness itself
- who gifts that goodness to creation to restore it

- who chooses to achieve 'his' saving work significantly with and through Israel and the church
- who makes this choice not because of human merits or abilities but because of 'his' generosity

The encounter with the grace of God is deepened, for many forms of Christianity, in the sacraments. Sacraments are a special way God has chosen to impart grace: to enable hope, to sustain believers, to give a taste of creation's eschatological future. Sadly, sacraments have also been the source of considerable controversy and division within the worldwide church. It may seem the height of theological abstruseness to find in sacramental theology such heated divisions over 'mere rituals'. But 'rituals' are only to be so dismissed if we view them as private inconsequential habits done by other people. Many people today assume that they have no rituals, or that they make their own sense of meaning without connection to any wider stories. We'll see that this often isn't really the case. The importance of sacramental theology and the passionate debates to which it gives rise flow from the sacraments' function – i.e. deepening the experiential journey into God's mystery. Sacraments are intensifications of the encounter of God in faith that bind believers to the Christian story of grace.

Savouring God, knowing ourselves

The sense of taste is more essential to knowledge, in particular theological knowledge, than we might at first assume. We are tasting creatures. Some of the first explorations we all made of our world were to taste, smell and touch. Before our eyes could focus or our brains make sense of the cacophonous noise coming to our ears, we knew the world and gained a sense of security through parental embrace, warmth, scent and the taste of milk. From milk to soil, baby toys to furniture, we all explored the substances of our world through taste.

The English language gives us a restricted sense of what it is to know. Our language shapes our expectations of what it is to know. The English language focuses on rational and disembodied knowing. That has not always been the case. The Latin *sapere* means both to understand and to have flavour, to experience taste. The Latin *sapientia,* translated as wisdom, means to know and to taste. Spanish is somewhat better at showing this intimate connection between knowing (*saber*) and savouring (*sabor*). We are *Homo sapiens,* that is we are wise, knowing, tasting creatures. When we talk of 'having taste' we tend to frame this in terms of aesthetic discernment, or understand it as an entirely subjective preference. Here too, Western societies have tended to regard intellectual knowledge as having primacy over aesthetic knowledge.

Sight has also been regarded as more important than taste. However, this unduly separates the experience of knowing – not least because in traditional Christian thought God is truth, beauty, goodness and being in their utmost. In God there is no separation of knowledge and beauty, truth and taste. The multisensory knowledge of God is an encounter of love. As we will see in Chapter 6, for St Augustine human knowledge of God is a practice of love in which 'I love a light of a certain kind, a voice, a perfume, a food, an embrace' (Augustine, 2009: 10.vi.8: 183). For the Psalmist, humanity is enjoined to 'taste and see that the Lord is good' (Ps. 34:8). For Friedrich Schleiermacher (1768–1834) the essence of religion is 'a sensibility and taste for the infinite' (Schleiermacher, 1988: 23).

While we understand ourselves as having five senses, previous generations regarded taste as an intensification of touch. There is an intimacy to taste not shared with some other senses. In taste the barrier between knower and known, us and the rest of the world, is fully permeable. The sensitivity of taste can detect nuances invisible to the eye. Ingesting nutrients constitutes our bodies, which are determined in their health, size and shape by the transformation of food into flesh. The philosopher Ludwig Feuerbach is said to have been the originator of the saying 'we are what we eat'. For Feuerbach, the phrase was meant to assert a pure materiality without a spiritual dimension: we are not driven by big ideas or spiritual goals, but are just eaters driven by the need to sustain ourselves, wandering through a landscape of scarce food with incessantly rumbling stomachs. For Christianity, it is equally true that we are what we eat, but this is understood in a very different way. As eaters we are creatures of a superabundant God, embodied in a material world gifted to us for our own delight in the beauty of the divine, and restlessly hungry until sated in worship of 'him'.

The Orthodox theologian Alexander Schmeemann (1921–83) thus states:

> Man must eat in order to live; he must take the world into his body and transform it into himself, into flesh and blood. He is indeed that which he eats, and the whole world is presented as one all-embracing banquet table from man. And this image of the banquet which remains, throughout the whole Bible, is the central image of life. It is the image of life at its creation and also the image of life at its end and fulfilment: ' ... That you eat and drink at my table in my kingdom'. (Schmeemann, 1973: 11)

The downplaying of smell, touch and taste as sources and types of knowledge stems back to ancient Greek philosophical traditions. Vision and hearing detect and respond to stimuli far outside the body, which allows critical distance and scientific objectivity. Smell, touch and taste are, by contrast, more intimate and bodily (Korsmeyer, 1999: 68). These 'lower' senses are therefore associated more with human tendencies for excess and vice. The irrational drive to gluttony is controllable in the balanced soul only through rigorous disciplining of desire. In our own day, both sides of this find their extremes. On the one hand asceticism in dieting reaches vicious excess in the false dysmorphic 'knowledge' of our bodies experienced in eating disorders. On the other hand, there is the toxicity of reaching for some synthetic or highly sugared 'treat' as a short-term alleviation of stress. Epidemic levels of depression and obesity curtail true knowledge and delight of ourselves and the world. Compared to sight, discernment is more central to taste. I cannot see much difference between a light and dark roast coffee, or between caffeinated and decaffeinated versions, but even the briefest of tastes will give me all this information and more. Taste is more than a highly sensitive apparatus for detecting chemical components, however. It involves a wider discernment, as in taste we cannot separate biology and culture. Our tastes have been formed by a variety of cultural factors, the types and quantities of food available, the cultural heritage that shape to those dishes, and the familial eating habits that we see around us. Ethnic, class and familial identities mix together in complex dietary expressions. Handed-down recipes provide lived continuities with distant or deceased relatives; 'comfort foods' reassure and relax us. Food practices from the complex symbolism of Japanese tea ceremonies to the most apparently utilitarian TV dinner say much about our values and identity.

Not surprising, then, that the embodied theatrical play of the Bible, as discussed in Chapter 1, can be read in a distinctly culinary complexion. It begins with a menu intended to delight: the garden of Eden 'enticing to look at and good to eat' with permission to eat all but the fruit of one tree. The fall is then represented as the loss of this bounty. In the story of Israel, food functions both as an identity marker of a distinctive vocation among the nations and as an encapsulation of God's gracious provision. In Christ we see a teacher whose parables and language are deeply agricultural and whose eating practice breaks down social stigmas. In the church there is the definitive thanksgiving of the eucharist, which also anticipates the final heavenly banquet at the culmination of history. From beginning to end, the Bible, and the forms of life it generates, is a story shaped by the deep connections between food and faith.

When Adam and Eve eat of the tree of the knowledge of good and evil, the near limitless bounty of the Garden of Eden is replaced by an inescapable scarcity. As Norman Wirzba points out, the Edenic human condition is not one of:

> luxurious ease – a state in which we simply pluck fruit without effort or understanding – but by the attention and practical discipline that enables us to know deeply where we are and who we are with. ... To eat, Adam must garden rather than simply shop. Food is not simply a 'resource' to be mined. Adam's work, and the insight that comes from gardening disciplines, enables him to eat with a deep appreciation for what he is eating. It is this appreciation that enables him to experience the Garden of Eden as paradise, as a 'garden of delights'. (Wirzba, 2011: 47)

That appreciation requires a sense of the complexity and challenge of producing food. The novelist, poet and farmer Wendell Berry insists that 'eating is an agricultural act' (Berry, 2010: 145). Eating is inextricably linked to practices of farming, not to mention processing and packaging and preparation in the kitchen. Yet we tend, he suggests, to see ourselves as consumers, distinct from the practices of agricultural production. But this is a false distinction which desensitizes us from our own contribution to the demand that drives agricultural practices.

Key points

- Taste is a form of intense knowing.
- There is an intimate connection between food and practices of faith.

Reflecting on food

Look in your kitchen cupboards, your larder, your fridge and freezer. Select at random various foods there. The quantity and type of food will depend on how recently you shopped, your income, the nature of your living accommodation, etc.

- What does the range of foods you have say about your lifestyle and your tastes?
- Do you have any food you grew or produced yourself? Would you know how to grow these foods? Would you want to?
- Do you have foods you have to prepare yourself, or are they prepared for you? Do you know how to prepare them all? Do you need to know?
- What factors make you decide to buy a particular food – e.g. price, flavour, health benefits, convenience, appearance?
- Do you know where your foods come from? Have you bought any direct from the producer? Are they ethically sourced? How can you find out?
- What is added to those foods – colourings, preservatives, other additives? Why are these added?
- Do you eat your food with anything like the 'fullest pleasure', to use Berry's phrase?
- After asking all of these questions, do you feel differently about your food or yourself? Do you often ask such questions of yourself?

Even if reflecting on the source and form of our food is unusual and perhaps even interesting, it may not yet be obvious why doing so might be pertinent to a textbook on

Christian theology. For Berry the connection is profound. He elaborates in distinctly sacramental terms:

> Eating with the fullest pleasure – pleasure, that is, that does not depend on ignorance – is perhaps the profoundest enactment of our connection with the world. In this pleasure we experience and celebrate our dependence and our gratitude, for we are living from mystery, from creatures we did not make and powers we cannot comprehend. (Berry, 2010: 152)

He concludes by citing the poem 'The Host' by William Carlos Williams (1953) in which all food, wherever it is found, of whatever type, is to be regarded eucharistically as the body of Christ.

Sense and story: Sacrament in ordinary

Not all eating is mundane and not all foods are ordinary. But even those that are can have enormous personal value. Cooking can be a chore, a time-pressured necessity towards the end of a demanding working day. Equally, it can be leisure. There is luxury in the leisurely perusal of a market of fresh produce and there is creativity both in trying a new recipe and in experimentally diverting from it. There is delight, noise and a great deal of mess in growing food and cooking with children, intimacy in a romantic meal for two and celebration in a birthday party. Eating structures our day and is central to the moments of celebration, commemoration and mourning that structure our year.

We give expression to our deepest held beliefs and values through our habits, eating practices and calendars. Sometimes the values revealed here come into tension with our own self-description. The rituals of our daily lives might be so habitual that they no longer appear to be choices. Whether it is supporting a football team or going shopping, these habits give expression to our identity. The Saturday ritual of watching the match, the pilgrimage to the sacred site of the home ground, the songs that narrate past glories, the shirts, scarves or tattoos that express the team's identity. Or perhaps ritual observance takes the form of weekly attendance at the consumerist temple of the mall; a year of festivals noted on a calendar demarcating the cycle of new seasons' product releases and sales. As meaning-making beings, humans will construct their habits around what matters to them most. For Christianity, as for Judaism, whatever takes centre stage in our lives is what we worship. For worship is not about the singing of songs or the silence of prayer, but about our love and desire. Avowedly secular habits, calendars and rituals remain practices of worship, in this fuller sense. Much of this goes unnoticed, but it structures our lives.

Reflection – Habits and culture

Our habits form our own personal sense of normality. It is only when I encounter someone who lives differently that I realize that my 'normal' is not the only normal out there. Perhaps as a child you visited a friend's home, or at some point in your life you travelled to a different country or encountered a different culture. You may have experienced some culture shock, perhaps because of the surprise of different food, or a different structuring of daily life.

Think of a time you encountered a different way of living. It could be something small, like a different approach to household chores; or something larger, like a different family or social structure. It could be a household with different norms. For example, in some homes interrupting may be a normal part of the cut and thrust of conversation; in another, interrupting may be disrespectful. In one home raised voices or swearing are commonplace, at most minor infractions; in another they are heinous acts that lack basic civility.

- Did the experience make you think differently about your own approach to daily living?
- Reflecting on it now, what might some of these everyday differences express about deeply held norms and values?
- Of course it is not just daily routine that carries meaning. We often have weekly, monthly or annual cycles of practices that structure our lives.
- What events, visits, or meals do you look forward to each year?
- Are there any such times that are more of a burden than a delight?
- Why do you engage in these? Is it to meet some external expectation, to remember, mourn or celebrate, to express your own identity as part of something bigger than yourself – a family, a faith, a nation?

Just as, in theological language, we are all worshippers of something, so we are all also liturgical. 'Liturgy' is another term whose meaning has become unhelpfully narrowed. Some Christian denominations will regard themselves as non-liturgical or anti-liturgical. By this is often meant a repudiation of ritualism – of the dry, formal, habitual repetition of particular words or ceremonial gestures. But in the fuller sense of the term even a community that has no formal calendar of practices, rites and readings will have common patterns of life – events, songs, stories, sayings and often meals – which bind it together and give expression to its story. The Greek word *leitourgia* simply means a public service, which originally could have involved sponsoring a public event, or donating time or money for some communal good. It came to mean the complete range of services, rituals and practices of a priest in a temple. Thus the word was used in the Greek version of the Hebrew Bible, the Septuagint, to refer to the rites and practices of the temple (Exod. 38:27 – though the term cannot be spotted easily in English translation). In the New Testament it is used in the same way (Joel 2:17) but is also used to contrast the 'better liturgy' (Heb. 8:6) of the new high priest, Jesus, in contrast with the temple practices.

In Chapter 1 we saw how the biblical story, in all its complexity, invites participation. Liturgies are the way in which the embodiment of that story occurs. Particular rituals, often meals, connect Christians to earlier parts of the story, and anticipate later parts. As with many religious practices, Christian liturgies use the eating of food to bind believers together and to remind Christians of their place in the story. In a society where most people grow up with little to no experience of the Christian church, childhood participation in a harvest festival may be one of only a handful of contacts with church that someone has in their lives. The Harvest Festival, as we have it now, is a nineteenth-century English invention. Nevertheless it does connect with more ancient agricultural festivals of annual thanksgiving, sacrifice and recognition of God's providence. God feeds 'his' people and 'he' gives them distinctive practices and rules for eating which serve as a mark of their chosenness by God. The complex dietary regulations of the *kashrut,* found in Leviticus and Deuteronomy, prohibit some foods – pork and shellfish, mixtures of meat and milk, etc. – and prescribe certain methods for slaughter and preparation. These prescriptions and proscriptions served to mark out Israel from 'the nations'. However, this distinctiveness was not about sealing Israel off from the rest of humanity, but about making Israel a conduit of blessing to others. Through Israel the nations were to be blessed (Gen. 22:18). This vocation created a strong duty of hospitality (Gen. 18:1-16, Lev. 19:33-34, Heb. 13:2), including provision of food for the widow, the stranger and the orphan (Exod. 22:21-24, Lev. 19:9-10, 23:22, Deut. 24:17-18).

Israel, and now also the church, is therefore called to be a conduit of God's gracious provision. Israel is enjoined to hospitality with a reminder that God's action in history delivered them from Egypt and provided for them in the desert. God is a super-abundant giver who nurtures 'his' world and sustains 'his' people. Emblematic of this is 'his' provision of sustenance during the exodus in the form of manna (Exod. 16:1-36). Along with quails and water from rocks, God miraculously provided for forty years of wandering in the wilderness. The fact that the manna could not be stored up without spoiling emphasised the daily and inescapable dependence of creature on creator. This is not just about physical sustenance: it is a model of God's wider provision, including his provision of his word – 'one does not live by bread alone, but by every word that comes from the mouth of the Lord' (Deut. 8:3-4).

There is a common (but perhaps now declining) habit of gratitude which recognizes dependence on the providential activities and care of God: the saying of a prayer of thanksgiving before a meal. It allows for a moment of reflection on scarcity and hunger in our own day – whether personally, within one's family and network of friends, or globally – and also acknowledges publicly that the world is permeated by the presence of God. Similarly, the Lord's Prayer's petition to 'give us this day our daily bread' may seem to be a request for the most mundane of dietary staples and nothing more. There are deeper theological resonance of God's daily provision of manna in the desert and the harsh reality of frequent bread shortages in the ancient world (Jn 6:25-35).

Within a church, Christian liturgy orders believer's lives around experiences of encounter with God. This takes place even in ostensibly non-liturgical traditions. In most denominations there is a focus on both 'word' and 'sacrament'. The 'word' refers to preaching and the hearing of scripture and the liturgical practices that embody these pivotal narrative moments are sacraments. There are hugely diverse accounts in Christian theology as to what sacraments are, and their necessity, centrality and function. A simple and more or less agreed upon definition comes from Augustine, who is said to describe sacraments as 'visible signs of an invisible grace'. Importantly for our emphasis in this book these are 'signs' that are 'sensible' (Westminster Shorter Catechism), instituted by Christ and are not just 'seen', but also heard, smelt, touched and tasted.

One key question is how many sacraments there are. In both Catholic and Orthodox traditions there are seven sacraments: baptism, confirmation, ordination, marriage, penance and reconciliation, anointing for healing and Holy Communion. For protestants only two of these, baptism and communion – also often called Mass, the Lord's Supper or the eucharist (from the Greek *eucharistein* – a meal of thanksgiving) – are sacramental. That is because only these two are explicitly instituted by Christ (Mt. 28:19 and Lk. 22:19, respectively).

Equally, for some Anabaptists the practice of foot washing (Jn 13:14-15) may also have been instituted by Christ as a sacramental practice (though many now prefer terms like 'ordinance' or 'ceremony') of mutual care and service. For the Society of Friends (Quakers) and the Salvation Army no particular sacraments are practised, because all of creation is, or can be, sacramental. Anything can be a visible means of experiencing the grace of God. This view recognizes the extent of God's grace throughout all of creation. It also focuses attention on the dangers of ritual becoming ritualism, thereby drawing focus from the signified to the sign itself. In many of these traditions, while not a developed ritual, a 'peace meal' – a fully shared meal of fellowship – harkens back to the '*agape* meal' of the early church, and to the last supper itself (which was, of course, a more varied menu than just bread and wine).

Activity – Early Christian eucharistic practice

The *Didache*, a first-century document providing guidance on worship and fellowship, speaks of this *agape* meal and shows the deep connection between food and fellowship with Christ.

Read chapters 9 and 10 of the *Didache*. There are many versions of this text online.

- What do you notice about the connections drawn between the eucharist and Jesus himself?
- What do you notice about the connections between the eucharist and the church?

There is considerable debate about practices of 'open table'. On the one hand, Jesus himself practised a radically open hospitality, enjoying and enjoining table fellowship with the excluded, dirty, shameful and downtrodden. He fed multitudes without attaching conditions. On the other hand, the last supper and the meal at Emmaus were shared with just his disciples. What restrictions (in somewhat uncomfortable language) did this early community place on access to the eucharist?

We saw in Chapter 1 that tradition (i.e. that which is handed on) permits the continuation of the story of salvation and the believer's alignment with God's activity in the world. It is worth noting that the first thing that Christ 'hands on' is a meal rather than a doctrine, creed or distinctive idea (1 Cor. 11:23-26). Both baptism and eucharist entail very ordinary stuff: water, bread, wine. These are set apart to carry special meaning. But how, we might ask? We should be attentive to both what sacramental theology affirms (what is happening) and what it denies (what it claims is not the case). The material elements of the sacrament – the water, the bread, the wine – are not, in pointing 'beyond' themselves, gesturing to a God otherwise hidden from this world. Rather in them participants experience materiality in a deeper way. In the eucharist, there is a kind of intensification of the significance of sensory experience as it becomes a site of localized encounter with the God who is embedded in every fibre of 'his' creation. Sacraments are a means of grace in that they are a place of encounter with God. They are practices initiated by God and enabled and empowered by God. Thus they are regarded not as human inventions, but human responses; not a technique to capture God, but a gift to help believers enjoy 'his' divine presence. The consecration of the elements is not the moment at which their materiality is separated from the mundane. Rather, in some respect still in their original ordinariness, they become special elements, chosen by

God and hallowed by the church, which yet indicate the sacramental character of all matter (Eph. 4:5-6). This is not to say that they are mere signs and indicators. For much sacramental theology, these practices do not simply re-enact past events of union with God; they are themselves a special moment or means of such encounter. The eucharist is itself a participation in God's being and activity in the world. It is a distinctly trinitarian celebration, in which believers are enabled by the empowering and transformative work of the Spirit to give thanks (eucharistein) for the incarnation of the Son (his life, death and resurrection) to the Father who sent him. In this way the eucharist, for some, constitutes the very being of the church. In the next two sections we will explore in more detail this sacramental connection between Christ and church. First, we will look at participation and initiation in baptism. Then we will consider the nature of the presence of God in the worldwide church and the world, as encountered in the eucharist.

Key points

- All patterns of living can be regarded as liturgies.
- Christian liturgy recalls and enacts God's superabundant gracious love for 'his' world.
- Liturgies usually include visible and sensible signs that centre on the most fundamental beliefs about the world and humanity's place in it. In Christianity these are called sacraments.
- Christians differ considerably in how many sacraments there are, how they work and what they achieve.
- Christian sacraments are special sites of encounter with God.

The waters of baptism: Participation and initiation

Celebrating Christian sacraments is to delight in the gift of incorporation into the narrative of divine sustenance, 'his' gracious provision of food; to identify with and get caught up in God's act of love and solidarity with 'his' world; and thus to find in that gift a call to feed a world beset with real and metaphorical hunger. That is to say, it is a gift that entails a significant calling – sacraments are inseparable from ethics – for becoming Christian is both an identity and a vocation. Baptism is the rite of incorporation into that gift and calling. Like many other ritual practices, baptism is a moment of transition in life. In Christianity it replaces circumcision as the identity marker of the people of God (Col. 2:11-12). The 'newness of life' enjoyed by Christians entails a sacramental participation first in the death of Christ (Rom. 6:3-5). Water is a potent symbol of death, cleansing and life. In biblical imagery water is connected to both creation and chaos and so, as so often in this book, we need to loop back to the creation stories of Genesis 1–3. We have already seen in them accounts of the goodness of materiality and the nature of gender and sexual identity. The richness of those stories can also be seen in the way they use images of water. Water is primordial matter – a swirling deep chaos (Gen. 1:2) and a monstrous destructive power (Ps. 74:12-17, Job 41). Yet God brings life from death. Water produces life (hydration) and food (irrigation) (Gen. 2:10-14). The four rivers flowing in the Garden of Eden are more than pleasant landscape gardening. Revelation picks up on this to describe the river of life bringing healing (Rev. 22:1-3). The imagery of the firmament of the sky may remind us of the gaseous atmosphere around the planet, but that would not have been the understanding of the first generations hearing the texts. For ancient Near Eastern cultures the firmament was a solid barrier holding back the waters of chaos. In the destructive flood of Genesis 6–9, the firmament is split open, creation is reset and begun again. Likewise in the exodus, Yahweh's separation of the waters from the land in creation is echoed at the Red Sea, when the Spirit of God again blows as a wind to divide water from land (Exod. 14:21-31). This definitive moment is then recapitulated by Jesus, when he miraculously walks on water (Mt. 14:22-36).

Activity – Christ's baptism and Christian baptism

Christ's baptism is foundational for Christian baptism. Mark's gospel begins with Christ's own baptism, and this moment has a central place in all the other gospels, where it is caught up in webs of rich theological allusion. For this activity we will focus on Luke chapter 4, but you could do a similar exercise with the other gospel texts. Read the text. Can you detect allusions to:

Creation
Exodus
Ritual cleansing
The Holy Spirit
The expected future

Now search online for the baptismal rites of two or three different Christian churches. Some will set a more prescribed text to be read out, others will allow greater scope for local adjustment and embellishment.

- To what extent do the themes listed above appear in their liturgy?
- What actions, symbols or gestures are also indicated?

After being baptized in the River Jordan, the Spirit descends on Christ in the form of a dove. This is an allusion to the dove that returns to Noah when land is finally emerging from flood waters (Gen. 8:6-12). Christ then journeys into the wilderness, just as Israel had done in their convoluted journey to the Promised Land. But note that the term used is not one of volition. Jesus 'is driven out' into the wilderness, perhaps evoking the way that Adam and Eve were driven out of Eden (Gen. 3:22-24), and the people of Israel were pursued by the forces of Pharaoh through the chaos of the sea. In the latter example, wind and water are once again indicative of the Spirit bringing new creation out of turmoil.

In addition, it is important to recall that water cleanses. Ritual impurities are washed away by water (Lev. 15–16). Baptism therefore signifies both a descent into chaos and death and a rising out of the water as a new creation. As an acknowledgement of the need of cleansing and a commitment to a new form of life, baptism is an act of repentance – as taught by John the Baptist. Jesus, as sinless, was not required to be baptized for the sake of individual purity, but he underwent this rite in order to identify with the historical activity of God and as a gesture of public obedience to God's calling for 'his' whole people to return to 'him'. As the one in whom God is 'well pleased' (Mt. 3:17), Christ is both Son and servant of God's kingdom work. Psalm 2:7, Isaiah 42:1 and 62:4 all use the title 'Son' to refer to the creation of a newly restored Israel that will 'bring justice to the nations'. As such, Christ's baptism begins a new phase for the people of God. It marks the start of the age of the Messiah, who serves as a second Moses.

The issues surrounding baptism are passionate and complex. Baptism is a hub for different conceptions of Christian belief, the life of discipleship, the way God acts in the world and especially the way God saves. A view of baptism also contains within it a certain ecclesiology – an account of the mission and ministry of the church, and correlatively its appropriate structures of ministry and authority. When the interpretation of baptism changes, so does ecclesiology – and vice versa.

Reflection – How to baptize

Ask yourself:

- Does it matter where baptism takes place? Must it take place in a church building, in a river or the sea, in a bathtub or in a paddling pool?
- Does baptism require full immersion in water or a sprinkle over the head?
- Does the person conducting the baptism need to be ordained or in some kind of recognized ministry?
- Does it need to take place publicly, where the church community is gathered, or it can take place privately?

Pictures of divine activity are entailed in your preferences here: To what degree is a sacrament our work or God's? Is it a response by us, and if so, in what power and ability is that response made – is it our own creatureliness and/or the empowering sanctifying work of the Holy Spirit? Need we separate these two? These are big, and here, at least, somewhat rhetorical, questions. You may feel able to answer some questions, you may not have a preference on any of them. The point is not so much to get you to answer these definitively, but to understand that these questions are all intertwined.

Baptism is a practice which contains within it many potential answers to the deceptively simple question: What is it to be a Christian? Baptism unites believer and Christ. In it the baptized person participates in the death of Christ, and only thus in his resurrection (Lk. 9:23-26). Just as baptism inaugurates Jesus's discipleship of God, his public mission and ministry, so a Christian's baptism begins their commitment to participating in God's work in history. Baptism was central to the continuation of the story after the resurrection of Jesus. When the early Christian community wanted to know how to go on, what to do, the answer Peter gave is a continuation of the call issued from the mouth of John the Baptist and Jesus himself: 'Repent and be baptised every one off you in the name of Jesus Christ, so that your sins may be forgiven; and you will receive the gift of the Holy Spirit' (Acts 2:38). Baptism in the power of the Spirit is more than an individual initiation, as it creates the church itself. This is because, as the book of Acts shows throughout, the coming of the Spirt and the baptismal invitation are of a piece. The church is the community of the renewed creation, and baptism is the way to join in fully in the enjoyment of this reality.

Activity – Liturgies of baptism continued

Returning to the liturgical descriptions of baptism you looked at earlier:

- What does the rite indicates is the purpose of baptism?
- How might you connect this to what you have learned about Christian theology?
- What particular roles and undertakings do you notice?
- Who does what?
- What promises are made?

Paul makes much of the parallels between the liberation of Israel from Egypt and the ensuing exodus, on the one hand, and Christian baptism, the coming of the Spirit, and the reality of the new creation on the other. This is particularly clear in

Romans 3-8, which is worth reading in full. Just as Israel passes through the waters to emerge (eventually) into freedom and blessing in the Promised Land, so in baptism the Christian passes through water to emerge in and as a new creation (Gal. 3:26-28, Eph. 2:4-7, Col. 2:11-13). 1 Corinthians 10:1-4 ties these stories together both in baptism and in eucharist – in water and in food. 1 Corinthians 10 and Romans 6 are pivotal texts for baptismal theology. In both of these passages the appeal to sacraments connects the community to the story of God's dealings with creation and history. In both texts this leads to an exhortation of ethical integrity, costly discipleship and cooperation with the work of the Spirit in sanctification.

There is also a distinct tension between the language of blessing and enjoyment and that of costly commitment. This in turn raises one of the most pressing, complex and divisive of theological debates surrounding baptism: May one baptize infants or only those who profess a faith for themselves? This is sometimes described as the difference between credobaptism ('credo' denotes believers) and paedobaptism ('paedo' from the Greek *pais* referring to a child). On the one hand, discipleship is risky, costly and demanding – not the kinds of adverbs and adjectives that create an impression of being suitable for children. While the lived reality of Christian discipleship varies enormously, at its root the New Testament portrays it as a life of 'taking up one's own cross and follow Jesus' (Mt. 16:24-26, Mk 8:34-38, Lk. 9:21-27). Sometimes this is understood as a broad metaphor for all types of pain and discomfort. In its context though it focuses very specifically on the deep risk and costly self-giving that sets believers at odds with powers of injustice and vested interest. Baptism therefore faces believers with the prospect of ridicule, dishonour, mistreatment, imprisonment and death. That is to say, it entails the kinds of activities and risks that would not be suitable viewing for a child, let alone for a child to undertake for themselves. But on the other hand, the language of blessing, enjoyment, inclusion and delight are clearly precisely the things that all would want children to enjoy. A community which excluded children from the central constituting reality of its experience would be distinctly unappealing to young people. Not just that, it would seem to run counter to the claim that in Christ something expansive, exciting and gratuitously generous has begun.

Then, of course, there is the question of freedom to choose. An infant is not able to choose to enter the life of Christian discipleship. Does this mean that infant baptism violates the freedom of the infant baptized? Defenders of infant baptism might respond that baptism is then made one's own in a rite of confirmation, when the child reaches an age where they can fully understand the commitment that they are making for themselves. This would track – with arguably greater significance – the way that parents may choose, for example, to raise their children vegetarian, to encourage engagement in sport and exercise, or to expose their children largely to left-wing political views. Children remain adept at rejecting their parents influence and may just as well turn out to be carnivorous, obese conservatives. Likewise, infant baptism cannot guarantee later 'adult' commitment to the faith. Thus infant baptism is closer to making a public promise to nurture the child in the light of God's prior and ongoing loving of that child, in hope of a future confirmation of that commitment. The question then becomes whether baptism is necessary at that early stage. Credobaptist churches will often have services of dedication which include naming and welcome, promises by parents, godparents and community, and a note of future hope of individual decision for discipleship. They will not, however, incorporate a baptismal rite into that service.

Exegetically, the case is complex. The vast majority of New Testament texts clearly indicate 'believer's baptism'. But, as we have stated above, baptism replaces circumcision as an identity marker of belonging to God's covenant people (Col. 2:11-12) – and circumcision was a rite performed on male infants at eight days old. While there is no explicit mention of the baptism of infants in the New Testament, there are references to the baptism of entire households (Acts 16:15, 33:1, 1 Cor. 1:16). These are complex texts. Commonly those who defend infant baptism will argue that Colossians 2 fully equates baptism and circumcision – see, for example, John Calvin's *Institutes* 4:16. Paedobaptists would elaborate that household baptisms would necessarily entail baptism of infants. A first-century household is not the modern Western nuclear family, but included children, parents, grandparents, servants and often slaves. On the other hand, a credobaptist might argue that Colossians 2 sees baptism as an identity marker, but does not say explicitly that it applies to children. Nor, of course, does circumcision apply to female infants. They may also point to 1 Corinthians 7, in which the unbelieving members of the household are said to be made holy through the baptized spouse. Unbelieving household members could not have been baptized.

Extended task – Baptism of infants

First, gauge your reactions to the arguments about credobaptism and paedobaptism. Which do you initially think is most appropriate and why?

You are likely to have assumptions and theological gut instincts, and it is important to be able to identify these. Theological discourse can often be characterized by rancorous disagreement. Key to arguing well is the ability to state sympathetically the views of those with whom you disagree, no matter how profoundly.

Using a variety of sources, compile the three strongest arguments you can think of for the view you find yourself least drawn to.
Either

- Hold a debate on the topic with others in the class.

Or consider individually

- How might a defender of the view you find yourself more intuitively drawn to respond?
- Has the process of working through two perspectives on an argument led you to modify your own view at all?

Eucharistic presence: God and matter

If, as we have argued, the sacraments are a site of encounter with God then a question arises about the nature of divine presence in the elements of water, wine or bread. Many answers have been given to this question. In the earliest days of the practice of the eucharist, the intense bodily language of Christ's Last Supper led to some misunderstanding among believers and especially critics. The charge of cannibalism, of literally eating human flesh and drinking human blood, was highly prevalent in the first centuries of Christianity. Justin Martyr (100–65) sought to give an account, a defence known as an 'apology' that avoided such charges and still gave a full account of the presence of Christ:

> We do not receive these things as common bread or common drink; but just as our Saviour Jesus Christ, being incarnate through the Word of God, took flesh and blood for our salvation, so too we have been taught that the food over which thanks have been given by the prayer of the Word who is for him, from which our flesh and blood fed by transformation, is both the flesh and blood of that incarnate Jesus. (Martyr, 1997, 66.2)

It is worth noting a fundamental connection between incarnation and eucharist. As God has made 'himself' present in Christ in the flesh, so consequently God is present in bread and wine. Note though that this is a process of *transformation*. The elements were not always more than simple food and drink. While many followed Justin in linking eucharist with incarnation, others focused more on Jesus's death, resurrection and ascension to heaven as creating the conditions for the presence of Christ in the eucharistic elements. By the ninth century increasing controversy led to the pursuit of greater precision. Some sought to provide an unflinching affirmation of the 'is' in Christ's declaration 'this is my blood … this is my body'. On this view, Christians quite literally imbibe blood and chew human flesh. For others, the bread and wine are not so much physically transformed, as they become signs or figures of a spiritual presence. Thomas Aquinas provided something of a middle ground by arguing that Christ is present, but that this is a 'sacramental' presence rather than merely a symbolic claim. In other words, there is indeed a real transformation, but it is one that leaves intact the appearance, texture and flavour of the bread and wine.

This may come as some relief, given the natural squeamishness at the notion of cannibalism. Thomas, citing Augustine's claim that the flesh and blood are 'invisible things' honoured 'under' the bread and wine, argues:

> It is obvious to our senses that after consecration all the accidents of bread and wine remain. And, by Providence, there is a good reason for this. It is not normal for people to eat human flesh and to drink human blood; in fact they are revolted by this idea. Therefore Christ's flesh and blood are set before us to be taken under the appearances of those things which are in frequent use, namely bread and wine. (Aquinas *Summa Theologiae IIIa q.75, a.5*)

To this day, the Roman Catholic catechism continues to teach Aquinas's view of the nature of this transformation, named transubstantiation. Transubstantiation relies on a philosophical distinction made by Aristotle (384–322BCE) between 'accidents' (such as the size, texture, shape, taste, or colour of the bread and wine) and 'substance' (the essential or inner nature of the bread and wine). Substances may be retained despite changes to accidents, and vice versa. For example, an oak tree retains its substance as 'tree', regardless of how old, tall, wide or in leaf it may be. Conversely, while the eucharistic accidents remain unchanged, the substance of bread changes into the substance of the body of Christ.

Protestants regarded transubstantiation as lacking biblical justification. They were cautious about any explanation that required the church to commit to Aristotelian philosophy. Indeed, for Martin Luther (1483–1546), it is important that Christ is present not just in the invisible substance behind the accidents, but that he permeates both bread and wine. The 'real presence' of Christ is 'consubstantial' with the eucharistic elements in the same way that both fire and iron are intermingled in a red-hot poker. Thus in no way does the presence of Christ annihilate the bread or wine. This view also had everyday implications, as it combatted aspects of common piety that the protestants regarded as superstition. It meant that outside of the church service, the consecrated elements were not to be worshipped or venerated, as they would be in the transubstantiation model. While Luther's approach appears to avoid tying Christianity to a philosophical system, it leaves unanswered the question about how Christ's body and blood are consubstantial with bread and wine.

For others, such accounts of physical change diminish the ability of the material to signify the spiritual. They make the spiritual all too literal. For John Calvin (1509–64) the elements signified the reality of events known by faith. The cross, resurrection and ascension of Christ may be past events – indeed, the ascension must mean that Christ's body is no longer literally present on earth – but nonetheless, in receiving bread and wine the Holy Spirit acts upon believers so that they are made new with Christ in heaven. Yet other views, stemming from the Swiss reformer Huldrych (or Ulrich) Zwingli (1484–1541) but found also in Baptist, Anabaptist and other evangelical traditions, focus purely on the elements as signs, without any physical transformation. The sacraments are simply memorials that are no different materially to bread or wine in any other context. They take on extra significance, however, in evoking the memory of Jesus's teaching and the historical breaking of his body and shedding of his blood. Just as we may hold dear some gift, photograph or memento of a deceased loved one, so the eucharistic elements provide a material focus for the act of remembrance.

In somewhat parallel ways recent movements in Catholic thought have sought to focus more on the event of encounter with God, and thus on the strongly symbolic nature of the sacraments. However, they also want to avoid the tendency in Zwingli to a purely intellectual non-experiential eucharistic knowledge – that the elements are merely effective communicators of an idea graspable without them. They seek to retain a commitment to the divine transformation of material things, while also re-establishing stronger connections with the wider project of God's restoring the world in Christ. Thus Christ himself is the *ursakrament* – the primordial sacrament on which other sacramental practices are based. These sacraments then embody the redemption of the world. The Roman Catholic theologian Edward Schillebeeckx (1963–2009) argued that Christ is present personally, but not physically, in the eucharist. The transformation of the elements is not so much a change of substance as a change of significance. This 'transsignification' does not change the matter of the elements (they remain baked flour water and, perhaps, yeast, and fermented grape juice), but it alters their significance and function. For such views it is important that we don't dismiss signs as of lesser standing than 'reality' or 'matter' – 'mere symbols'. For meaning-making creatures like human beings, the context and use of an object is as real and important, as its size, shape, texture or material. The symbolic, social, cultural aspects of bread, its meaning, purpose and perception, are just as much the 'reality' of the bread as is its ingredients or chemical properties. In transsignification, God transforms the mundane elements. This is important, for it is not an act of human will, a simple choice to regard bread and wine as a trigger for memory. God causes the elements to function in a fuller way than they otherwise would. They go through an essential change in that, in their final reality (transfinalization), the bread and wine make present the reality of the ascended Christ. Bread is not anonymous flesh, wine not generic blood; together they are the symbols of the sacrifice of Christ. Here is a sacrificial gift from God that is reciprocated, but never balanced out, by the church's offering of thanks and praise (*eucharistein*).

Key points

- Explanations of the simple but enigmatic phrase 'This is my body ... this is my blood' shape and give expression to wider accounts of how God is present and active in the world.

- Christian theologians have drawn on widely differing understandings of the nature of matter to account for the eucharistic presence of Christ.
- These differences have often been the source of significant division, and are often a focus for ecumenical efforts to heal division.

Questions for discussion

- Which, if any of the above accounts of eucharistic presence, do you think makes best sense of the central claim 'This is my body … this is my blood' (Mt. 26:26-27)?
- Why do you think this often quite technical set of debates has divided Christianity as significantly as it has?
- What do you think your preferences identified in answer to question 1 say about your broader account of the nature of the relationship between God and the material world?

Taste and the richness of knowledge

We can see, therefore, that a complex series of philosophical, cultural and theological factors have shaped differing accounts of how Christ is present in the eucharist. In different ways these ideas seek to preserve the surprising strangeness of worshipping a God who gives 'himself' to us as food (Jn 6:22-59). John Calvin places the symbolic presence of Christ in the light of Christ's remarkable statement: 'I am the living bread that came down from heaven. Whoever eats of this bread will live forever; and the bread that I will give for the life of the world is my flesh' (Jn 6:54). For Calvin faith itself is fundamentally about eating, rather than seeing:

> It is that we are quickened by the true partaking of him; and [Christ] has therefore designated this partaking by the words 'eating' and 'drinking' in order that no one should think that the life that we receive from him is received by mere knowledge. As it is not the seeing but the eating of bread that suffices to feed the body, so the soul must truly and deeply become partaker of Christ that it may be quickened to spiritual life by his power. … In this way the Lord intended … to teach not only that salvation rests for us on faith in his death and resurrection, but also that, by true partaking of him, his life passes into us and is made ours – just as bread when taken as food imparts vigour to the body. (Calvin, *Institutes,* Book IV, Ch. XVII.V)

Despite the differences in Christian understanding of the eucharist a common emphasis is that sacramental eating and drinking is not so much about believers taking Christ into their bodies, but about the way that believers are incorporated into his body. Essentially, by participating in Christ in the eucharist, believers become the church. Our emphasis in this book has been on participation as performance, a participation in an ongoing story of God's active engagement with his creation. The emphasis on participation in eucharistic theology points not to a static interpenetration of divine and human substances, but to the anticipatory denouement of God's providential initiative in Christ.

Activity – Intertextual analysis

The dramatic language of the fourth gospel draws heavily on this motif.
  Read Exodus 16:1-36.
  Read John 6:22-59. Highlight or note down the parts of this text that seem to refer to the Exodus text.
  How is John drawing similarities and contrasts with the Exodus text?

As we have already noted, the New Testament presents Jesus as a new Moses. His public ministry begins in the fourth gospel with a sign of abundance – turning water into wine at the wedding in Cana (Jn 2:1-11). The feeding of multitudes appears in all gospels – whether four (Mt. 15:32-39, Mk 8:1-9) or five thousand (Mt. 14:12-21, Mk 6:31-44, Lk. 9:12-17, Jn 6:1-14) – and recalls God's feeding the people of Israel in the desert. In the Gospel accounts, Jesus's provision of food is such that the disciples gather together leftover bread into twelve baskets. This is clearly an image of God's re-gathering the twelve tribes of the people of Israel, just as Israel had harvested manna in the desert. However, there are also significant contrasts between Moses and Israel on the one hand and Jesus on the other. In the temptation narratives, when the Spirit leads Jesus out into the desert and Satan tempts him in his hunger to make bread out of stone, Jesus quotes Deuteronomy 8:3-4: 'One does not live by bread alone but by every word that comes from the mouth of God.' Where the people of Israel grumbled and complained both of hunger and then of the manna provided, Jesus is seen as a paragon of trust and faithfulness. Indeed, the resonance reaches back beyond Moses to the start of the story of eating. Where Adam eats prohibited fruit, despite the abundance that surrounds him, Jesus remains faithful even in acute hunger. Thus where the bread brought through Moses's intervention only gives temporary sustenance, in John 6 the bread that *is* Jesus yields eternal life.

The eucharist is therefore a remembrance of the full narrative arc of the biblical redemption story. It is the practice which places the whole of believer's life in the flow of God's grace throughout history – a grace that restores the divine image in humanity. Just as eating is at the centre of creaturely life, so too eucharistic eating is at the heart of many Christian visions of the life of the world. As Norman Wirzba puts it, in the eucharist, 'to remember Jesus is to join in a *re-membering* of a world *dis-membered* by sin' (Wirzba, 2011: 150).

Activity – Interconnected doctrines

Read the following extract from the Orthodox theologian Alexander Schmemann (1921–83), and identify how the eucharist is placed in relation to a great many elements of Christian theology: the nature of God, the nature and work of Christ, the condition of humanity and the mission of the church.

> For we already know that food is life, that it is the very principle of life and that the whole world has been created as food for man. We also know that to offer this food, this world, this life to God is the initial 'eucharistic' function of man, his very fulfilment as man. We know that we were created as *celebrants* of the sacrament of life, of its transformation into life in God, communion with God. We know that real life is 'eucharist,' a movement of love and adoration toward God, the movement in which alone the meaning and value of all that exists can be revealed and fulfilled. We know that we have lost this eucharistic life, and finally we know that in Christ, the new Adam, the perfect man, this eucharistic life was restored to man [sic]. For He himself was the perfect Eucharist; He offered Himself in total obedience, love and thanksgiving to God. God was His very life. And He gave the perfect and eucharistic life to us. In Him God became our life.
>
> …Remembrance is an act of *love*. God remembers us and His remembrance, His love is the foundation of the world. In Christ, *we remember*. We become again beings open to love, and we *remember*. The Church, in its separation from 'this world,' on its journey to heaven, *remembers* the world, remembers all men, [sic] remembers the whole of creation, takes it in love to God. The eucharist is the sacrament of cosmic remembrance: it is indeed a restoration of love as the very life of the world. (Schmemann, 1973: 34–6)

Chapter summary

- Food is central to decisive moments in the Christian reading of the biblical narrative.
- The eucharist, as the sacrament of food, is central to most forms of Christianity.
- Christians have formulated varied accounts of how Jesus is present in the elements of the eucharist.

- As with communal eating more generally, the eucharist connects people together, building social bonds and giving a sense of identity.
- Unlike other forms of eating, Christians see the eucharist as a means of the grace of God; the grace which unites us with God, restores humanity and brings believers into the narrative arc of the biblical story of food and fellowship.

Recommended reading

Berry, Wendell (2010), 'The Pleasures of Eating'. In *What Are People For?* 145–52. Berkeley, CA: Counterpoint.

Davison, Andrew (2013), *Why Sacraments*, London: SPCK.

Schmeeman, Alexander (1973), *For the Life of the World: Sacraments and Orthodoxy*, New York: St Vladimir's seminary press.

Wirzba, Norman (2011), *Food and Faith: A Theology of Eating*, Cambridge: Cambridge University Press.

5
Smelling: Mysticism and memory

Reflective exercise

If possible, use some olfactory stimuli (e.g. incense, coffee, fresh bread, perfume). If such items are not available, simply reflect on the powerful link between smell, imagination and embodied memory, and the evocative way that smell can impact mood, disposition and action. Share some examples, if you wish.

Starter questions

What slang phrases do you use that suggest that you have learned from smell? Does 'smell' have generally positive or negative connotations in Western culture? Why do you think this might be?

Theology of smelling?

Many readers are likely to be taken aback by a 'theology of smelling'. Such surprise might itself be a symptom of an insufficiently embodied understanding of knowledge of God. Others may struggle with the theological 'bridge' of smelling because this sense is more powerfully associated with animals such as dogs. Their noses are so sensitive that they can detect the odour of ovarian cancer in plasma samples. The human sense of smell is not as acute, but it is much better than we might imagine and works even on a subconscious level. As any chef or wine buff will say (perhaps at length …), smell is also strongly integrated with the other senses. Approximately 80 per cent of the dynamism and range of flavour comes from smell rather than taste. Smell is therefore a profound part of the human sensorium. Yet other readers may be aware that compared to other senses, such as sight, there are fewer references to smell in the Bible. In the Hebrew and Greek, however, it becomes clearer that biblical writers 'think through' the sense of smell in striking ways. We will touch on some examples later.

Perhaps the most significant barriers to taking a 'theology of smelling' seriously are the devaluation of smell in Western social history (Classen, Howes and Synnott, 2002), the deodorizing of much modern life and a post-Enlightenment preference for intellectual over affective (i.e. experiential, heartfelt) knowing. Consequently, knowledge that is gained through cognitive processes such as analysing and evaluating has become more highly prized than knowledge that is formed by a response to an olfactory stimulus. In stark contrast to our ancient forebears, smells are now more likely to be associated with instinct, memory and emotion, rather than reason and spirituality (Classen, Howes and Synnott, 1994: 36). Yet if theology is 'full-bodied' thought, as this book maintains throughout, then the sensory experience of smell has its place in religious epistemology. Admittedly the contribution of smell to theology has yet to draw the kind of academic interest that has been stimulated by other senses and so what follows is necessarily more tentative than the work presented in previous chapters. Even so, it aims to help us realize that our sense of smell continues to impact our thinking and behaviour and that there is much to learn from Christianity's relationship to scents and smells.

Smell: Delight and disgust

The reflective exercises at the start of this chapter will hopefully have elicited examples of the connection between smell and mood. Perhaps you mentioned the perceived benefits of aromatherapy, which incidentally often draws upon scents that are mentioned in the Bible (e.g. frankincense, hyssop and sandalwood). Certainly, the global perfume/body spray industry depends heavily upon the emotive nature of smell and on associated deep-seated psychological factors, from social anxiety to sexual desire. Whether you want to feel relaxed or revitalized, or simply have people drawn helplessly to you, there is a smell that can be co-opted to your purposes. Perhaps you have also discovered or recalled that there is an individual component to our perception of smell (one person's 'intoxicating' might be another person's 'nauseating') and theorized that this may be down to how our emotional response to smell is governed by association. Everyone – we would hope! – is aware that embedded in our human evolutionary history are definitive bad smells, such as stagnant water or rotten food, which signal 'Danger!' to our survival instincts. These smells result in a universal reaction of disgust.

Much of your discussion may have centred on the ways in which smells can evoke powerful, perhaps long-forgotten memories. It is striking how a smell can take us straight back to a moment, setting or person, and reconstitute other types of sensory memories and emotional states. The physical structuring of the sense of smell holds the key to such experiences. When someone with full olfactory capability smells something, the olfactory neurones lining the upper part of the nose detect the chemicals in the air and generate an impulse. This impulse travels up the olfactory nerve into the part of the brain called the olfactory bulb, which is located high up in the nasal cavity. Here, the signal is processed and the information passed onto other structures in the brain, which are known collectively as the limbic system. The scientific consensus is that the limbic brain has an ancient evolutionary history and it deals with three core functions: emotion, memory and arousal (or stimulation). The fact that smell is hooked into the 'old' part of the human brain helps to explain why it is so strongly linked to these responses.

The biblical writers had no way of knowing that the human olfactory system is strongly connected to the amygdala and hypothalamus – the areas of the brain that are critical to the processing of emotion – but they certainly appreciated the effect of the link. It was perfectly natural for them to link pleasing smells with divine pleasure and enjoyment. The theological status of such sensory language – i.e. whether it is metaphorical or substantial and literal – is not something that we can resolve in this chapter. A divine olfactory sense will probably be a metaphor for most contemporary readers, but this could be because biblical texts are being overlaid with views of transcendence and non-corporeality which would not necessarily have been shared by the original hearers. Other ancient Near Eastern flood narratives (e.g. atrahasis, enuma elish) show the gods as irascible because of sensory offense, such as humans making noise. There is therefore some ambiguity on this point.

That said, the sense of smell is in fact well-suited to conveying relational warmth between God and the creatures in whom 'he' delights. If we recall that in detecting a smell, we are taking chemical compounds into our own bodies, we quickly realize that smell is one of the most intimate of all the senses, as it requires us to merge, to some extent, with our surrounding environment. This makes the nose a place of conjoined otherness. The Israelites thought 'through' the nose in a similar way. They were more aware than perhaps we are that smell is the only sense dependent on another bodily function: breathing. For them, to have life is to smell and vice versa. We can readily detect this link in the Hebrew. *Reï'ach* means 'scent, odour, smell, aroma'. And as scents are breathed in through the nose, *reï'ach* is related to *ruach*, which means 'spirit, breath, wind'. It follows that God's Spirit was thought to reside in human nostrils – and not the heart, as we might imagine today. See, for example, Genesis 2:7 ('Then the Lord God formed man from the dust of the ground and breathed into his nostrils the breath of life; and the man became a living being') and Job 27:3 ('as long as my breath is in me and the Spirit of God is in my nostrils'). We could also think of how God delights in the 'pleasing aroma' of the sacrifices which were central to Israel's cultic worship. We will consider this in more detail later on in this chapter.

In the New Testament, Paul also operated within a framework of olfactory delight. Writing to the Ephesians, he said, 'Therefore be imitators of God, as beloved children, and live in love, as Christ loved us and gave himself up for us, a fragrant offering and sacrifice to God' (5:1-2). Incense is not explicitly mentioned here, but the echoes of the Levitical sacrificial codes make Paul's meaning clear: Jesus's loving self-sacrifice on the cross was a 'pleasing aroma' to God. Elsewhere, when Epaphroditus brought supplies to Paul from the church in Philippi, Paul wrote, 'I am fully satisfied, now that I have received from Epaphroditus the gifts you sent, a fragrant offering, a sacrifice acceptable and pleasing to God' (Phil. 4:18). But possibly one of Paul's most famous evocations of scent is found in his second letter to the Corinthians, where he describes the relationship between God, Christ and humanity in terms of fragrance:

> But thanks be to God, who in Christ always leads us in triumphal procession, and through us spreads in every place the fragrance that comes from knowing him. For we are the aroma of Christ to God among those who are being saved and among those who are perishing; to the one a fragrance from death to death, to the other a fragrance from life to life. (2 Cor. 2:14-16)

The scholarly consensus is that Paul is borrowing an image of a triumphant Roman procession, thrown for those who had recently won a significant military victory. Participants would have burned aromatic herbs and frankincense along the route, as offerings to the Roman gods. In Paul's hands, this image becomes a procession thrown for Christ, who leads in victory those who witness to him, and evangelists are the incense bearers, wafting the fragrant smoke of the knowledge of God wherever they go. This world-changing pungency of Christ-aroma delights God.

The other side of God's delight in 'pleasing aromas' is that God also recoils from the stench of human sin. For instance, the prophet Isaiah hears God speaking to the rebellious Israelites: 'who say, "Keep to yourself; do not come near me, for I am too holy for you." These are a smoke in my nostrils, a fire that burns all day long' (65:5). This might sound strange, until we appreciate that there is a semantic link between smell and divine displeasure. The word translated as 'nose' in Hebrew is 'aph, yet most of its appearances in the Hebrew Bible are translated as 'angry' or 'anger' as 'aph is derived from the root anaph, meaning 'to be angry'. To understand the connection, we need to appreciate that the Hebrew Bible uses language in concrete and figurative, rather than abstract, ways. This means that ideas and words are related to something that can be sensed using the five senses. The close association between 'anger' and 'nose' in the Hebrew lexicon makes sense when we think about what happens when humans get angry. It can show in several ways in our bodies: faces become red, hands and voices get shaky, breathing patterns change, nostrils may flare, heart rate increases and blood pressure is raised. And such reactions are not unique to humanity. Many other creatures (think of raging bulls) tend to snort and breathe heavily when angered. Thus, when the Hebrew literally describes someone as 'short of nose' (Prov. 14:17) or 'short of breath' (Mic. 2:7; Exod. 6:9), it means that they are angry. The inflection of God's wrath/nose is likewise found in Jeremiah 32:31 ('This city has aroused my anger and wrath, from the day it was built until this day, so that I will remove it from my sight') and Ezekiel 6:12 ('Those far off shall die of pestilence; those nearby shall fall by the sword; and any who are left and are spared shall die of famine. Thus I will spend my fury upon them'). In contrast, someone who is 'long of nose' (Prov. 14:29) or 'long of breath' (Eccl. 7:8) is patient. The same reasoning applies when God is described as in Exodus 34:6 as 'merciful and gracious, long of nose [= slow to anger]'. The divine characteristic of 'length of nose' (*'arek 'appayim*) is echoed later in the story of Jonah (4:2). In this context it is because God is slow to anger that Jonah anticipates God's forgiveness of the people of Ninevah. In all the above examples, anger is somatized – i.e. it is connected in various ways to the nose and the sense of smell – rather than internalized, as it tends to be in the West (Pilch, 1999: 11).

Just as God finds sinful human thoughts and actions to be irritants in 'his' nose, so the scent of the Gospel can smell vile to some. To return to Paul's image of a victory parade for Christ (2 Cor. 2:14-16), there were also captives present in a Roman procession. They would have known that they were most likely on their way to their deaths. For them, the incense would have 'stunk' of defeat and condemnation. Paul points out that, analogously, the incense – the knowledge of Christ – has a divisive effect on those who smell it. For those who do not respond to Christ, the 'smell' of the Gospel stinks as it is a scent that announces their death. This text must be read, of course, in the context of the whole narrative arc of the biblical story, which for Christians centres on the redemptive person and work of Jesus Christ. At the very start of his ministry, Jesus publicly identified himself with a passage from Isaiah: 'The Spirit of the Lord God is upon me, because the Lord has anointed me; he has sent me to bring good news to the oppressed, to bind up the brokenhearted, to proclaim liberty to the captives, and release to the prisoners' (61:1). Jesus's mission is to set prisoners free; to save rather than condemn. That said, according to Paul some people are repelled by his smell of freedom.

Reflective task – Does God have a sense of smell?

Ask yourself: At what point does anthropomorphizing God (i.e. imagining God to have human-like traits) start to diminish both a Christian view of God's transcendence and a healthy Christian theological anthropology (i.e. the consideration of human beings as made in the image of God, but are not themselves God)? No matter the strength of your views, ensure you try to do justice to the opposing perspective.

To start you off, the question of whether God can 'smell' in anything other than a symbolic way is part of a wider discussion about how Christians understand divine transcendence to relate to corporeality. There are several ways to think about the properties of God's 'sensual' action:

- Ancient Near East religions thought that each god had an individual fragrance and could discern through smell as much as the other senses.
- Many current theologians consider God's act of 'smelling' to be a sensory metaphor for spiritual realities – such as intimacy.
- Panentheists are often drawn to spiritualize the world, with all its sensuousness, as the 'body of God' (Sallie McFague's work is briefly discussed in Chapter 7).
- Process theologians argue that God 'experiences' the world because God has one 'pole' that evolves through intimate interaction with the world.

Key points

- The language of smell often communicates an intensity and immediacy of sensory experience: delight or disgust.
- God delights in 'pleasing aromas' of sacrifice and is repulsed by the stench of sin.
- Humans can find the smell of the Gospel attractive or repugnant.
- Christian theologians understand the relation of transcendence to corporeality in a range of ways.

Smell: Discernment

Introductory reflections

1. Have you ever used pleasant smells as part of a placatory gesture? Why did you do this?
2. Has your sense of smell ever helped you to discern the truth of a situation?
3. Can you recall a time when smells gave you knowledge that other senses would have missed?

If you are unlucky enough to suffer from hay fever or allergies, you will know more than most that human nasal passages are extremely sensitive. This anatomical feature is understandable, given how critical our noses are for survival (smelling danger or food), breathing and to a lesser extent, guarding our immune system. Even when there is an odourless threat our noses may react to protect us, either by making us sneeze or by giving us a runny nose and/or a warning sensation of burning. Perhaps less well-known and more controversial is the suggestion from some scientists (such as Tamara Brown, GenePartner) that body odour helps us on a subconscious level to choose our life partners or spouses. The idea is that we are more likely to be attracted to people who have an immune system that complements our own, and the genes that regulate immunity also produce certain smells, which act as secret signals of compatibility (or not). (It is important to remember, though, that there is more to sexual attraction than DNA.) What is certain is that our noses and sense of smell have a vital role to play in discernment.

Susan Ashbrook Harvey points out (2006: 1–2) that the cultures of the ancient pan-Mediterranean regions valued smells even more overtly and for a much wider range of reasons than we tend to today. Different smells helped to demarcate physical spaces (public events, celebrations and ceremonies, different rooms in a home) and they were a vital component of many aspects of everyday life. Scents helped people to protect, structure, understand and advance their lives. 'Good' smells were associated with immortality, divine presence and favour as much as tasty food and healthy relationships. 'Bad' smells were connected to decay, mortality and destruction as much as ill health. But more than this, it was believed that odours could create the very situations that they represented. They could cleanse or contaminate; purify or pollute; heal or endanger. In other words, they were legitimized by science and medicine, had the capacity to influence environments and could order human relations and human–divine interaction (Ashbrook Harvey, 2006). When Martha protested that the tomb of her brother, Lazarus, should not be opened because of the four-day stench (Jn. 11:39), she was concerned that they would all be made unclean simply by the odour of putrefying flesh.

It was in the realm of religion where smells and scents reigned supreme. The sense of smell was taken to be an indicator of truth and was therefore associated with knowledge (Smith, 2007: 60), and the smoke of incense, in particular, was believed to act as a conduit between human and divine worlds. All these elements are in evidence within the forms of worship laid down in the books of Exodus, Leviticus and Numbers. Smells – particularly the smells of incense and burnt offerings – helped the worshippers to discern a Holy transaction: human sin in exchange for God's forgiveness. This means that there are significant connections between the olfactory sense and the Hebrew Bible sacrificial rites which inform atonement theology. (Atonement is discussed in detail in the next chapter, but as a working definition, we can say that it brings about harmonious 'at-one-ment' between God and 'his' errant people.)

We have already touched on how the smoke of burnt sacrifices was a 'soothing aroma' for God. To go a bit deeper, we can consider how the Hebrew word *nicho'ach*, meaning 'soothing, quieting, tranquilizing', is derived from the verb *nuach*, which means 'to rest, to settle'. *Nicho'ach* therefore carries the literal meaning of something that is disquieted subsequently being made to be at rest. In the context of 'pleasing odours' (e.g. Num. 18:17, Lev. 8:21), it expresses how the obedience behind the offering of sacrifices calms the anger of God, offers protection against God's wrath and/or pleases him. It is important to realize that God delights in unchanging love (Mic. 7:18) rather than anger (Ezek. 18:23), but, nevertheless, the destructive nature of sin is an offense to God's love and is opposed to God's desire for the flourishing of creation. The sacrificial system – which Christians believe prefigured Christ's offering of himself on the cross – was given by God to the people of Israel so that atonement for sin could take place and holiness and right relationship with God restored. Soothing aromas were vital to the liturgical discernment of souls that had become 'at rest' through God's atoning work. (We will explore the different levels of meaning of 'at rest' in Chapter 7.)

The Day of Atonement

The Hebrew word that is translated as 'atonement' is the verb *kaphar*. It means 'to cover, purge, make reconciliation.' In a confluence of sensory experiences sin is 'covered over' and dealt with on this day, so that God no longer sees or smells it. Immerse yourself in an imaginative reading of Leviticus 16 and then consider the questions below. Doing an internet search for images of the Tabernacle might help you to picture the scene.

- What divine strictures enable the High Priest's sacrifices to smell pleasing to God?
- What different functions does incense have?
- What other senses are being drawn upon in this ritual?
- Do your answers to the questions at the beginning of this section help you to understand these practices, which in so many ways seem alien to us?

The importance of scent to the worshipping life of the Israelites is displayed in Exodus 30 (echoed later in Lev. chapters 2 and 16) where there are detailed divine decrees about how to build the incense altar and where it is to be placed; how often incense is to be burnt and by whom; and how to blend the oil which would be used to anoint Levites to the Priesthood and consecrate the furnishings of the Temple. Both the oil and incense could not be used for any other purpose: they were 'holy to the Lord' (Exod. 30:37). The fragrance of incense evoked the presence of Israel's Holy God (Is. 6:3) and symbolized prayer rising to God (Ps. 141:2l). (The New Testament picks up on the latter tradition in Revelation, which speaks of the sweet incense of prayer filling heaven – Rev. 5:8, 8:3 15:8, 18:13.) Incense was therefore a means of encounter and dialogue between earthly and heavenly realms. It also demarcated the sanctity of the Temple space (which was itself built of aromatic woods), set the Priests apart and, as a thick cloud of smoke, protected the High Priest on the Day of Atonement (for no one could see God and live – Exod. 33:20). On this day, the smell of blood from sacrificed animals, offered as substitutionary deaths for sin (Ezek. 18:4), was mixed in with these heady fragrances. Having made atonement, the High Priest laid hands on a live goat (Lev. 16:8). In biblical symbolism, the laying on of hands always entails the transmission of something. In this case, all the 'iniquities of the people of Israel' (Lev. 16:21) were transferred to the goat's head. In the sight of the whole community, the goat was released into the wilderness, as a reminder that Israel's sin was removed by God 'as far as the east is from the west' (Ps. 103:12). This day of deliverance was also ordained as a day of Sabbath rest (Lev. 16:31). All of these sensory actions (smell, sight, touch, rest) were powerfully associated – in the case of the incense and Temple blend of oil, uniquely so – with recognizing God's holiness and the holy calling of Israel, perceiving God's love and mercy and provoking memories of God's redemptive action.

Sacrifices could however become malodorous to God. During Isaiah's time, the Israelites were disobedient to God in many ways while keeping the Temple rites with all due rigour. Through Isaiah, God said, 'What to me is the multitude of your sacrifices? says the Lord; I have had enough of burnt offerings of rams and the fat of fed beasts; I do not delight in the blood of bulls, or of lambs, or of goats. ... bringing offerings is futile; incense is an abomination to me' (1:11, 13). God's nose can 'sniff out' false sacrifices and wrong intentions – something that can also be done by the Jewish Messiah, the expected Saviour, who Christians believe is Jesus Christ. Isaiah 11 anticipates the Messiah arising from the stump of Jesse (a small family grouping within the twelve tribes of Israel) and says that the Spirit of the Lord rests upon him (v.2) and that 'His delight will be in the fear of the Lord' (v.3). Calvin suggests that verse 3 can also be translated literally as 'he smells [*riach*] in the fear of the Lord'. He writes: 'We ought to learn from the metaphor in the verb *smell*, which means that Christ will be so shrewd that he will not learn from what he hears, or from what he sees; for by *smelling* alone he will perceive what would otherwise be unknown' (1850: 376). The Messiah's keen sense of smell, which Calvin includes within the gifts of the Spirit (1850), will enable him to discern the hearts of all people, beneath their outward religious appearance and practices, and enable him to govern God's people.

The ancient association between smell and the spirit continued into the early Christian period, when olfaction was treated as an acute instrument of discernment and the tradition of 'odour of sanctity' reached its height. It was thought that when a Christian saint died, the smell of their 'sweet soul' leaving their body could be detected. This odour was not disease-spreading; it was a healing scent, released by God's grace. The practice was denounced by protestants at the reformation, as part of their belief that miracles were confined to the biblical era. This meant that the revered, holy aroma of St Teresa of Avila's death, for instance, was debunked and ascribed to the sweet smell of diabetes instead. Due to the additional de-mythologizing of the world during the Enlightenment – when philosophers concluded that 'smell was an insignificant, "animal" sense, incapable of serving as a medium for the intellect or spirit' (Classen, [1994] 2002: 57) – the tradition was no longer mainstream by the late nineteenth century.

Key points

- In the ancient world the sense of smell was an important tool for discerning truth and attaining knowledge.
- Smells on the Day of Atonement helped the Israelites to discern: God's Holiness, God's acts of forgiveness and redemption, and their God-given identity as God's people.
- God's 'nose' discriminates between true and false sacrifices and God's Messiah similarly judges by smell.
- Medieval Christians thrived on the discernment of 'mystical' scents.

Fragrance of worship

There is a huge array of elements in the worshipping life of the universal church – in the use of music, silence, liturgy, bells and incense, physical postures, types of prayer, the number of practices considered sacramental and how they are practised and by whom – but there is considerable agreement about what worship means. The word comes from 'worthship' – literally, to give worth. So Christian worship fundamentally entails giving God 'his' worth, recognizing 'his' value. It is also a vehicle for the ecstatic response of human beings to God's invitation to join 'his' life of love and be transformed into the likeness of 'his' Son, Jesus Christ, through the power of the Spirit. It inspires Christians to enjoy God's presence and live a life that honours 'him', and it is based within, and flows out of, Christian community – both earthly and heavenly (Heb. 11:40).

When it comes to thinking about the use of smell in worship Christian theology strikes a complex balance between the danger of reducing sensory experience to an idol and doing justice to the incarnate, full-bodied vibrancy of God's involvement with creation. There have been widely different emphases and practices down the centuries. As we have seen, the immediacy and intensity of smell are central to the biblical imagination of God's delight in creation and in righteousness, and it is likewise central to how 'his' image-bearers praise and know God. In the Hebrew Bible it is not that God possessed a predilection for the smell of roasted animals, so much as God approved of the attitudes behind the worship offered: authentic contrition (Ps. 51:15-17), obedience (1 Sam. 15:22) and mercy (Hos. 6:6). In the New Testament, the gift of frankincense to the infant Christ signalled his divinity (Mt. 2:11) and was bound up with the first recorded instance of worshipping him. While Paul's use of olfactory language is highly metaphorical, he clearly validates the experience of smell as a means of penetrating theological truth (e.g. 2 Cor. 2:14-16) – even though he is writing to audiences largely without access to the sacrificial practices of the temple in Jerusalem and for whom the smells of incense were strongly connected with pagan worship.

Early Christian thinkers (i.e. pre-Constantine), on the other hand, were generally negative about deploying fragrances as part of worship, as there were concerns that scented altars and rituals were too closely associated with pagan and Jewish belief and would therefore draw believers away from faith in Christ. Even so, Christians at this time had an ambivalent relationship with scent, as it was used in carefully limited ways (e.g. fragrant anointing oil was used in baptismal, healing and burial rites). Smell was, however, recognized as an important metaphor for reflecting on the role of worshippers. Clement and Origen treated fragrances as powerfully symbolic and spiritualized many mentions of incense-burning in the Hebrew Bible – i.e. the only incense due to God was that of prayer. Following Christianity's shift to establishment religion under Constantine, Christian beliefs remained the same, but Christians became more comfortable with 'claiming the physical world as a realm of positive spiritual encounter through the engagement of physical experience' (Ashbrook Harvey, 2006: 58). The sense of smell and scent-producing materials were accordingly granted new value and consequence. Odiferous substances – primarily oil (often perfumed) and incense – were introduced more prominently into Christian worship, the latter taking longer to reach acceptance due to its strong affiliations with pagan devotional practices. The fragrance of incense came to be appreciated as an 'active agent of divine presence' (Ashbrook Harvey, 2006: 96) and as a pedagogical device that could help Christians better apprehend the elusive nature of God. (We will explore the latter point in the next section.)

Activity – The scent of worship

The sense of smell is highly valued today within different traditions of Christian worship. Type 'use of incense in Christian worship' into video websites like YouTube and watch videos put up by the Eastern Orthodox, Anglican and Roman Catholic Churches. Try to avoid any videos that verge on diatribes; these may not be representative of their traditions.

- How do these Christians understand their sense of smell to aid their understanding of, and practice of, worship?
- What teachings about God does incense reinforce?
- How is the experience of incense enhancing the worshippers' memory of God's redemptive work and their emotional response to this recollection?
- Is the use of incense associated more with liturgical or non-liturgical churches (usually, but not always, associated with pentecostalism). Why do you think this might be?
- Does the worship connect with other senses as well?

There is evidently something about smell that helps it to set the scene. A 2019 survey, commissioned by the Independent Network in the UK, found that it takes people well under a minute to judge a house when visiting – and that smell is the first thing that they notice, ahead of room temperature or messiness (Knight, 2019). Perhaps for this reason, a quarter of the respondents admitted to buying new candles or air fresheners before expecting a new visitor! For people who want to sell their home, the smell of white tea and figs could help secure a sale. Apparently, this combination emits a more subtle aroma than coffee and bread (the previous estate agent favourites) and provides a freshness that enhances new-build homes, in particular (Woollaston, 2014).

In the same way that we might select fragrances for our homes to make them appeal to visitors or potential purchasers, Christians can use fragrance to bring new depths to worship. Sometimes Christians burn incense in their own homes as part of their rhythm of daily prayer, but for the most part incense is reserved for public religious ceremony, as an olfactory indicator that materiality is suffused with divine presence. At these times, incense is often put into a censer, which is essentially an enclosed chamber attached to long chains. When swung, scented smoke is distributed. This action is called censing and it can occur at key points during worship. It can take place in front of the clergy and choir processing into church at the start of a service, as a symbolic reminder that King Jesus is entering for the act of worship; priests might cense people as a sign that they are blessed by and claimed for Christ (so it might occur during an ordination service, during which people are set apart for public ministry); the Bible might be censed when the Gospel is read. Incense might also be used during times of prayer in a church service and, given its heritage as an expensive gift, as a way of proclaiming the costly sacrifice of Jesus during eucharistic celebrations. If we recall that when we see, hear or touch something, we process the stimulus but remain physically unchanged (unless we are damaged by the experience in some way), yet when we smell and taste something we are taking in otherness, it helps us to appreciate why incense is used in these ways during acts of worship: it heightens Christians' awareness of intimacy with God and intensifies the physicality of the time and moment. Using incense therefore gives Christians two important reminders of place, for when believers meet with God through worship, they are taken more deeply into materiality and are located more clearly within the eschatological arc of redemption history.

Smells also, of course, connect us strongly to emotion as well as memory. Worship is a heartfelt matter – recall God's scathing retorts after 'sniffing out' false worship – and scented worship can be a strongly affective experience. To understand what this means we need to appreciate that affection, theologically understood, is not about fond attachment, and emotions and affections are not interchangeable as terms. It is rooted in the Augustinian spiritual tradition of affective theology, which developed out of Augustine's study of the Bible. Essentially the affections are the strongest inclinations of the soul (to paraphrase the evangelical affective theologian, Jonathan Edwards). They bring together our thoughts, feelings and behaviour, and engage us in the willed, tenacious pursuit of whatever we desire the most. Affections can therefore include emotions, but they are much more than emotions. Sam Storm explains:

> Emotions can often be no more than physiologically heightened states of either euphoria or fear that are unrelated to what the mind perceives as true. Affections, on the other hand, are always the fruit or effect of what the mind understands and knows. The will or inclination is moved either toward or away from something that is perceived by the mind. An emotion or mere feeling, on the other hand, can rise or fall independently of and unrelated to anything in the mind. One can experience an emotion or feeling without it properly being an affection, but one can rarely if ever experience an affection without it being emotional and involving intense feelings that awaken and move and stir the body. (2007: 45)

Augustine argued that the heart was the centre of the affects. When God encourages someone's heart to seek and find 'him', it leads to the transformation of their desires and, from there, to the transformation of their behaviour. In other words, someone's affections (will, emotions, conduct) are changed by God, as a result of encountering 'him'. Worship – whether church-based or part of private devotions – is a gift from God to humanity that enables believers' affective knowledge to be honed. The sanctifying work of the Holy Spirit is integral to this process. The Spirit enables, empowers and infuses the worship with the love, presence and authority of God, binding believers to 'him', and progressively changing them into the likeness of Christ. This can be a challenging process, as emotions can be stretched and educated, memories of the believer's place in salvation history examined and strengthened, and decisions to serve God and 'his' purposes in the world tested and renewed.

In this way, the believer's affections become better aligned with the perfect will of God. At its best, Christian worship – far from being a narcissistic affair – can be a disciplining in discipleship. Many Christians find that using incense during these times heightens the intensity of the affections and encourages them all the more to savour and to disseminate the ineffable fragrance of Christ. As already said, this can happen when Christians come together as a church body (Heb. 10:25) – affective knowledge is far more effective (and interesting!) when it is built up within structures of accountability and community – but Christians also benefit from regular periods of solitude with God, just as Jesus did (Lk. 5:16, Mk. 3:7).

Sarah Coakley argues that through prayer, we are also able to gain doctrinal knowledge affectively. Through the working of the Spirit we learn that the divine persons are one-in-being, we are incorporated into the life of God, and we understand the nature of trinitarian relations. Namely that the Father is the 'source of all'; the Spirit is the 'infinite desire of God for God', who 'yearns' for the Father, 'goads' us in our restlessness towards the Father and purifies our desires and longings; and the Son is the 'divine prototype' of perfected creation, with whom we are united through prayer (2013: 114). Our 'total experience' of God is therefore 'ineluctably tri-faceted' (2013). We learn more about this dynamic at the end of Chapter 3.

Key points

- In the Hebrew Bible, smell was an integral part of worship; it continued to be valued in the New Testament.
- Christians were reticent about the use of aromatic scent until the time of Constantine and deep scepticism continues to surround their use in some Protestant traditions in particular.
- In primarily Eastern, Roman Catholic and High Anglican Churches, scented practices of worship unite Christian believers to the memories, emotions and affective knowledge that flow through acts of worship.

Extended task – Does emotion have theological value?

Some may argue that while the emotional responses that may follow religious experience are important, they do not qualify as content for Christian theology. Discuss – drawing on the texts below.

Text 1 – Wolfhart Pannenberg, Anthropology in Theological Perspective

'Christian thinkers could not accept the Stoic condemnation of the affects for the simple reason that Scripture repeatedly speaks of the sorrows and joys of the devout. Referring to Paul, Augustine explained that even the good could experience sadness. The Gospel reports that even the Lord himself became angry, felt joy, wept over Lazarus, "desired" to celebrate the Passover with his disciples and was troubled in the face of his own death. The question therefore is not so much whether the devout mind can feel anger, but rather why it feels anger; not whether it grows sad, but at what it feels sadness; not whether but why it is afraid. … According to Augustine, on our journey to God the affects are the feet that either lead us closer to God or carry us farther from him; but without them we cannot travel the way at all' ([1985] 2004: 259).

Text 2 – Gerald McDermott, Seeing God: Jonathan Edwards and Spiritual Discernment

'Emotions (feelings) are often involved in affections, but the affections are not defined by emotional feeling. Some emotions are disconnected from our strongest inclinations. For instance, a student who goes off to college for the first time may feel doubtful and fearful. She will probably miss her friends and family at home. A part of her may even try to convince her to go back home. But she will discount these fleeting emotions as simply that – feelings that are not produced by her basic conviction that now it is time to start a new chapter in life. The affections are something like that girl's basic conviction that she should go to college, despite fleeting emotions that would keep her at home. They are strong inclinations that may at times conflict with more fleeting and superficial emotions' (2000: 32–3).

Negative and mystical theology

Introductory reflections

1. How might the diminishment of, or complete loss of, the sense of smell effect someone's life? What does this tell you about the 'reach' of this sense?
2. Imagine the smell of coffee (or even better, sniff some if you have some handy). How would you describe this smell to someone? If this is hard to do, why do you think this might be? And is this a problem or a positive?

The experience of the loss or inability to smell (anosmia) is frequently described as deprivation of the savour of life. Anosmiacs often speak of feeling cut off from the world around them – a feeling which is made worse by the invisibility of their disability. They also miss the loss of triggers for memories and feel that their emotions have become 'blunted', all of which can negatively impact their relationships. As the loss of the olfactory function can result in the loss of important neural pathways, the onset of anosmia in someone who previously had a strong sense of smell can be an early sign of the onset of diseases such as Parkinson's or Alzheimer's. Smells therefore give us an intense sense of space and memory, of relationality and identity, even though they can be hard, if not impossible, to describe. If you have ever had to choose a colour to paint a wall, you will know that paint charts can, rather impressively but often awkwardly, describe many shades of one kind of colour. Yet as Martha S. Jacobi reminds us (2016: 28), we struggle to put smells into words. We tend to describe smells in terms of something else: a smell is like freshly mown grass, rosewood, cinnamon. There is a sensorial distance that cannot be collapsed or pinpointed by our language, even as we experience it. Smell's linguistic openness is echoed in the way that it also straddles the material and the non-material. They are produced by bodies and yet they are inherently enigmatic. We could say that smell is central to the forms of affective knowing that are hardest to express – i.e. those that cannot be contained in language.

Placing the intensity and inexpressibility of smell at the culmination of our exploration of the sensorious nature of theological knowing helps us to reflect on the limitations of theological language. The philosopher Ludwig Wittgenstein once famously said: 'Describe the aroma of coffee. Why can't it be done? Do we lack the words? And for what are words lacking? But how do we get the idea that such a description must after all be possible? Have you ever felt the lack of such a description? Have you tried to describe the aroma of coffee and not succeeded?' (2001: 610). This raises a critical theological question: If something like the smell of coffee is beyond our description, then how on earth can we speak of God? Perhaps we should shut up and say nothing. When it comes to olfactory experiences, however, we accept that we can know something even if cannot be epistemologically precise about it.

This gives us a bridge to something called negative theology (otherwise known as apophatic theology, from the Greek word *apophasis*, meaning 'denial' or 'negation', and *via negativa*, meaning 'negative way'). In the broadest sense, this is a form of theology that celebrates how God will always exceed human understanding and language. Speaking analogically, we might be able to discern 'his' fragrance, but we cannot fully pin down 'his' scent within our human frame of reference. God also eludes capture not because 'he' is utterly unknowable, but because there is so much to be known we will never reach the end of 'him'. To keep this perspective in view, emphasizing the limits of our language reminds theologians of humanity's finitude and creaturehood. To aid such cautiousness, apophatic theologians make negative statements (saying what God is not) instead of positive statements (saying what God is). Eagle-eyed readers will spot that even this can become problematic, however, as denials can still communicate the nature of God, albeit in a different way. In which case, they are simply a back door for kataphatic theology (kataphatic theology, from the Greek word *kataphasis*, meaning positive or affirmative).

Pseudo-Dionysius the Aeropagite, who wrote in the early sixth century, was acutely aware that negatives can hem God in as much as affirmations – indeed, can become affirmations if we stop and rest at the point of negation. His apophaticism therefore took the form of an unceasing saying and unsaying. In his highly influential work *The Mystical God*, Dionysius gave order to the perpetual motion between affirmation and negation, a motion practised in contemplation rather than reached through reason or the senses. To paraphrase Stang (2012: 238), one begins by contemplating the divine names, working from the highest to the lowest (even contemplating God as a sleepy drunk, Ps. 78:65). This descent mirrors the descent of God, who is above being, into the being of creation. One then works back up the chain, this time denying all the names just affirmed. This contemplative ascent reflects the yearning of creation to return to its source. Crucially, the divine names are denied 'not because God is not, for instance, good, but because God surpasses the good: God is so superabundantly good that the notion of good no longer has full purchase' (2012: 239). Thus, even the negations are negated. In all this, Dionysius keeps in mind the example of Moses on Mount Sinai (Exod. 19), who, having realized that God transcends anything that might be said of 'him', is brought into mystical union with God in a 'cloud of unknowing'. This experience gives Moses a form of affective knowledge – i.e. he feels that he knows something, but he knows that he cannot put it into words. Nor is Moses left unchanged by Dionysius's *via negativa*, which Stang views as an ascetic exercise (2009: 15-18). Being united to the unknown God requires the self to strip away its categories of self-understanding and step outside itself in ecstatic yearning for God. While this brings suffering, it clears the way for the self to be conformed to the God who is even beyond being.

Thinking about smell can also take us into mystical theology, which learns from practices of contemplative prayer and asceticism. These practices teach Christians to be selfless and to yearn for and experience God as the source of all love. Mystical theologians argue that knowledge of God gained in these ways is to be valued more highly than rational knowledge produced by reason, as contemplation leads to the direct intuition of God. How, though, is such a thing possible? The Bible uses plenty of sensory language that suggests that 'perception-like contact with God is possible' (Coakley and Gavrilyuk, 2012:1): as we have already seen, Paul writes that Christians are to breathe in the 'sweet aroma of Christ' (2 Cor. 2:15). Biblical writers give us other tantalizing hints that our senses can grant us some knowledge of God. In Deuteronomy 4:28 and Psalm 115:4-8, YHWH (Yahweh) derides false idols and ridicules them as being insensitive and inert by pointing out they lack any senses. So in addition to the lifelessness of idols and the lifelessness that idolatry brings, there is a suggestion that the wider knowledge of God involves all human senses – perhaps even that the more evanescent senses like smell are superior, given that there are other Hebrew Bible references to the connection between aroma, truth and wisdom (e.g. Ecclus. 24:15). Yet the Bible also says that, in trying to look at God, we are looking at 'what cannot be seen' (cf. 2 Cor. 4:18, Heb. 11:27) (Coakley and Gavrilyuk, 2012). What are we to make of this quandary?

Christian thinkers down the centuries have wrestled with the non-physical perception of God, who is utterly ontologically distinct from creation. One diverse tradition is that of the 'spiritual senses'. An important theologian who engaged with this tradition was Bonaventure (1217–74). In his hands, the spiritual senses are a fivefold way that God can be distinctively experienced as present. In his book *The Soul's Journey into God* he charts the Christian soul's growth into a likeness of God and the believer's progression to mystical union with God. He suggests that just as human souls delight in our five physical senses and their union with objects in the corporeal world, so there are five corresponding spiritual senses which delight in the non-material reality of Divine Wisdom – e.g. what is most beautiful, harmonious, fragrant, sweet or delightful. Bodily sensation involves apprehension, delight and judgement (and we can see God 'in the mirror' of these sensory processes); spiritual sensation follows God's work of grace and involves our apprehension of a spiritual object – Jesus Christ, the incarnate Word (LaNave, 2012: 164). Bonaventure describes the stages of the spiritual senses in this way:

> When by faith the soul believes in Christ as the uncreated Word and splendour of the Father, it recovers the spiritual senses of hearing and sight: its hearing to receive the words of Christ and its sight to view the splendour of that Light. When it longs in hope to receive the inspired Word, it recovers through desire and affection the spiritual sense of smell. When it embraces in love the Word incarnate, receiving delight from him and passing over into him through ecstatic love, it recovers its senses of taste and touch. Having recovered these senses, when it sees its Spouse and hears, smells, tastes and embraces him, the soul can sing like the bride of the Canticle of Canticles [Song of Songs]. (1978: 89)

Bonaventure is here using positive sensory language for the immediate, apprehension of God, which nevertheless goes beyond any form of intellectual knowing. In so doing he deliberately inverts the usual hierarchy of senses. Sight and hearing, which are traditionally associated with the intellect, come first rather than last, and are subordinated to the affective and higher form of sensual apprehension of taste and smell, culminating in the intimacy of taste and touch in union with God. Bonaventure ranks touch as the highest of the spiritual senses as it refers to the close encounter of bodies and the experience of love; it therefore aptly refers to union with the incarnate Word. The spiritual senses together prepare the way for the Christian believer's ecstatic union with God:

> *No one* grasps this *except him who receives* … , since it is more a matter of affective experience than rational consideration. For in this stage, when the inner senses are restored to see the highest beauty, to hear the highest harmony, to smell the highest fragrance, to taste the highest sweetness, to apprehend the highest delight, the soul is prepared for spiritual ecstasy through devotion, admiration and exultation. (1978)

Such non-cognitive spiritual ecstasy is itself a mode of knowing – that of affective cognition. It is grounded in the body and bodily practices as much as the love and grace of God, as shown in the incarnate Word; and it calls believers into unending comprehension of God, who is always 'beyond' and always calling people forward into union with 'him'. Contemplative prayer is therefore a profound work of the Holy Spirit (discussed in Chapter 4) – which is extremely apt here, given the biblical connections between the Spirit, life, breath and the nose.

Extended task

Write either a paper on the relationship between affective and intellectual knowledge or put together a web-profile of a major mystical theologian.

Chapter summary

In this chapter we have:

- Explored biblical metaphors for smell as delight, disgust and discernment
- Explored the fragrance of worship and showed how practices of Christian worship shape and form affective knowing
- Used the ineffability of smell to help us reflect on negative and mystical theology, and to connect theology with prayer, contemplation, embodiment and pneumatology.

Recommended reading

Mysticism

Hollywood, Amy, and Patricia Z. Beckman, eds. (2012), *The Cambridge Companion to Christian Mysticism*, Cambridge: Cambridge University Press.
McIntosh, Mark (1998), *Mystical Theology: The Integrity of Spirituality and Theology*, Oxford: Wiley-Blackwell.
McIntosh, Mark (2008), *Divine Teaching: An Introduction to Christian Teaching*, Oxford: Blackwell Publishing.

Negative theology

Davies, Oliver, and Denys Turner (2002), *Silence of the Word: Negative Theology and Incarnation*, Cambridge: Cambridge University Press.

Spiritual senses tradition

Coakley, Sarah, and Paul L. Gavrilyk (2012), *The Spiritual Senses: Perceiving God in Western Christianity*, Cambridge: Cambridge University Press.

McInroy, Mark (2014), *Balthasar on the 'Spiritual Senses': Perceiving Splendour*, Oxford: Oxford University Press.

Worship

Wainright, Geoffrey, and Karen W. Tucker, eds. (2006), *The Oxford History of Christian Worship*, Oxford: Oxford University Press.
White, James F. ([1980] 2000), *Introduction to Christian Worship*, Nashville, TN: Abingdon Press.

6

Loving: Politics and/of salvation

It's often said that religion and politics should never be discussed in polite company. If that is so, then in this chapter we will examine how impolite theology must be. We reject the cliché that religion and politics are so inflammatory and potentially divisive that they may upset a middle-class dinner party, and more problematically, challenge the intimacy of our relationships with others. Instead, we shall argue that theology and politics alike are all-encompassing. Indeed theology tries to articulate the ways in which Christianity claims the whole of the life of the believer; and every area of life – from what we eat to how we perform our gender roles, from how we shop to how we raise our children – is essentially political. 'The earth is the Lord's, and all that is in it, the world, and those who live in it' (Ps. 24:1). There won't be space to deal with those complicated everyday tasks here; instead our guiding motif will be one of the most political, and most theological, of human actions – loving and being loved.

The chapter progresses through three ways of relating theology and politics – the antithetical (theology vs. politics), the mode of encounter (theology through politics) and then the shaping of action (theology as politics). We begin by noting how our particular historical and cultural context may shape our assumptions about the relationship between 'religion' and 'politics'. Having shown, second, that theology is inherently political, and politics often implicitly theological, we'll examine how theology, particularly the doctrine of salvation and the atonement, enacts and enables political concern.

Antithesis: Theology vs. politics

We all have structures of thought and models of action which impact our approach to the world. One of the most unsettling things about theological study, or any other academically rigorous study, is its capacity to subject our thinking to a thorough examination. In this chapter we will show that we must significantly widen both the conception of religion as essentially private belief and the common assumption that 'politics' is about the actions of nation states or political parties.

In popular discourse, especially in the media, religion 'intervening' in politics is associated with particular controversies (abortion and gay marriage are often prominent issues) and a particular form of religion (perhaps 'political Islam' [*sic*] or the fundamentalist Christians of the American 'Religious Right'). Such assumptions are limited and problematic. The notion of 'getting involved' implies a transgression of boundaries – of moving from one territory to another. This idea can develop into the complaint that religious communities 'get involved' in politics or ethics only so that they can 'impose' their views on others and sow seeds of division.

This is the type of picture painted by popular, but less than satisfactory, models of contemporary culture. Samuel Huntingdon's 'clash of civilisations' thesis, for example, claims that in a post–Cold War world, as conflicts from Rwanda to Northern Ireland to Iraq show, people's cultural and religious identity will be the primary agent of conflict. Why is that? Because, says Huntingdon, religious identity works by separating those who are 'in' and 'out', and then justifying abhorrent tactics in dealing with the latter (Huntingdon, 1996). Other secular critics lament the loss of the 'great separation' between religion and politics (Lilla, 2008), and express frustration at the stubborn refusal of public religion to ebb away.

Behind these objections lies a norm about what religion and theology *should* and perhaps more importantly *should not* be concerned with. That norm is carried by verbs like 'getting involved', 'imposing', etc. That norm is open to question. It is part of the common political story of our times. It may seem obvious to you that religion is a matter of private preference, and politics a matter of public importance. But that is only obvious within the story of modern Western politics. The decision to frame this as a boundary question between two distinct realms or activities is itself a powerful political act. The definition and relationship of religion and politics could be, and often has been, framed very differently. Historically, religion and the secular have been defined, and distinctions between the private and the political have been drawn, in such a way as to exclude, domesticate or simply ignore challenging elements of diverse theological traditions (Asad, 2003). The British theologian John Milbank stridently denounces the modern invention of 'the secular', seeing it as an attempt to 'police the sublime' and defang theological critiques of the dominance of capitalism and late modern liberalism (Milbank, 2006).

From time to time the background assumptions that shape public debate come to the fore. For example, in June 2013 an editorial in one British newspaper, *The Independent*, protested at what it held to be an inappropriate intervention by the newly appointed Archbishop of Canterbury, Justin Welby, in two political issues of the day: the crippling debt burden incurred by those desperate enough to use 'payday loan' companies, with an annual interest rate of up to 5,853 per cent, and a proposed cap on state benefit payments to rises well below inflation. Both were identified by the Archbishop as having a highly damaging impact on the poorest and most vulnerable in society.

While anxiety over child poverty is admirable, public pronouncements on purely political issues in which his organisation has no direct involvement are as unconstructive as they are inappropriate. The question is neither Archbishop Welby's motivations nor his capabilities; ... he has both the background and the acuity to make an informed contribution. The question is whether he should do so.

For *The Independent*, even when we agree with him, the answer must be no. ... Archbishop Welby is still the unelected leader of a minority institution which enjoys disproportionate influence on the basis of history alone. His efforts to reclaim the initiative and make the Church relevant again are understandable. But they are also erroneous.

This is no swipe at religion, but such matters are a private affair, and spiritual leaders – for all the authority they may have among their own – have no business in mainstream politics. That bishops still sit in the House of Lords is an anachronism that makes a mockery of British democracy. If Archbishop Welby wishes the Church of England to support credit unions, it is his prerogative to act accordingly, but there his legitimacy ends (*The Independent*, Friday, 26 July 2013).

Leaving aside the irony of an unelected newspaper editor complaining at the political interventions of an unelected churchman, the rhetoric that the church should stick to 'spiritual' matters and keep out of politics is a persistent refrain in public discourse. However, it would be a mistake to think that the privatization of religion, and hence of theology, is predominantly or solely a fault-line in the debate between religions and secularists. For many Christians the separation of religion and politics is also axiomatic (i.e. a definitional principle which we can use as a foundation for our worldview). They may appeal to a 'common sense' understanding of the famous passage from all three synoptic gospels, where Jesus says, 'Render unto Caesar the things that are Caesars, and to God the things that are God's' (Mt. 22:15-22, Mk 12:13-17, Lk. 20:20-26). This phrase, if not the whole passage, has permitted a variety of accounts of the complementary separation of church and state. However, in its original context and function it is not likely to have been interpreted in this way. As N. T. Wright points out:

Jesus gets his interlocutors to produce a coin, ... with its blasphemous inscription and its (to a Jew) illegal image, a portrait of Caesar himself. Whose is it? he asks. Caesar's, they answer. Well then, says Jesus, you'd better pay back Caesar in his own coin – and pay God back in his own coin!

The closest echoes to this double command are found in 1 Maccabees 2.68. Mattathias is telling his sons, especially Judas, to get ready for revolution. 'Pay back to the Gentiles what is due to them,' he says, 'and keep the law's commands'. Paying back the Gentiles was not meant to refer to money. I am sure that some of Jesus' hearers would have picked up that revolutionary hint. Because he was standing there looking at a coin, his surface meaning was, of course, that the tax had to be paid; but underneath was the strong hint that Caesar's regime was a blasphemous nonsense and that one day God would overthrow it.

The setting and the saying show decisively ... that Jesus did not mean it as indicating a separation between the spheres of Caesar and God, with each taking responsibility for a distinct part of the world. ... the saying must have meant that God claimed the whole of life, including questions about taxes. Of course, Jesus acknowledges, you may have to pay taxes to the pagans, just as Jews in exile had to pray to God for the welfare of Babylon; but that doesn't mean that God is only concerned with a different, 'spiritual' world. God is present in the ambiguity, summoning people to an allegiance which transcended but certainly included the position they found themselves in vis-a-vis the occupying power (Wright, 2004: 163–4).

So far we have questioned a commonly held, but by no means universal, account of the separation of religion and politics. It may be that you hold to a version of a 'great separation'; you may find it theologically untenable; or you may dislike defining the relationship of abstract nouns such as 'religion' and 'politics' – preferring instead to take things on a more ad hoc issue-by-issue basis. Whatever your starting position, it can be helpful to identify your own assumptions and definitions. One way to do this is to question the ways in which your views on political theology are shaped by the cultural assumptions of your current context.

Questions for discussion

We have deliberately provided a slightly dated example above. What more recent examples can you find? Search online news media, newspapers and television news for stories in which religious groups or figures have made comment or engaged in political action. Discuss in groups:

1) How is such participation in politics conceived? Our assumptions are often shown in our verbs: 'intervene', 'pronounce', 'lecture' and even 'preach' may have negative connotations; 'speak out', 'criticize', 'defend', 'take a stand' may have more positive associations.

2) To what extent are political engagements expressed and justified in relation to central theological claims of Christianity? Is the theology explicit or implicit?

3) What connections can you see between Christian political action and concern for social justice, and the various doctrines discussed so far in this book?

We are now going to look more closely at how political visions carry theological claims with them, and how theology issues in political claims.

Key points

- The nature and relationship between religion and politics are contingent and open to question.
- The separation of religion and politics is itself a political move.
- Theological claims frequently have political consequences.

Theology through politics: Love in the city

Christian thought has often tied together salvation and the political by envisaging the Christian life as the chastening and shaping of love. We most often associate 'love' with the fleeting emotional and hormonal state of 'being in love'. We have seen throughout this book that theology entails affective as well as more cerebral forms of knowing, yet tying 'love' to the transitory, albeit meaningful, intensity of 'being in love' can be misleading. Christian love is not episodic. Stanley Hauerwas deftly identifies the tension here: 'When couples come to ministers to talk about their marriage ceremonies, ministers think it's interesting to ask if they love one another. What a stupid question! How would they know? A Christian marriage isn't about whether you're in love. Christian marriage is giving you the practice of fidelity over a lifetime in which you can look back upon the marriage and call it love. It is a hard discipline over many years' (in Cavanaugh, 2002: 13 and 46).

We see that love is profoundly central to politics in Jesus's summary of the law and the prophets as love of God and neighbour (Mt. 22:36-40, Mk 12:30-31, Lk. 10:27-28), and in the constant Johannine refrain that connects love and knowledge (e.g. 1 Jn 4:8). Such passages suggest that if the goal of human action is found in the loving embrace of God, the Christian life is caught up in the mutually constitutive love of God and of God's creation. As we saw in our discussion of *agape* and *eros* in Chapter 3, there is therefore no competition between an appropriate love of others, the world or ourselves, on the one hand, and love of God on the other. When those loves become competitive, things have gone wrong. Religion and politics have become unduly separated. This is given influential expression in Augustine's *City of God* XIV.28:

> Two cities have been formed by two loves: the earthly by the love of self, even to the contempt of God; the heavenly by the love of God, even to the contempt of self. The one, therefore, glories in itself, the other in the Lord; the one seeks glory from men, the other finds its highest glory in God, the Witness of our conscience. The one lifts up its head in its own glory; the other says to its God, 'Thou are my glory, and the lifter of mine head'. In the Earthly City, princes are as much mastered by the lust for mastery as the nations which they subdue are by them; in the Heavenly, all serve one another in charity, rulers by their counsel and subjects by their obedience. The one city loves its own strength as displayed in its mighty men; the other says to its God, 'I will love Thee, O Lord, my strength' (1998: 632).

Augustine's writings can be misread in two ways. First, he could be understood to only say that the coercive exercise of governmental power is a necessary concession to sin; it's there to keep order. That is only part of the picture. Augustine sees loving as fundamental to all human action, and so governmental power is there to encourage civic virtue as well as restrain sin. Second, he is sometimes seen to be saying that loving God requires disdain for bodily life, where actually he is warning believers about flirting with idolatry. The point to grasp is that Augustine argues for the proper balance of desires and loves. The goods of this world are 'common objects of love', properly ordered to desire for God but used to different ends by the earthly city. The heavenly city pilgrimages through mortality, making use of the temporary and imperfect order and peace of political society. This involves the heavenly city in a cooperative enterprise with the earthly city, but it doesn't automatically follow that the latter will regard the former in a positive light.

Discussion activity – Varied readings of Augustine

Various political theologies have used Augustine's *City of God* to justify their own policies. Read the extract below from *The City of God* XIX.17

> Therefore, for as long as this Heavenly City is a pilgrim on earth, she summons citizens of all nations and every tongue, and brings together a society of pilgrims in which no attention is paid to any differences in the customs, laws, and institutions by which earthly peace is achieved or maintained. She does not rescind or destroy these things, however. For whatever differences there are among the various nations, these all tend towards the same end of earthly peace. Thus, she preserves and follows them, provided only that they do not

impede the religion by which we are taught that the one supreme and true God is to be worshipped. And so even the Heavenly City makes use of earthly peace during her pilgrimage, and desires and maintains the co-operation of men's wills in attaining those things which belong to the moral nature of man, in so far as this may be allowed without prejudice to true godliness and religion. Indeed, she directs that earthly peace towards heavenly peace: towards the peace which is so truly such that – at least so far as rational creatures are concerned – only it can really be held to be peace and called such. For this peace is a perfectly ordered and perfectly harmonious fellowship in the enjoyment of God, and of one another in God. When we have reached that peace, our life will no longer be a mortal one; rather, we shall then be fully and certainly alive. ... This peace the Heavenly City possesses in faith while on its pilgrimage, and by this faith it lives righteously, directing towards the attainment of that peace every good act which it performs either for God, or – since the city's life is inevitably a social one – for neighbour. (1998: 946–7)

How successfully does this text justify the following:

1. A cosmopolitan international community beyond national identities
2. The establishment of the church, or some other legal recognition of the special place of the church to the good of society
3. The constitutional separation of church and state
4. A human right to freedom of religion, whereby all are free to determine for themselves how to 'enjoy' God
5. A duty for some Christians to participate in military service in order to contribute to the peace of the earthly city
6. A theology which prioritizes the spiritual over the mundane, the 'next life' over this life
7. An endorsement of Christians cooperating with secular and other religious communities for the betterment of society
8. The view that the state is only legitimate and functioning properly when it endorses worship of the one true God.

Augustine's thought can be difficult to understand. The above text needs placing in its broader context if its meaning is to be grasped, and simplistic interpretations ruled out. Fundamentally, Augustine's intention in narrating the two cities is not to permit some easy assimilation of Christianity and Rome. Instead he wants to show how the Christian virtue of humility exceeds the Roman virtues of pride, honour and glory – going so far as to describe the latter as not virtues at all but 'splendid vices'. Indeed, for Augustine's Christianizing and innovative account of the classical cardinal virtues, love (*caritas*) is the prime virtue in which the more specific, and perhaps for us the more obviously political, virtues of prudence, temperance, fortitude and justice find their source and home – that is in God 'himself'. A failure to ground our politics in God is thus a failure of love. Thus he says in *On the Morals of the Catholic Church* I.15.25:

> As to virtue leading us to a happy life, I hold virtue to be nothing else than perfect love of God. For the fourfold division of virtue I regard as taken from four forms of love …. The object of this love is not any thing, but only God, the chief good, the highest wisdom, the perfect harmony. So we may express the definition class: that temperance is love keeping itself entire and incorrupt for God; fortitude is love bearing everything readily for the sake of God; justice is love serving God only, and therefore ruling well all else as subject to man; Prudence is love making a right distinction between what helps its towards God and what might hinder it. (Augustine, 1887b: 48)

Augustine's critique of the Roman Empire was that in failing to love fully it had failed to be genuinely political: it failed to be a genuine *res publica* – genuinely public. Consequently it was unable to maintain stability, equality and unity. Rome's 'peace' was not genuine peace. Augustine's great innovation, placing love at the heart of politics, has considerable consequences for how we see human action. Perhaps the most fundamental question of political theology is not, 'who should we be?', nor even, 'what should we do' but 'what/whom do you love?' In answering this question we will name those people and institutions we value most, that we would die for, perhaps kill for, certainly spend our money on, and devote our time and energy to. All of these actions are thoroughly political. Through these political actions and views, one encounters fundamental claims about the nature and limits of human action, our individual and collective identity, our role in the world – and consequently the purpose of human life and of the world itself, and thus of God's presence and action in and through the action of human beings. Political thought and action are a mode of theological encounter.

Having placed love at centre-stage in politics, we still need a concrete sense of what this looks like. The short answer is that the love of God for the world, and God's present initiative in restoring that world, takes on a very particular shape: Jesus. To develop this answer we will now explore how three theologians have depicted Jesus's preaching about non-violence and his embodiment of loving enemies, and consider how these portrayals may connect with divergent political 'applications'. Then we'll unwrap the complex ways in which diverse, and perhaps conflicting, political visions issue indirectly from different conceptions of the atonement.

Key points

- Following Augustine, much political theology places love at the centre of its account of what it is to be political.
- Augustine's vision of two cities moved by two loves has been interpreted and used to support a wide range of different, and perhaps even conflicting, political visions and agendas.

Theology as politics: Loving enemies

We have just seen, in relation to Augustine's political writings, that we have a tendency towards eisegesis (i.e. reading our own meanings into a text – the opposite of exegesis). This is even more the case with interpreting Jesus. Which of the range of messiahs is genuine? There is immense political–theological debate surrounding the action of the love of God-in-Christ. The issue of violence and non-violence is fundamental to this debate.

There can be no doubt that Jesus's teaching placed on his followers a radical, perhaps even counter-intuitive, set of demands: anger is equivalent to murder, a lustful glance constitutes adultery, one should love not only one's neighbour but also one's enemy. Throughout Christian political and ethical thought, there has been a wide variety of ways of approaching these demands. Some have downplayed their radical nature, but in doing so are the demands of the Gospel diluted for the sake of an easier life? Others take such injunctions to be a clear stipulation of Jesus's ethic, but are they simply rhetorically tone-deaf and unable to recognize hyperbole (exaggeration for effect)?

We can open up these questions by briefly considering three interpretations of Jesus's teaching on non-violence and presenting common theological critiques of each position.

Dirty love: Reinhold Niebuhr (1892–1971)

Niebuhr strongly criticizes how some forms of Christian political thought can drift into naivety and idealism. In response, he argues that the unconditional love preached in the Sermon on the Mount is poorly suited to responsible political life. Like Nygren's absolute split of *agape* and *eros* (which we criticized in Chapter 3), Niebuhr identifies this love as radically demanding: it endorses a complete sacrifice of the self. Unlike Nygren, Niebuhr holds that God's pure *agape* can build upon and influence the less perfect loves of the human condition. In this he was shaped by Augustine's doctrine of original sin – that love is conditioned by human contingencies – and the more pessimistic elements of Augustine's political vision. Niebuhr combined these thoughts with a strong split between public and private life (potentially depoliticizing the latter).

In private face-to-face relations the action that gets us close, but not all the way to, loving enemies is 'mutual love' – i.e. love that is conditional and reciprocal (Niebuhr, 1943: 69). Here the grace of *agape* may stimulate greater patience and forgiveness when reciprocity fails – such as when one feels exhausted, betrayed or undermined; when the 'return' of love is not forthcoming. In other words, fragments of *agape* may prevent mutuality from becoming diminished.

Niebuhr is pragmatic about the limits of human capabilities. For him, the starting point of Christian political reflection is the impossibility of enacting *agape*, and hence enemy love. It is 'justice' – the pursuit of equilibrium between the claims of every person – which must be the guiding norm of political life. Neither self-giving love nor even the 'mutual love' of personal relationships can be attained in politics. The brutality of groups means that the best that one should aim for in political society is not the achievement of any substantive good, but the counter-balance of self-assertions whereby 'self-interest and power must be harnessed and beguiled rather than eliminated. … forces which are morally dangerous must be used despite their peril' (Niebuhr, 1976: 59). In other words, sometimes we need to get out hands dirty.

The imperative of loving our enemies may chasten our actions here. Justice may be compromised when a preference for our own group (nation, race, class, gender) or own beloved pulls our gaze away from the demands of those we find less appealing, or less easy to identify with. While enemy love is an ideal present only as an 'impossible possibility' (Niebuhr, 1935: 19), nonetheless, it spurs us on to a productive dissatisfaction with anything less than justice.

Critique of Niebuhr: The challenge of balance and completeness

The political implications of our theology depend on how we hold together the cocktail of doctrines. So, for example, Niebuhr accuses early-twentieth-century liberal versions of Christian pacifism of an indifference to justice, born of a failure to take original sin seriously. Whereas critics of Niebuhr have said that he emphasizes sin at the expense of grace and redemption, downplays central tenets of Christology and almost entirely ignores the role of the church in history and the divine economy (i.e. God's project of redemption and restoration of the world).

For many, Niebuhr's attempt to balance this world and the next, and to avoid either idealism or cynicism, is intuitively appealing. Others question his depiction of the law of love. For Niebuhr, enemy love is a form of pure passivity. Any activity is morally and theologically compromised by the impossibility of purity. Given this starting point, there can be no genuine social ethic in Jesus's preaching, 'precisely because the ethical ideal is too rigorous and perfect to lend itself to application in the economic and political problems of our day' (Niebuhr, 1992: 30). Thus for Niebuhr it is no accident that Jesus's radical non-violence led him to the cross. That is where it would lead any of us. However Jesus's path of radical passivity is precisely what Christians must *not* follow. His ethic only pricks the conscience; the law of love 'hover[s] over every social situation as an ideal possibility' (1986: 115). Yet as David Clough has dryly remarked, 'given that [Niebuhr's] Christian realism led him to judge that the atomic bombing of Hiroshima and Nagasaki by the United States could be justified, this hovering seems at quite some altitude' (2009: 203).

Niebuhr's theology is also deficient when it comes to Christology and eschatology. Regarding the latter, his disconnection of everyday life from the eschatological in-breaking of God's kingdom may be too strong. As H. Richard Niebuhr, Reinhold's younger brother, notes, this has a tendency to make not just the fullness of the kingdom, but also its first fruits (1 Cor. 15:20) after the resurrection an ahistorical reality. It also encourages us to think that God is more hidden than orthodox Christianity has claimed (H. R. Niebuhr, 1996: 100).

For John Howard Yoder, who we'll turn to next, it is here that Niebuhr's Christology falls down. Niebuhr regards the cross as a sign of the ineffectiveness of Jesus's messianic pacifism. We see 'love triumphant in its own integrity' (Niebuhr, 2013: 82), but this is not a triumph in the world. Christ's victory over sin and death does not yield a Lordship in history. Indeed, Niebuhr reads the resurrection as only a symbol of the theological demand that 'the suprahistorical triumph of the good' (Niebuhr, 1943: 308) must, in some as yet unspecified way, transform and rescue the processes of human history. What, then, is Yoder's alternative?

Engaged love: John Howard Yoder (1927–97)

Both Niebuhr and the liberal pacifists he criticized assumed that genuine love of enemy entailed complete non-resistance in the face of injustice. Conversely, Yoder defends Christian non-violent resistance against evil. The indiscriminate, self-sacrificial love of Jesus's political life is to be emulated precisely because this is how God acts in human history to overcome evil. This means that equating politics solely with coercion or violence (and thus only with what governments and states do) is questionable. Yoder could not be clearer:

> [Jesus] refused to concede that those in power represent an ideal, a logically proper, or even an empirically acceptable definition of what it means to be political. He did not

say …, 'you can have your politics and I shall do something else more important'; he said, 'your definition of *polis,* of the social, of the wholeness of being human socially is perverted'. (1994a: 107)

For Yoder, the possibility of loving enemies is grounded in the cross, which shows us the genuine effectiveness of self-sacrifice as the non-violent absorption of human hostility to God. 'This death reveals how God deals with evil; here is the only valid starting point for Christian pacifism or nonresistance. The cross is the extreme demonstration that *agape* seeks neither effectiveness nor justice, and is willing to suffer any loss or seeming defeat for the sake of obedience' (1998: 59). As opposed to Niebuhr, Yoder has a strong reading of the historical impact of the resurrection, for on the cross 'effectiveness and success had been sacrificed for the sake of love, but this sacrifice was turned by God into a victory which vindicated to the utmost the apparent impotence of love' (1998: 60).

This is not to say that effectiveness and justice don't matter, but that these things can only genuinely occur if the faithful love of enemies is pursued. They may not even be immediate or within our lifetimes; martyrdom is a meaningful possibility. Nonetheless, love of enemies will be vindicated, for it moves through the world in the same way God does. 'We do not, ultimately, love our neighbour because Jesus told us to. We love our neighbour because God is like that. It is not because Jesus told us that we love even beyond the limits of reason and justice, even to the point of refusing to kill and being willing to suffer – but because God is like that too' (Yoder, 1998: 52). In Yoder's evocative phrase, obedience to the non-violent love of God enacted in Christ moves 'with the grain of the universe' (1988: 58). This focus on the non-violent character of God leads Yoder to say – again, in direct contrast to Niebuhr – that Christ is only to be imitated at one point: the cross (1994a: 95). Loving our enemies, as exemplified by Christ on the cross, is 'the political alternative to both insurrection and quietism' (1994a: 96 and 36).

Christian political thought has often sought to find some way of avoiding radical demands such as these. For example it can stress the difference between Jesus's context and ours: Jesus lived in a situation of powerlessness under empire, we live in democratic political structures; Jesus dealt with small-scale rural societies where everyone knew each other, many of us live in less intimate urban environments; Jesus expected the world to come to an end very soon, we have to look after it for our own good and the good of future generations. Or it can focus on christologies which stress the 'spiritual' or 'existential' significance of Jesus as 'spiritual' saviour and friend. These approaches all deny the normativity (i.e. the binding norm of practice) of Jesus's non-violence, and thereby get caught in ever-renewing forms of ancient christological heresies. Setting aside the normativity of Christ because of Jesus's limited context undoes the full divinity of Christ whereas divorcing the cosmic Christ of faith from the Jesus of history compromises the fullness of Christ's humanity. For Yoder, a full and orthodox account of Christ as fully God and fully man leads one to non-violence.

Critique of Yoder: Questioning connections and consequences

In Yoder's theology the practicability of loving enemies is built on the relationship between Christology, eschatology and ecclesiology. His argument for non-violence would be vulnerable if any one of these constituent doctrines is found wanting. Yoder's ecclesiology has been subject to some vociferous critique: he presents a naïve account of human action, an idealized picture of the church and a sectarian vision of the role of Christianity in society (i.e. a church that's more interested in maintaining clean hands than in serving the common good). Each of these criticisms falls short. First, the faith that loving enemies is ethically possible does not make that faith cheap or easy. It is not cheap because refusing violence does not prevent one from being its victim. Active, non-violent resistance of evil can mean putting oneself in harm's way. It's not easy because of the sinful habits that shape us all. Yet while Yoder recognizes the sinfulness of the church in all its forms, he still regards it as being caught up in the sanctifying work of the Holy Spirit. Thus Yoder's ecclesiastical vision is what one of us has elsewhere called a 'becoming Church' (Bourne, 2009: 129). This is why Stanley Hauerwas's appropriation of Yoder frequently appeals to a strong account of the Christian community as a place of character formation. Christians need the community of discipline and grace to shape themselves in the light of Christ's demand. Hauerwas puts it provocatively:

> I say I'm a pacifist because I'm a violent son of a bitch. ... part of what nonviolence is – [is] the attempt to make our lives vulnerable to others in a way that we need one another. To be against war ... is a good place to start. But you never know where the violence is in your own life. To say you're nonviolent is ... to make your life available to others in a way that they can help you discover ways you're implicated in violence that you hadn't even noticed. (in McCarthy, 2003: np)

For Yoder, the everyday life of the church creates a community of witness. In contrast to Niebuhr's 'futurist' eschatology (i.e. the Kingdom of God is a purely other-worldly future event), Yoder adopts an 'inaugurated' eschatology: the Kingdom of God has begun, and the Church is tasked with showing the world God's rule. 'The church does communicate to the world what God plans to do, because it shows that God is beginning to do it' (1994b: 126). This means that the church's life exemplifies 'a renewed way of living within the present' (1994a: 185). It exists in the reality of, and therefore takes its cues from, the claims of Christology and eschatology. This means that the quintessential fact of Christian politics is the victory of God in Christ, over the principalities and powers.

When the church seeks to love enemies, it bears witness to the victory of the Prince of Peace. In Yoder's terms, 'The people of God are called to be today what the world is called to be ultimately' (1992: ix). There is no basis for self-righteousness or pride here, for the division of 'church' and 'world' runs through the heart of every believer. Thus the criticism of sectarianism may miss the mark, as it attributes both the wrong motivations and the wrong model of action to Christian non-violence as enemy love. The motivation is never one of purity; the movement not one of protectionist withdrawal. Rather non-violent enemy love is seen as a mode of action shaped by the ontological conditions of reality as it has been transformed in Christ.

Our final approach to loving enemies affirms with Yoder and against Niebuhr that such a love is possible in this world; but denies that which both Yoder and Niebuhr affirm – that enemy love entails non-violence.

Violent love: Nigel Biggar (b.1955)

Nigel Biggar (b.1955) defends violence in war as a viable enactment of a conditional and discriminate love of enemies. There are three stages to his argument (2013). First, Biggar seeks to demonstrate that Jesus does not reject violence per se, but only private unauthorized violence driven by Jewish religious nationalism. Second, Biggar claims there are key indications in the New Testament that lethal violence, while never enjoined, is implicitly accepted. Here he places great emphasis on the 'faith' of the Centurion at the foot of the cross (Mk 15:39), the positive depiction of the Centurion Cornelius (Acts 10:1-33) and a reading of Romans 13 which takes lethal violence to be legitimate when enacted by a government in the exercise of its divine mandate as an agent of God's wrath. Finally, Biggar claims that engaging one's enemy with lethal violence may constitute an act of love – albeit only in certain limited circumstances (i.e. by applying the Just War tradition).

While both Niebuhr and Yoder focus on the radical demands of enemy love as *agape*, Biggar does not engage with the term. Instead he analyses the ethics of forgiveness and questions whether Jesus's ethic of love is to be construed as unconditional and indiscriminate (2013: 23). He suggests a distinction between two stages of forgiveness: unconditional compassion, sometimes followed by an absolution (conditional upon repentance). Only forgiveness-as-compassion is pertinent to loving enemies. 'Even wounding or lethal coercion can be compassionate at least insofar as it refuses vengeance, intends to stop the wrongdoer doing wrong, intends that he should not resume it, would be content to achieve that by persuading him to surrender, and restrains its use of violence according to its intentions' (2013: 75). He argues that such compassion is central to Augustine's claim that love of enemies does not prohibit a certain benevolent but 'unpleasant severity' (Augustine, 2001: 222).

Benevolence includes large-scale use of lethal force. Such tragic violence is understood as a form of punishment which does the wrongdoer 'the service of constraining him from further wrongdoing and encouraging him to repent and embrace peace' (Biggar, 2013: 61). It retains the selflessness commonly associated with *agape* in that 'forgiveness always involves the absolute self-sacrifice involved in swallowing one's impulses to vengeance and in suffering discipline by the motive of compassion and the intention of peace, I do not think that it must or should involve the bypassing of justice, appropriate resentment, and proportionate punishment' (Biggar, 2013: 74).

Critique of Biggar: Reading politics and the politics of reading

So far we have focused on Jesus's injunction to love enemies, as found in the Sermon on the Mount. However within the New Testament many other texts appear pertinent to this debate. Those who argue in defence of non-violence would claim that the thrust of the New Testament narrative as a whole encourages believers to eschew violence. For example, the temptation narratives (Mt. 4:1-11, Lk 4:1-13) show Jesus renouncing any resort to armed resistance (Hays, 1996: 322); Jesus's injunction to 'turn the other cheek' encourages a form of profound non-violent resistance to imperial humiliation (Wink, 1992: 75–7); Jesus rebukes the disciple who is said to cut off the ear of the High Priest's slave (Mt. 26:51-53, Mk 14:47-48, Lk. 22:49-53, Jn 18:10-11); Stephen emulates Christ in praying for his enemies (Acts 7:60); and Christians are enjoined by Paul never to take vengeance, but to bless their persecutors (Rom. 12:19). Additionally, there is the incarnational motif of *kenosis* (Phil. 2:5-8), which is taken to indicate vulnerable self-giving and service, the like of which is incompatible with the use of lethal force (Hays, 1996: 330); the pastoral epistles urge patient suffering on the model of Jesus, rather than retaliation and the return of abuse and violence (1 Pet. 2:21-23); and even the most dramatically divisive genre of apocalyptic in Revelation endorses non-violent conquest of evil through 'the blood of the lamb and by the word of their testimony' (Rev. 12:11).

Those who seek to ground a defence of lethal violence in the New Testament often place substantially greater weight on apparently exceptional texts. For example, how John the Baptist (Lk. 3:14-15) Jesus (Mt. 8:5-13, Lk. 7:1-10) and the Apostles (Acts 10:1-11:18) endorse the faith of Roman soldiers without any explicit imperative to give up military service (should such have been an option). Other common texts are regarded by defenders of non-violence as metaphorical – e.g. Jesus's comment, 'I came to bring not peace but the sword' (Mt. 10:34 – the Lukan parallel says 'division' rather than 'sword', Lk 12:51), the Pauline use of military imagery (Rom. 6:13, 2 Cor. 10:3-6, Phil. 1:27-30), or Ephesians 6:10-20. As in so many theological debates, there is no alternative but to engage in careful, critical and open exploration of the texts.

This raises a broader hermeneutical question of how to give due weight to each of these texts. In turn, this generates a complex doctrinal question, demanding both christological considerations and an account of the function of biblical authority (discussed in Chapter 1): To what extent are the particularities of Jesus's ministry (a context of oppression, marginalization and an expectation of an imminent eschatological deliverance) an obstacle to the identification of continuing norms of Christian political action?

Key points

- Political theologians draw on divergent readings of doctrine to make sense of Christ's imperative to love your enemies.
- A theological politics must do justice to a variety of Christian doctrines.
- It must be fully aware of the actual sinfulness of the church.
- It must be mindful of the political nature of its practice of reading and applying scripture.

Questions for discussion

1 Do you think love of enemies is an unconditional and indiscriminate imperative?
2 How do Niebuhr and Yoder differ in their view of Christian political action? Which do you think is most persuasive?
3 How do Yoder and Biggar differ in their account of the normativity of Jesus? Which do you think provides the stronger theological rationale?
4 How might some of the ideas outlined earlier in this book inform our reflections on the relationship between God's love of the world through Christ and through us? For example, might the idea of resonance from Chapter 2 help us understand the nature and limit of our emulation of Christ's love of enemies?
5 What other New Testament texts on love could be held to have significant political importance? For example, in what way might the famous claim that 'the love of money is the root of all kinds of evil' (1 Tim. 6:10) be pertinent to global capitalism and consumerism? Might the assertion that 'perfect love drives out all fear' (1 Jn 4:18) have something to say to a political culture saturated with discourses of fear (of crime, of immigrants, of terrorism) and a corresponding 'need' for robust surveillance and security measures?

Having thought about how Jesus's preaching and embodiment of loving enemies shapes political action, we'll now consider another aspect of 'theology as politics' – the politics of a particular area of Christian doctrine at the heart of many theologies – the nature of salvation.

The politics of salvation

In this section we'll explore the theme of atonement, that is the ways in which in Christ God takes the initiative to restore humanity to a right relationship with 'him'. In particular, we will see how different conceptions of the atonement contribute to different political visions. When seeking ways to express and conceptualize Christian belief, we reach for analogies and metaphors from around us, including from political and social structures. This is necessary but dangerous work, especially in theological areas where the church has never sought to provide a definitive account. The nature of the atonement is one such area. Many of the metaphors and images used to express salvation and atonement have political connotations. This is evident even in the word 'redemption' (Gk. *lutron*, Heb. *padah*), which refers to the way God redeemed Israel from slavery in Egypt (Deut. 7:8). Yet sometimes, especially when metaphors originate in a distant culture or time, our use becomes anachronistic, constraining their power or imposing later preferences. Metaphors can become domesticated by familiarity, and lose their ability to unsettle the structures of thought and action that determine our lives. Our selection and use of metaphors is itself a political act, for theological language must be chastened against the tendency to make God in our own image.

Motifs of liberation and freedom are central to Christian imaginings of atonement. While we often think of freedom in terms of individual choice – the 'freedom' to choose a political party, a school, an iPad – freedom in the Christian sense isn't the ability to make a brand choice. From the New Testament perspective, human beings are going to serve a master, be it pleasure, money or God. The question is, which master will we choose? The metaphor of slavery to Christ is a way of saying that by being 'slaves of Christ' believers can be truly free, Christians can have 'life in abundance' (Jn 10).

'Justification' (Gk. *dikaiosis*) is often taken to be a 'federal' metaphor, set in the law courts. Hence Martin Luther famously sees justification as concerned with an individual's standing before God the judge. For N. T. Wright, though, 'justification' refers to four interrelated things – the law court, the covenant, the coming kingdom and the church (1997, ch. 7). If the term expresses the legal status of a believer, the setting is the cosmic trial of 'the nations' (Is. 43-44). It is therefore tied into the covenant that God made with Abraham and fulfilled in the incarnation, life, death and resurrection of Jesus. Justification is therefore about recognizing the believer's membership of the community to which God has pledged 'himself'. It is something that God has done in the middle of history in anticipation of completing the work at the end of history. It is about how the church sees itself as part of the covenant people, witnessing to God's reconciling work.

With something as pivotal as the question of *how* Christ achieves atonement, the appropriate quest for clarity can blur into the less helpful desire for a final and definitive account. This can happen when Jesus's crucifixion is extracted from other elements in the drama of salvation; when the brute fact of his death is understood to be the thing that saves, or – most dangerous of all – when the intense pain of crucifixion is thought to be salvific. Against these tendencies, the church uses a blend of evocative metaphors to express something of the mystery of reconciliation with God. If we restrict how these metaphors can work together, or elevate one metaphor to a shibboleth (i.e. it becomes a distinctive marker for identity, see Judg. 12), the Christian vision of salvation is diminished.

What about the political impact of different metaphors and models of atonement? We only have space to work through one example: penal substitution (whereby the work of Christ is conceived as 'taking on' the punishment we deserve as sinners). The popular song, 'In Christ Alone' (2001) by Keith Getter and Stuart Townend, has been caught up in the wider Evangelical furore on this, notably in refusing to licence an amendment to the second verse, which would replace 'wrath' with 'love'. Search for the song online – read the verse – what difference would it make to indicate that it is God's love, rather than 'his' wrath, which is satisfied on the cross?

All metaphors and models carry with them a raft of exegetical, theological and practical issues. Can the transfer of punishment to an innocent third party constitute a just punishment? Is righteousness an imputable (transferable) credit? Is sin best understood by analogy with criminal wrongs? It is commonplace to begin discussions of substitution with the argument put forward by Anselm of Canterbury (c.1033–1109). More than preceding accounts, he focuses strongly on the satisfaction of debt and demands of God's wrath. Importantly, Anselm's setting was feudal, not federal. The offended party was owed restitution of honour, not the satisfying spectacle of punishment. In terms of atonement, Christ the God-man gives the honour due to God through his substitutionary death on the cross, and so fulfils justice. Only a human should make this payment, but only God-made-man could achieve this restoration once and for all.

It is not until the sixteenth century, when feudal structures were a thing of the past, that many influential theologians (including Luther and Calvin) shifted at least some of their understanding of substitutionary atonement from a framework of honour and shame into the metaphorical setting of the criminal courtroom. With this shift came even greater potential for the caricature of a cruel God, extracting rough justice from an innocent to placate 'his' burning rage. Removing substitution from the biblical texts which depict the triumph of God's merciful justice in Jesus's kingship over the earth (Is. 53, Mk 10:45, Rom. 8:3, 2 Cor. 5:21), then contorts 'God the vindicated reconciler' into 'God the vindictive punisher'. When the metaphor of substitution is pulled from its roots in this way, it is vulnerable to the caricature of the Father as a 'cosmic child abuser', who is satisfied by punishing 'his' child for the ills of the world.

In Chapter 5 we considered the notion of worship as a smell pleasing to God. Building on the notion of sacrifice covering over the stench of sin, and soothing the nose of an angry God, two distinct but related terms are influential in understanding the nature of a substitutionary sacrifice: that it either means a 'propitiation' in which wrath is placated or 'expiation' in which uncleanness is removed and sin is covered over. From the earliest Christian use of sacrificial language there has been concern to explain sacrifice in a way that does not reduce it to 'pagan' forms of propitiation – the aromatic soothing of a raging deity. Whether the ideas of propitiation or expiation are deployed, the same challenge faces both proponents and critics today.

Penal substitution therefore creates a variety of theological problems, the most pressing of which is the way that justice and mercy are pitted against one another. An alternative would draw on the ways in which God's wrath (*orge*) pertains to the destructive consequences of human sin, rather than divine vindictiveness. God's wrath then becomes a way into his mercy, as it invites humanity to repent.

Furthermore, penal substitution has political ramifications. Timothy Gorringe has persuasively suggested that the modern culture of increasingly retributive punishment and large-scale penal vindictiveness flows from the ways in which penal substitution shaped the social imagination of European and North American societies (Gorringe, 1996). If justice is achieved through the infliction of suffering – if pain itself is the currency of redemption – then the state must inflict hard treatment to achieve justice. If, however, 'wrath' is about communicating censure and inviting repentance, punishment could be understood as restorative – as a mode of penance. The state is then viewed as a structure mandated by God for the pursuit of the common good. It will create space for the genuine and necessary pains of remorse and repentance to be worked through, and it will be oriented towards reconciliation between the victim and the community. That might mean the vast expansion of community sentencing, victim–offender mediation and a very substantial reform of imprisonment (Bourne, 2014).

Restorative justice does not render substitutionary language inappropriate, however. The claim that Christ died 'for us' or 'in our place' can be fruitful if it is governed by an appreciation of how such metaphors only make sense when framed within the loving mercy of God. God's mercy does not demand our obedience as the cost of entry into salvation. Instead God invites our obedience – the fragmentary recovery of our own full humanity, enabled by the Holy Spirit – as a grateful recognition of God's grace. To quote Katheryn Tanner 'the cross simply does not save us from our debts to God by paying them. If anything, the cross saves us from the consequences of a debt economy in conflict with God's own economy of grace by cancelling it' (Tanner, 2001: 88).

The condition of forgiveness, that is having been forgiven, produces significant and costly imperatives for Christians. If, with the French cultural critic René Girard, we see atonement as the unmasking of the ways in which we construct our identity and create fleeting feelings of security by scapegoating vulnerable groups in society, then our forgiveness becomes a calling to repudiate these unmerciful 'sacrifices' (Hos. 6:6, Mt. 9:13). As Rowan Williams puts it:

> So to live a forgiven life is not simply to live a happy consciousness of having been absolved. Forgiven-ness is precisely the deep and abiding sense of what relation – with God or with other human beings – can and should be; and so is itself a stimulus, an irritant, necessarily provoking protest at impoverished versions of social and personal relations. Once we grasp that forgiveness occurs not by a word of acquittal but by a transformation of the world of persons, we are not likely to regard it as something which merely refers backwards. (Williams, 1982: 52)

Key points

- The dominant images used to express our claims about God often rely upon, and shape, our political structures and struggles.
- Being concerned about politics gives us a way into theology, and theology issues in political claims and demands.

Questions for discussion

1 How might other interpretations of atonement impact the practice of criminal punishment?
2 How might our claims about salvation challenge our everyday patterns of living? For example, what might it mean to:
   a) believe in the once-for-all sacrifice of Christ in a society where the environment is sacrificed for our appetites (for meat, energy or consumer electronics)
   b) believe Christ has paid the price 'for us' in a land where government budgets and the lives of young men and women are expended in pursuit of geo-political dominance
   c) understand ourselves as recipients of grace, while wearing clothes produced by children serving as an unwilling substitute for our own labour
   d) name ourselves as redeemed in a world where bonded labour, enforced prostitution and human trafficking enslave others?

Chapter summary

In this chapter we have:

- Identified some of the ways in which our cultural and historical context shape and constrain our account of politics and theology
- Explored the fundamental political importance of loving and being loved
- Wrestled with three ways of understanding Jesus's teaching on love of enemies
- Examined some prominent ways of engaging in critique of political theologies
- Delved into the way in which the theology of salvation can inform, shape and lead to political action.

Extended task – Blog or column on Christianity and politics

In the first part of this chapter we gave an example of the Archbishop of Canterbury's speaking out on a social and political issue. We deliberately chose an issue where disagreement is limited – not many people would argue for higher interest rates on payday loans. By contrast, more recently the Archbishop of Canterbury has commented on issues including Britain leaving the European Union, a scandal in the Royal Family and controversial claims of anti-Semitism in a major political party – claims made during a general election campaign.

Write a blog post or newspaper column reflecting on the extent to which the complexity of political divisions among Christians should shape the ways in which influential figures speak out on contemporary issues? Should the church only speak out where there is consensus? Should it avoid any appearance of endorsement of a political party?

Recommended reading

Bretherton, Luke (2010), *Christianity and Contemporary Politics: The Conditions and Possibilities of Faithful Witness*, Oxford: Wiley-Blackwell.

Cavanaugh William T, and Peter, Scott, eds (2006), *The Blackwell Companion to Political Theology*, Oxford: Blackwell.

Cavanaugh, William T., Jeffrey W. Bailey, and Craig Hovey, eds (2011), *An Eerdmans Reader in Contemporary Political Theology*, Grand Rapids, MI: Eerdmans.

Cooper, Thia (2007), *Controversies in Political Theology*, London: SCM Press.

Pecknold, Chad (2010), *Christianity and Politics: A Brief Guide to the History*, Eugene, OR: Cascade.

Phillips, Elizabeth (2012), *Political Theology: A Guide for the Perplexed*, London: Continuum.

7

Resting: The Sabbath of all creation

This chapter uses your experiences of rest to help you form an eschatological conception of restful embodiment. (The word 'eschatology' comes from the Greek *ta eschata*, meaning 'the last things'.) For some readers, 'having a rest' may feel a long way away at the moment. This is actually reminiscent of one of the ways that eschatology can be misunderstood: people think that it is only about what happens at the end of the world. However, eschatology also recognizes that true rest has already begun. Christ's resurrection and the sending of the Spirit have established the Second Creation as a present-day reality (2 Cor. 5:17) as well as a future hope (Rom. 8:20-21, 1 Cor. 15). To use theological language, God's Kingdom is both 'now' and 'not yet'; to use Jesus's language, it is both 'drawing near' (Mk 1:15) and still to 'come' (Mt. 6:10). This is called an inaugurated (or 'unfolding') eschatology. Most scholars today think that this approach is the best fit for the biblical material.

In what follows we aim to give an overview of what restful embodiment involves; universal creaturely delight and flourishing, the presence of justice, wholeness and peace, the joyful reconciliation of all things with God, peace of salvation – all in and through Christ and the Spirit. We consider two variants in eschatological belief and two types of Christian ecology, and a playful theology of Sabbath helps to frame theological questions about the status and treatment of non-human creation. Only when all these markers are in place do we return to this book's theme of human embodiment, now set within the cosmic context of redeemed creation. As we progress it will become clear that eschatology connects with many issues that have already been discussed in previous chapters – e.g. the person of Christ, the sacramental nature of the world, politics, culture and the diverse ways in which Christians read the Bible. Some of these issues are entwined in our first topic: a theological system, prevalent in (particularly North American) Evangelical Christianity, called premillennial dispensationalism.

Premillennial dispensationalism

Glorious Appearing: The End of Days is the twelfth book in the phenomenally popular *Left Behind* series by Tim LaHaye and Jerry B. Jenkins. It sits in the literary genre of apocalyptic fiction (from the Greek *apocalypsis*, meaning 'unveiling' or 'revelation'). In one scene, Jesus returns to earth to cleanse it of all non-Christians. During the ensuing genocide he causes immense suffering by sending a plague on people and horses that dissolves their flesh, eyes and tongues while they are still alive. If you have not already done so, reading Chapter 1 will help you to think through your answers to these questions:

1. Does this presentation of Jesus align with the Jesus of the gospels? If so, how? If not, how is the *Left Behind* Jesus different and is the mismatch a problem?
2. The above scene recalls Zechariah 14:12, which speaks of terrible divine judgement falling on those who oppose the settlement of Jews in their own land. Should these verses be interpreted literally, and if so, why? Is there an alternative reading?

The *Left Behind* books are imaginative accounts of the end of the world, as set out in premillennial dispensationalism. As a doctrinal system it is late to the theological scene (emerging in the 1870s) and it has two straightforward elements. First, it always interprets biblical prophecies in a literal way. Special prominence is given to the closing chapters of Revelation, which are read as anticipating Christ's return to earth before establishing his thousand-year reign (hence 'premillennial'). Second, history is divided into different periods of history (hence 'dispensations'), each of which contains different covenants between God and humanity. Combined, these two elements produce an End Times chronology:

(i)   Humanity currently lives in the Age of Grace, which will end with the Rapture. True believers will be 'caught up in the clouds' to meet Christ (cf. 1 Thess. 4:15-17), as dramatized in the 2014 film *Left Behind* (average rating of 2.2/10 on rottentomatoes.com – you have been warned).

(ii) The Rapture inaugurates The Great Tribulation (a seven-year period of divine judgement and intense suffering, cf. Dan. 9:24-27) and the rule of the Antichrist.

(iii) The Antichrist will be defeated by Christ at the Battle of Armageddon (Rev. 16:16).
(iv) Christ begins a thousand-year reign on earth (Rev. 20:2), during which time Israel rules the earth's physical realm. Christians rule spiritually in their new, eternal bodies.
(v) Christ ends rebellion once and for all and brings in the New Heavens and New Earth (Rev. 21-22).

Premillennial dispensationalism grew in influence when it was disseminated throughout the United States. Of particular importance here is the strongly dispensationalist Scofield Reference Bible (the first edition was published in 1909 and it is still a bestseller), Christian radio and TV, and books by dispensationalist authors, which sell by tens of millions. Its influence is waning in university settings, but, even so, it is still the dominant form of conservative eschatology in the United States and it gives strong support to American foreign policies that protect Israel. Unfortunately, as Harry O'Meier points out (2010: 251–2), since dispensationalism's conception it has (not always, but in the main) evolved in such a way as to have a negative impact on how creation should be viewed and treated. If the world is destined for destruction, creation care slips down the list of priorities. It has also tended to veer towards quietism – of accepting the climate crisis without trying to do anything about it – in order not to be distracted from the main work of 'getting souls into heaven'.

Key points

- Premillennial dispensationalism promotes a literalist eschatology which anticipates the destruction of the world.
- This belief can undermine environmental concern and shape political participation.

Discussion questions

1 One criticism of premillennial dispensationalism is that it can present the world as a transitory, even dark and evil, place from which we must escape. Looking back to Chapter 2, does this attitude remind you of a type of teaching?
2 How might this belief system help Christians to feel 'at rest' in their lives and in the world?

Restorative eschatology

When we think of feeling 'restored', we might imagine feeling well-rested, refreshed; someone who has the energy to help others and can enjoy the day rather than just stumble through it. This starting point might promote the idea that a 'restored creation' – which is the beating heart of restorative eschatology – is a 'reset'; a going back to the Garden of Eden of Genesis. However, restorative eschatology requires more imagination, as God is in the business of 'making all things new' (Rev. 21:5). It is closer to people being transformed into the best possible version of themselves; they are continuous with who they are now yet have never existed in this way before.

Task – Creation and re-creation

Read Genesis 2:7-10, John 20:11-16 and Revelation 22:1-3.

1. How are these passages connected? What do they say about the value of creation and ecological action?
2. Connect these passages with theological themes from Chapters 1 and 2.

Those who maintain that the restoration of creation is the best eschatological model would plant a tree the day before a mass extinction event. On one level this might seem nonsensical: surely ecological efforts are pointless whether the earth is destroyed or re-made. Yet a restorative mindset means, in part, that God grants all matter eternal worth, and all good things – from friendships to freshly planted saplings – will be gathered up and taken forward into an ever more gloriously embodied future in the Second Creation (cf. 1 Cor. 15). Restorative eschatology is therefore wrongly interpreted if it is taken to mean that the renewed world will be non-material, impersonal and non-bodily. The details of this transformation are hazy (1 Cor. 13:12), but Paul gives assurances that 'in the Lord your labour is not in vain' (1 Cor. 15:58).

Such an inaugurated eschatology is both ecologically hopeful and demanding. Through the Spirit, the 'pledge of our inheritance' (Eph. 1:14), Christians receive a taste of the life to come; and eucharistic (Chapter 4) and Sabbath practices (which we explore in this chapter) structure how they live towards the Second Creation, in anticipation and embodiment of that future. Participating in the 'rest' of salvation (Heb. 3–4, Eph. 2:8-9) gives believers renewed vision for the earth and strong resources for hope. This is not to say that eschatological rest is passive; it has a purpose, albeit a playful one (we come to this in more detail later). For being grounded in, and looking to, the Second Creation has the effect of sinking believers more deeply into this creation – to perform more valiantly the line from the Lord's Prayer, 'thy Kingdom come, thy will be done, on earth as it is in heaven'. And therein lies the challenge.

N. T. Wright is one of the leading exponents of restorative eschatology. Together with New Testament scholars E.P. Sanders and James Dunn, N. T. Wright is associated with the 'New Perspectives on Paul' movement. Their shared hermeneutic is to situate Paul and Jesus within the thought-world of first-century Judaism. Doing so, they argue, makes the 'big story' of the Bible (its 'metanarrative') come more clearly into view. Wright's 'new-covenant' theology holds that Jesus, as Israel's representative, gave himself up to death on the cross (Phil. 2:8) and was raised to a new type of physical life, in order to defeat the powers of darkness and initiate God's plan of new creation. In this way, Jesus launched the 'age to come' in the middle of history. Wright has been concerned that the Bible's holistic vision of a Second Creation has become dangerously devalued, if not lost, in some parts of the Western church. Too many people have been fed a mixture of Gnosticism (outlined in Chapter 2) and moralism as shoddy substitutes for the Christian fundamentals of 'redemption, sanctification and renewal' (Torrance, 1997: 107). He desperately wants the church to recover the biblical arc of cosmic restoration through Christ, as prophetically anticipated by John in his vision of the New Jerusalem descending to earth (Rev. 21 and 22). To paraphrase Wright, it is not so much that 'we go up' to heaven (as in the 'rapture' teaching of premillennial dispensationalism) so much as God 'comes down' to reign on a renewed earth. In recent years, however, this vision of transformed creation has been challenged, particularly by North American Evangelicals in the Reformed tradition, who are wary of the 'New Perspective on Paul' project in general. Christians elsewhere in the world, however, find that it ties in well with their own experiences.

Key extract – Restorative eschatology as a present reality

'Jesus is a liberator. Liberation here must be understood in its totality, as removal of all that which keeps the African in bondage, all that makes him less than what God intended him to be. It connotes the total idea of liberation from fear, uncertainty, sickness, evil powers, foreign domination and oppression, distortion of his humanity, poverty and want. … Jesus' own self-identification with the poor and needy makes his proclamation – "I have come that they may have life and have it more abundantly" [John 10:10] – more meaningful to the African Christian. This ties in neatly with his traditional idea of religion, which strongly repudiates the complacent Euro-American doctrine of "Pie-in-the-sky-when-you-die", which is a distortion of the message and person of Christ. … Eschatology as understood in the western world does not form part of the African thought-form. For many, the experience of salvation is a sign that with the coming of Jesus, suffering and death are eliminated, and these will have no room in the Kingdom of God established here on earth.' Kofi Appiah-Kubi, 'Christology', extracts (1976) (In Ford and Higton 2002: 454).

Appiah-Kubi, a Ghanaian, was writing from within an African context, where he thought eschatology was far more of a lived experience than in 'the West'. What might account for this difference?

Key points

- Restorative eschatology claims that the Second Creation is both 'now' and 'not yet'.
- Christians witness to this restored reality by taking care of the environment.

Discussion questions

1 Do you find restorative eschatology's idea of eternal (albeit transformed) embodiment exciting, disappointing or something else?
2 What experience, teaching or hermeneutic is influencing your answer?

Activity – Restful creation

Watch a variety of nature clips online – for example, soothing meditative videos, examples of excellent landscape and nature photography. Then think about how our world, in its entirety, could become even more restful.

Christian ecology

At the time of writing, Australia is on fire and Jakarta is under water. According to the IPCC, extreme weather events like these will become the new normal if carbon dioxide output is not aggressively reduced by 2030. Humanity's long-term abuse of land, sea and air is deepening the climate crisis further. Scientists and environmental pressure groups are ringing every warning bell they can find and eco-anxiety is on the rise (Beddington, 2019), especially among young adults and parents of small children. Perhaps you can relate to these worries.

In such unsettling times, what theological resources do Christians have to inspire them to protect the earth's community? We only have space here to introduce two strands of Christian ecology: stewardship and ecofeminism. They both place a high value on embodiment, but for different eschatological reasons. These views also connect to a political theology of the environment.

Stewardship

> ## Reflection – The blame game
>
> In 1967 a medieval historian named Lynn White published an article entitled 'The Historical Roots of our Ecologic Crisis'. It epitomizes the view that Christianity is largely responsible for our ecological problems because its advocacy of human mastery has encouraged humans to adopt an exploitative stance towards nature. White does, however, greatly admire St Francis of Assisi (c.1181–1226):
>
>> The key to an understanding of Francis is his belief in the virtue of humility – not merely for the individual but for man as a species. Francis tried to depose man from his monarchy over creation and set up a democracy of all God's creatures. With him the ant is no longer simply a homily for the lazy, flames a sign of the thrust of the soul toward union with God; now they are Brother Ant and Sister Fire, praising the Creator in their own ways as Brother Man does in his. (Beddington, 2019: 1206)
>
> Without a rediscovery of this kind of spirituality, White fears that things will continue to get worse and turning 'more' science and 'more technology' will not redeem our situation (Beddington, 2019).
>
> 1. Do you agree with this last point?
> 2. Have much faith do you have in science or technology to solve the climate crisis?

If White was alive today, he may well be encouraged by the 2015 Papal Encyclical *Laudato Si* (meaning 'Praise be to You'). This document is one of the most thorough appeals for Christian stewardship in recent times. Like White, Pope Francis argues that a spiritual dimension is needed if we are to understand the causes of environmental destruction and the means of their solution (33). Like his namesake, Pope Francis affirms a fraternal and sacramental view of creation ('our common home is like a sister' [1]; 'soil, water, mountains: everything is, as it were, a caress of God' [43]). Without such a framework, he argues, creation becomes objectifiable and therefore exploitable. All that exists is interconnected and has its own integrity and purpose, yet humans have forgotten both their creatureliness and their unique duty to look after nature. Consequently, 'The earth, our home, is beginning to look more and more like an immense pile of filth' (16).

Task – The exegesis of stewardship

Read Genesis 1 and 2. These chapters are central to theological debates about Christian ecology.

1. Which verses speak of humanity's responsibility to take care of the earth?
2. In these chapters, humans are said to originate from the earth *and* have a privileged position within creation. Can these two perspectives be reconciled? If so, how?
3. If one perspective is emphasized at the expense of the other, how might this affect the way that Christians treat creation?

Pope Francis notes that our culture has failed to find solutions to the environmental crisis for a whole host of reasons – including personal selfishness, over-confidence in technological progress and capitalism, and the disregarding of justice. Pope Francis argues that these problems stem from an inadequate Christian anthropology: 'dominion' properly means 'stewardship' (59).

Appealing to Genesis 1 and 2, Pope Francis calls for human beings to cultivate, with God's help, virtues like gratitude and generosity that buttress 'ecological citizenship' (100). This is part of humanity's calling to 'lead all creatures back to their Creator' (43). Taking this vocation seriously would renew the intimacy between God and creation and involve human beings joining with God to restore rest to creation. The latter entails 'recovering and respecting the rhythms inscribed in nature by the hand of the Creator', as shown in the law of the Sabbath (38) (cf. Lev. 25). Ecological restoration also involves bringing forth newness in the world. Humans can do this by working with the creative Spirit who has 'filled the universe with possibilities' (42). Cooperating with the Spirit in God's work of ongoing creation is a deeply eschatological act and, here too, rest is important – not least because when we are properly at rest we stand to become better ecologists. Contemplative rest 'prevents that unfettered greed and sense of isolation which make us seek personal gain to the detriment of all else'; it 'opens our eyes to the larger picture and gives us renewed sensitivity to the rights of others'; and it 'motivates us to great concern for nature and the poor' (111).

For Pope Francis, it is in the material depths of the eucharist that Christ – the Word for (Jn 1:3, Co. 1:16-17), and means of, creation-care (Col. 1:20) – is to be found.

> In the Eucharist, fulness is already achieved; it is the living centre of the universe, the overflowing core of love and of inexhaustible love. Joined to the Incarnate Son, present in the Eucharist, the whole cosmos gives thanks to God. … The Eucharist joins heaven and earth; it embraces and penetrates all creation. … [it] is also a source of light and motivation for our concerns for the environment, directing us to be stewards of all creation (110–11).

Key points

- Stewardship means that humans, while part of creation, bear special responsibility for bringing creation to eschatological perfection.
- It combines a sacramental view of the world with an awareness that creation's final fullness in Christ is yet to be revealed.
- It recognizes that rest is as important as work for humans.

Discussion questions

1 The stewardship model has been criticized for being anthropocentric and managerial. Why do you think this might be? Are these things necessarily wrong?
2 What type of sacramental theology connects the eucharist with stewardship of the earth? (Chapter 4 will help you here.)

Ecofeminism

Introductory reflections

1. What is the link between upskirting and plastic pollution; the gender pay gap and crashing insect populations?
2. What social attitudes or structures allow the link to exist?

The MeToo movement, which tries to help female survivors of sexual violence, began in Brooklyn, New York, in 2006. In 2017 the hashtag #MeToo went viral and raised awareness of just how many women around the world have experienced sexual harassment from men. This exposed a culture of abuse in Hollywood and shone a light on exclusionary male centres of power within organizations. This issue was, for a time, front page news. Ecofeminists go further still. They bring together insights from feminism, ecology and socialism to show how patriarchy has badly damaged the inter-relationships between humans, animals and the natural environment. If the whole society of creation is to be 'at ease', qualities like equality and diversity must be pursued as matters of justice and the earth viewed organically (i.e. not mechanistically).

Sallie McFague is a theologian who argues that traditional Christian theism trades on dualism and hierarchy – God is spiritual (eternal, perfect, superior); the earth is material (mortal, imperfect, inferior) – with dire ecological consequences. Its over-emphasis on divine transcendence (which she thinks has masculinist overtones), its desire for humans to imitate share in God's controlling power and its attempts to save people 'out of' creation – these things have contributed greatly to humanity's desecration of nature. (In the language of this chapter, authoritarianism is an improper form of rest: it runs against the Holy habits that the Scriptures seek to 'settle' us in.) Much of the problem, as McFague sees it, is that theological language (e.g. King) is irrelevant to current human experience and conjures up unhelpful images (e.g. ownership). McFague's answer is to draw on all kinds of experiences and biblical and extra-biblical sources. Together, they lead to new metaphors that can help humanity to adapt to the needs of the moment – such as climate crisis. In this respect, McFague especially sees a theological demand for metaphors that are inclusive, ecologically sound, non-hierarchical and 'immanental' (i.e. affirming of God's presence in the world).

In her book *The Body of God: An Ecological Theology* (1993), McFague reconceives the transcendence of God in an immanental way. (In other words, a 'traditionally' distant transcendent God is replaced with panentheism: literally translated, it means 'God-in-all'.) Essentially, McFague models 'the universe or world as God's body' (vii) whilst upholding God's agency – the Spirit is the 'breath of life' in all forms of life (131) – and the God–world distinction. Thus, God is 'in and through all bodies, the bodies of the sun and moon, trees and rivers, animals, and people' (133). As incarnation characterizes the whole universe, Jesus is not unique; he is a paradigmatic instance of divine embodiment.

Ecologically, McFague argues that creation should be cared for because it is God's body and because God cares for the whole world (not just humanity). This metaphor allows for extraordinary intimacy between God and the world. All of creation rests in God, without remainder – so much so that whatever happens in the world rebounds on God ('If the world is God's body, then nothing happens to the world that does not also happen to God', 176). God therefore suffers permanently with the world's pain. When humans overstep their place or forget their interconnectedness with the cosmos, they are acting against right relationships. McFague defines this as sin (114). Salvation, however, is conceived on a cosmic, rather than individual, scale. It is about all the bodies of the world being liberated from that which prevents their flourishing. The means of salvation is therefore immanentism: humanity is 'with God whether we live or die … our bodies … are within the body of God. God is not somewhere else … but with us in the earth, the soil, that receives us at our death' (176–177).

McFague's hope for a New Creation is that humanity, finally, takes stewardship seriously. Drawn to Isaiah's vision of a renewed world (65:17-25) as God's 'promise to us' (2006: 205), she sees that 'we are called to live in a different world, a world where the good of the individual and the good of the community are intrinsically and intimately related' (2006). She argues that this world can be realized if we would but repent and value creation's integrity; ask God to change our vision so that we can see our place in the eco-web of interdependency; and limit our wealth for the sake of others (2006: 210). Her advice to people who struggle with denial, apathy and indifference? 'Just do it' (2006: 207) and 'hang in there' because God does (2006: 212). McFague's hope is resourced by the resurrection, which is reconceived symbolically; it is an encouragement that God's passion for life triumphs over death. But so far as the world has a teleological (from the Greek *telos*, meaning 'end' or 'purpose') direction in McFague's thought (i.e. the world is going somewhere, for a reason), the emphasis falls on an embodied eschatology that encourages never-ending cooperation between God and humanity.

McFague does not explain why it is better to choose some metaphors rather than others and so her approach is arguably subjective. Additionally, her choice to value experience over and above Scripture and tradition has led to the criticism that her work is weighted towards anthropology rather than theology (Hampson, 1990: 159). McFague is content to say that 'the transcendence of God frees us to model God in terms of what is most significant to us' (1993: 193). And one of the most pressing needs, for her, is that people are inspired to live in ecologically responsible ways.

Key points

- Ecofeminists argue that patriarchal domination cuts across the relationality of life in ways that demean women and destroy the natural world.
- McFague proposes a panentheist, organic model of the world as the 'body of God'.
- In this model, creation, in all its joy and pain, rests in the 'body' of God; eschatology equates to working for more interconnected and respectful forms of embodied life.
- Creation care is essential.

Discussion questions

1 In comparison to classical theism, does McFague's eschatology give people more, or less, motivation to shape a better world?
2 Which model creates more hope that this will come about?

Group Activity – The impact of eschatology

Search for Christian action groups on the internet that aim to protect the environment. Can you work out what eschatologies are operating behind their agendas?

A playful Sabbath

Introductory reflections

What comes to mind when you think about 'play'? Brainstorm some ideas and associations.

Most people would happily accept that play has a strong role in human development and communal cohesion (Pellegrini, 2009: 2011). A love of play is also widespread throughout the animal kingdom. Play, it would seem, is a very important activity. Even so, at least in the West, the value of play is subordinated to that of work. This is gradually changing, as more people prioritize quality of life and make sacrifices in order to become FIREs (Financially Independent Retire Early). But for the most part, play is still thought to be a lightweight, even frivolous, activity. Christian tradition, too, has – with fairly miserable monotony – been negative about play. This may, in part, be due to a reluctance to theologize in an embodied way. Brian Edgar, for instance, observes that transcendent terms for God such as Lord, God and Creator do not create difficulties for Christians in the way that intimate terms like Lover, Friend and Playmate do (2017: 2). In such a *milieu*, speaking of a 'playful' God seems counter-intuitive, perhaps even disrespectful. Yet a theology of the Sabbath reveals a God who revels in delight, who makes and restores with joyous abandon, and who seeks playful intimacy with all of creation (not just humanity).

It is a common misconception that the high point of the creation narrative in Genesis 1 is the creation of humanity. However, the story in fact culminates on the Sabbath – i.e. the day for rest and re-creation. Robert Ellis makes an interesting link here with ancient customs (2014: 148). The original hearers of Genesis would have associated 'rest' with the practice of installing a god's shrine in a newly built home. The god was said to be 'resting' in residence, which meant enjoying the environment and blessing it with divine presence. In Genesis, it is male and female together that image God, and humanity is called to share in the Creator's Sabbath enjoyment. From this exegetical perspective, it is less that God is sitting back, satisfied, after finishing the work of creation; more that the Sabbath is sacred time when God enjoys the world and invites the world to participate in divine joy (Moltmann, 1993: 278–80).

Playful rest can also be active and productive. In Proverbs 8:24-26 the female figure of Wisdom (later linked to the Torah, and so, in Christian tradition, to the person of Christ) precedes the creation of everything and without her, nothing came into being. She worked at God's side and was 'filled with delight day after day, rejoicing always in his presence, rejoicing in his whole world and delighting in mankind' (8:30-31). Her relation to God's creative work, characterized in verse 30a, hinges on the translation of Hebrew 'āmôn. Some translations render this word as 'architect' (or comparable parallels), but it can also be translated 'little child' or 'darling' (Plantinga-Pauw, 2015: 53). On this translation, Wisdom exudes a child's delight, shares God's delight in creating the world and hints at the fullness of divine playfulness that is yet to come. Nor are biblical writers shy of using fun metaphors for the Second Creation. Images of raucous joy, song, feasting, dance and play are common. Zechariah 8:5, which gives us an image of heaven, says, 'And the streets of the city shall be full of boys and girls playing in its streets'. Jesus picked up this theme when he pointed to children and said, 'the Kingdom of Heaven belongs to such as these' (Mt. 19:14).

These thoughts may connect with your earlier brainstorming about play. If you came up with associations like 'carefree', 'self-forgetting', 'lack of obligation', 'interactive' and 'delighting in something for its own sake', then you are close to the heart of the Christian eschatological vision. Moltmann, who has reflected deeply on the theological significance of play, argues that the endpoint of creation is to be construed as a kind of newly innocent childhood: Christian tradition has 'painted' heaven in 'the colours of unhindered laughter' (2013: 55). Far from being something that humans need to outgrow, play is something humans are destined to grow into. It is part of creation's hopeful longing for consummation and restoration, where God plays delightedly with what 'he' has made.

Key points

- The theology of Sabbath reveals God's ongoing, playful delight in creation – both now and to come.
- The Sabbath is not just for humanity: it is for God and all of creation.

Questions for discussion

1 Do you find it easy or difficult to think about God delighting playfully in creation?
2 Is the aesthetic language of 'playfulness' (e.g. joy, delight) theologically viable on its own or does it need to be tempered by ascetic language (e.g. sacrifice, service, obedience)?
3 Is divine delight offensive in the light of suffering, or is it part of the offensive against suffering?

Animals at rest

Introductory reflections

1. If you have a pet of some kind, spend a few moments thinking about what it means to you. If you do not have a pet, imagine caring for one. Then think about how this animal might 'rest' in their life and help you to 'rest' in yours.
2. Different cultures have different ideas about which animals, if any, are acceptable to eat. How can we decide which animals are off-limits?
3. What connects Colossians 1:15-20, Ephesians 1:9-10, Hebrews 1:2-3 and 1 Corinthians 8:6?

Understanding God's playful delight in creation raises important questions about the place of animals in creation. We know that animals can help us to be at rest – pets are proven to lower blood pressure (Cusack, 2013: 65) and increase the longevity of patients with heart disease (Beck and Katcher, 1996: 8). Sadly, we also know that humanity, for the most part, does not value the rest of animals (even pets can be kept for utilitarian reasons). Intensive farming practices, deep-sea dredging and the destruction of animal habitats – these are just some examples of what happens when we believe that God is primarily, perhaps even exclusively, concerned with human life. How we use animals for labour, entertainment and medical research should also be scrutinized (see Clough, 2018). The holistic view of the Scriptures, however, is that creature care is a vital and just part of creation care (Job 12:10, Ps. 36:6, Ps. 104:29-30). William Wilberforce (1759–1833) saw this clearly. In addition to his pivotal work in abolishing slavery, he also co-founded the RSPCA (Royal Society for the Prevention of Cruelty for Animals).

The British theologian David Clough leads the field in giving special consideration to animals in theological ethics, in the context of Christian doctrine. For him, not only do biblical texts such as Colossians 1:15-20, Ephesians 1:9-10, Hebrews 1:2-3 and 1 Corinthians 8:6 direct our attention to the cosmic significance of Christ's life, death and resurrection for all forms of creaturely life, but John's Prologue speaks, in a way that Clough argues is quite deliberate (2012: 86), of God taking on 'flesh' (Jn 1:14). Clough concludes that the divine Word takes on creatureliness rather than human nature. It follows that if the incarnation is not species-specific, then Christ's humanity – like his gender – has no soteriological importance (2012: 98). The ramifications of this reading are significant.

For instance, after the death of a much-loved animal companion, many people wonder: Will I see them in heaven? Christianity has traditionally replied in the negative: the mandate of Genesis 1:26-27 (and 9:6) is that human beings alone are called to be 'image-bearers' of God. However this is the beginning, rather than the end, of the matter, as

> There has been endless debate about how the image is to be specified – intelligence? dominion? relationality? male-female relationship? physical appearance? Or some combination, corresponding to the Trinitarian nature of God? The crucial Christian criterion has been the person of Jesus Christ, but that too has led into ramifying discussions – what sort of humanity is that? in what ways might a 1st-century Jewish carpenter's son be normative for everyone else? is his maleness supposed to include femaleness? (Ford, [1999] 2013: 62)

Clough argues that imaging God is something that happens only in and through Jesus Christ (2012: 67). If it stands that Jesus Christ takes on creatureliness, then the way is open for other creatures to image God in their own way. In which case, non-human creatures are open to the transforming work of God, right on into the Second Creation. Ecclesiastes 3:18-21 would seem to leave this open as an option: 'Who knows whether the human spirit goes upwards and the spirit of animals goes downward to the earth?'

Read the texts below and then answer the questions. This exercise will encourage you to connect Christology and the imaging of God (by either humans or animals).

Text 1 – Rowan Williams, *Faith in the Public Square*, extracts

'Humanity, in the Genesis story, names the animals; the calling of the human person is to name the world aright, that is, to acknowledge it as God's gift and to work so as to bring to light its character as reflecting God's character, to manifest its true essence. Thus it is common to describe the vocation of human beings in this context as "liturgical": human beings orchestrate the reflection of God's glory in the world by clothing material things with sacred meaning and presenting the world before God in prayer. Worship is ...a foretaste of the God-related destiny of the world... in which everything can be clearly seen as bearing God's glory and love. And one signal and important aspect of sin is the refusal of human beings to undertake this calling, to refuse to act in a "priestly" way towards the environment – to refuse to bless and give thanks, to refuse right use of material things'. (2012: 178)

Text 2 – Extract: Richard Bauckham, *God and the Crisis of Freedom*

'All creatures, animate and inanimate, worship God. ... The creation worships God just by being itself, as God made it, existing for God's glory. ... There is no indication in the Bible of the notion that the other creatures need us to voice their praise for them. This idea, that we are called to act as priests to nature, mediating, as it were, between nature and God ... intrudes our invertebrate sense of superiority exactly where God will not allow it' (2002: 177).

1. Do these texts contradict each other?
2. Some scholars think that humans can have a 'priestly' function in creation – e.g. uniting the praises of the whole creation – without denying that elements of creation praise God in their own way. What connections do you see between christological debate (does Jesus take on humanity or creatureliness?) and imaging debates (do humans solely image God or can animals as well)?

Whether animals need salvation is another matter. Andrew Linzey says not, in the sense that animals 'are not moral agents with free will and are not therefore capable of sin' (2009: 52). Even so, a form of redemption is still valid and necessary for those animals that need to be saved from the 'effects of human cruelty' (2009: 2). Clough reasons differently. The fact that 'all things' are reconciled to God through Christ is an indication that 'all things' need to be reconciled (2012: 127). As an intrinsic part of their embodiment all animals are born into structural sin (i.e. an environment that turns away from God's purposes), although they may sin in ways that are unique to them, on a scale of responsibility that reflects how much each creature can respond to its environment and God (2012: 119). This pattern would fit with Scriptural recognition of non-human creatures being able to praise God (Ps. 145:5), acclaim 'his' rule (Ps. 103:19-22) and do 'his' will (Jer. 8:7) (Bauckham, 2010: 78).

It is hard to imagine what animals 'resting' in the Second Creation would look like, but there are prophetic hints in Scripture of newly irenic (i.e. peaceful) relationships. Isaiah 11: 6-9 is an important text in this respect:

The wolf shall live with the lamb,
      the leopard shall lie down with the kid,
the calf and the lion and the fatling together;
      and a little child will lead them.
The cow and the bear shall graze,
      their young will lie down together,
      and the lion shall eat straw like the ox.
The nursing child will play over the hole of the asp,
      and the weaned child will put its hand on the adder's den.
They will not hurt or destroy
      on all my holy mountain;
for the earth will be full of the knowledge of the Lord
      as the waters cover the sea.

This Scripture is often read as foreseeing peaceful relationships between creatures. Richard Bauckham suggests, instead, that it is an image of reconciliation between humanity and domesticated and wild animals (2010: 80). He connects this text with Jesus's forty-day fast in the wilderness before starting his ministry. It is easy to overlook Mark's line that Jesus was 'with the wild beasts' (1:13) during this time. According to Bauckham, Mark's use of the phrase 'to be with' carries a sense of close association: 'Jesus befriends [the wild animals]. He is peaceably with them' (2010). This offers a snapshot of how Jesus's Messianic mission of peace includes healing rifts between creatures – of all types.

God's renewal of creation through Christ can therefore inspire Christians to treat animals with compassion. For some Christians, the eschatology of animal theology results in a choice to be vegetarian or vegan; others are happy to eat meat but avoid the exploitation of animals for the testing of cosmetics. Either way, animal theology has done much to alert Christians to the wrong assumption that 'the purpose or *telos* of animals is … identical with human needs' (Linzey, 2009: 11). For if the 'incarnation is God's love affair with all fleshly creatures' (Linzey, 2009: 14) then, through Christ, animals and humans can be restful, peaceable gifts of divine welcome to one another.

Key points

- Animal theologians give a biblical and systematic account of the purpose, value and meaning of non-human creatures.
- Caring for animals demonstrates eschatological justice (it brings a future reality into the present), and connects to the doctrine of creation (all creaturely life is of intrinsic value to God) and the doctrine of redemption (God redeems all that God creates).
- These doctrines come together in the incarnation (the Word's assumption of creaturely flesh, for the sake of re-creating the whole earth).

Discussion questions

1 Charles Camosy suggests that 'some Christians believe that concern for animals means less concern for justice for humans' (2013: 15). What do you think?

2 Are there limits to how much of the eschatological Kingdom of God (the 'not yet') can break into the political realm of animal rights (the 'now')? If so, why?

3 Can the above arguments about the place of animals in God's creation and Second Creation be extended to vegetation? Are there theological reasons for not eating salad?

Activity

Explore Creaturekind (www.becreaturekind.org) and consider how you as an individual, or your institution or place of work, could take up some of their suggestions.

Humanity at rest

> ### Introductory reflections
>
> According to the sleep scientist, Matthew Walker, people in the West are experiencing a 'catastrophic sleep-loss epidemic' (2017). More than ever before, we understand the benefits of quality sleep (better brain function, emotional stability and immunity), and the costs of not getting enough sleep (increased risk of physical disease and poor mental health). Yet this new information coincides with us getting less sleep than ever before.
>
> How well-rested do you feel?
>
> What changes, if any, would you like to see?

We come at last to consider how collective human embodiment connects with a redeemed world. The emphasis on collective embodiment is important for two very simple, but easily overlooked, reasons: human beings are embodied in community and in diverse ways. And so, after introducing what it means for Christians to enter the Sabbath rest of God we will learn from the theology of disability, particularly with respect to redeemed time and life 'in heaven'.

Sabbath rest encompasses hope, humility, trust in God's provision and promises and the anticipation of the final redemption of all things. As we hinted at earlier, in our discussion of stewardship, in the Hebrew Bible the Sabbath was connected with freedom (slaves must be given free time every Sabbath – Deut. 5:12-15), justice (for the poor, slaves and animals – Exod. 23:11) and ecological concern (the land must enjoy a sabbatical rest, a Jubilee year, every seven years – Lev. 25:1-7). The Sabbath principle also widened out into the great Jubilee (Is. 61) – a festival of rest that, every fifty years, revealed God's intention to restore people's lives, bodies and land to health and vitality.

Extract – Sabbath restoration

'Restlessness is not limited to human beings; it torments all living things which want to live and have to die. Where is the harbour of happiness, ..., the place of rest? It is not far off in the "seventh heaven"; nor is it in the innermost part of the human being. ... It is on earth and easy to find in time: on the Sabbath day the eternal one is present in his rest, and those he has created can find him if they themselves come to rest. ... The Sabbath is not only the day of rest but also the day of no longer intervening in nature. In the Sabbath stillness, people no longer intervene in the natural environment through their work. With this, the view of the world changes; things are no longer valued for their utility and practical value. They are perceived with astonishment in their value as being. ... With this, the environment as it is related to human beings becomes the world as it proceeded from God's creation. There is no proper understanding of the world as God's creation without this way of perceiving it in the Sabbath stillness. In pure pleasure, without reason or purpose, things display their creaturely beauty. ... The fearful questions about the meaning of life and usefulness vanish: existence itself is good, and to be here is glorious.' Jurgen Moltmann, *Ethics of Hope*, extracts (2012:233).

1. In what ways does the Sabbath restore people? give them a sense of place in the world? change their relationship to their environment?
2. Pull out some key phrases from the above extract that connect with themes that we have considered in this chapter.

Christians believe that all the Hebrew Sabbath elements – justice, freedom and renewal – point towards creation's glorious eschatological future in Christ. When Jesus described himself as the 'lord of the Sabbath' (Mt. 12:8), he meant that the Sabbath is fulfilled in him. Hence his invitation to God's people to 'come to me, all you that are weary and are carrying heavy burdens, and I will give you rest' (Mt. 11:28). As risen Lord, he ushers in the reality of the Second Creation and now, through the Spirit, 'Sabbath stillness' is centred on him. In him, the 'restlessness' of creation (cf. Rom. 8) finds a 'harbour of happiness'. In this chapter, we have considered some of the qualities of this rest: joy, delight, playfulness, restoration, justice, easement, peace, community, reconciliation with God.

Task – Exegesis of Sabbath rest

The Letter to the Hebrews sees the new reality brought by Jesus in terms of a great Sabbath rest. Read Genesis 2:2, Psalm 95:7, 11 and Hebrews 4.

1. How does the writer of Hebrews make a case for who Jesus is and the eternal significance of what he has achieved?
2. How does the writer connect the Son's work and rest in Hebrews 4? What is the difference between humans imitating this pattern and participating in it?

The New Testament writers go noticeably quiet when it comes to advising Christians how to mark their day of rest on Sunday (the day of Christ's resurrection and therefore the first day of the Second Creation). This may have been because they saw it fulfilled in Jesus. How, then, can Christians best celebrate the 'rest' of Second Creation life? There are a variety of views. Some Christians feel that people should not work or cause others to work on Sunday; others additionally rule out taking part in activities such as playing sport or watching TV. Yet others might rest at any point during the week and see this as Sabbatical. A possible point of agreement between these views – taking our cue from the delight of God's Sabbath rest – is that, if Christians do work on Sunday, God desires them to work from a place of eschatological rest. The idea that our present is pregnant with eschatological hope – a theme that is prominent in twentieth-century political theologies – has greatly influenced liberation theologies around the world. But what difference does this make to Christians in regular life?

In his commentary 'The Literal Meaning of Genesis', Augustine wrote of Adam and Eve: 'You see, there was no stress or wearisome toil but pure exhilaration of spirit, when things which God created flourished in more luxuriant abundance with the help of human work. As a result the creator himself would be praised more abundantly' (2002: 356–7). Here is a triple joy: the enjoyment of the sacramentality of creation (its God-given ability to show us the delight of God), the joy of working with God to bring creation into ever-greater fullness of being and the joy of praising God in a deeper way. Working in an office, gardening, being artistic, raising children – these can all be forms of delight that '[take] us deeper into the world' (Clavier, 2015: 60). Work, of whatever sort, becomes wonderfully capacious if we can work out of being 'at rest' with God and the world.

This is often easier said than done, as family life can be stressful, work environments may foster presenteeism and holiday time can be compromised by our contactability. Nor does taking a day off work to catch up on something else constitute genuine Sabbath rest (it's a 'bastard Sabbath' to use Eugene Peterson's memorable phrase, 1993: 46). Those in Christian ministry are not immune to these problems. Archbishop Welby – who had a previous career as an oil executive – has admitted that being a parish priest was the 'hardest work I've ever done, and the most stressful' (in Sherwood, 2017). In the face of our frenetic 24/7 culture, the practice of intentional rest, of keeping Sabbath, is a 'subversive' practice (Swoboda, 2018) as well as a foretaste of heaven.

John Swinton – theologian, registered mental health nurse and registered nurse for people with learning difficulties – suggests that, in the West, we have largely lost the sense of living in divine rest. Instead, 'commodified clock time' (2018: 79) has encouraged us to treat time 'in ways that are grasping, utilitarian, instrumental, focused, selfish, and ultimately idolatrous' (2018: 57). The critique and constructive thought of disability theology has much to teach us about living within, and out of, Sabbath rest. First, we come to appreciate that Sabbath time is a way of being in the fullness of time. It has a quality of freedom, as it is not goal-directed and judged by productivity. Second, we gain a deeper sense of community. Disability theology values time given over to welcome, friendship and togetherness – qualities which are implicit in the reality of divine rest, where, as Walter Bruggemann has it, God and God's people are 'not commodities to be dispatched for endless production …. Rather, they are subjects in an economy of neighbourliness' (2014: 6). This way of timely love, taught to the able-bodied by the disabled, reformulates what disability even means:

> To give generously of one's time – to care, notice, value and appreciate time – is to adopt the attitude of Jesus and to begin to tune one's body into the cadence of God's time and the redemption of all time. To live into God's image is, at least in part, to learn what it means to live within the Creator's time. When the world is looked at in this way, those things that we name 'disability' begin to look very different. (Swinton, 2018: 65)

This change in mindset also has ecological implications, for in refusing to render disability as 'other', 'heroic' or 'sinful' we become more likely to accept the normal creaturely limits that all humans experience yet tend to deny (injury, illness, ageing, death). 'In these denials', warns Creamer, 'we live a lie, a lie that harms other people (those on whom we project and reject these limits), the environment (when we pretend that it also has no limits), and even our selves' (2009: 119).

Nancy Eisland, who relates her experience of lifelong disability to Christian tradition, sees the risen Christ as the image of the disabled God. With his impaired feet and a pierced side, he shows us that divinity is compatible with the limits of a broken body and, moreover, brings grace to broken humanity through it. That Christ keeps his scars in the Second Creation honours the difficulties of disabled embodiment and challenges normative notions about what it means to be a 'perfect' human. For Eisland it is crucial that her disability is somehow 'caught up' into her ongoing, albeit transformed, identity: 'My disability had taught me who I am and who God is. What would it mean to be without this knowledge? Would I be absolutely unknown to myself in heaven, and perhaps even unknown to God?' (2002: 10).

This is not an isolated example. The resurrection body may well be imperishable and glorious (1 Cor. 15:42-43), but living with disability shapes people's lives in 'substantive rather than incidental ways' (Yong, 2007: 269) and imposing narrow views of eschatological perfection, to the point where resurrected bodies are completely disconnected from people's lived experiences, is able-bodied colonialism. Amos Yong therefore argues, following Paul, that 'the resurrected body will … be both continuous and discontinuous with our current bodies, but the norm will be the resurrected Christ, not our conventions of able-bodiedness' (2007: 274). We know that God values diversity and particularity in this creation; these characteristics will surely be even better in the Second. Indeed, Christ's risen body cries out for eschatological imagery of inclusive embodiedness. In making this case, Yong's redemptive theology of disability aims to offer a 'more inclusive view of what it means to be human, a more hospitable image of the church, a more holistic understanding of divine salvation, and a more expansive image of God's eschatological hospitality – all driven by the conviction that Christian beliefs matter for Christian practices' (2007: 292).

In many ways, these aims match the concerns of this book. Traversing the ways in which we think theologically through sensory experience has meant journeying deeply into human embodiment and encountering a diverse range of Christian thinking in the process. Moreover, it has introduced how theology as full-bodied thought shapes our conception of the fullness of bodily life, in this world and the world to come. In closing, it is encouraging to recall that God entrusts the Gospel to this way of thinking. To hear again John's words from the introduction – 'We declare to you what was from the beginning, what we have heard, what we have seen with our eyes, what we have looked and touched with our hands, concerning the word of life' (1 Jn 1:1). To know God is indeed to know the world aright.

Extended task

Write a research paper on one of these topics:

1. A critical assessment of the theology behind the following attitudes towards Sunday rest: Calvinist, Seventh Day Adventist, Evangelical.
2. How different eschatologies might impact pastoral practice (e.g. bereavement or healthcare chaplaincy, dealing with sickness, ageing or disability).

Key points

- Prescriptions for Sabbath rest found in the Hebrew Bible – e.g. freedom, justice, delight and ecological concern – are fulfilled in Jesus, the Lord of the Sabbath.
- Christians mark Sabbath rest in different ways.
- Work can be related to eschatological Sabbath rest, with healthy consequences for humanity and the world.
- Disability theology can teach the able-bodied about how to rest in God, and how to frame human embodiment eschatologically.

Questions for discussion

1   What spiritual practices are available to Christians to help them 'rest' in Christ's finished work of redemption?
2   Are there any potential problems (theological or otherwise) with naming God a 'disabled God'?
3   How might the notion of eschatological perfection influence disabled rights?

Chapter summary

In this chapter we have:

- Introduced two eschatological models (premillennial dispensationalism and restorative).
- Introduced two forms of Christian ecology (stewardship and Christian ecofeminism).
- Interpreted a theology of Sabbath in terms of God's playful delight in creation.
- Reflected on the place of animals in this world and the Second Creation.
- Considered the collective embodiment of humanity within the context of redeemed creation, with a focus on disability theology.

Recommended reading

Eschatology

Menn, Jonathan (2013), *Biblical Eschatology*, Eugene, OR: Wipf and Stock Publishers.

Ecofeminism

McFague, Sallie (1993), *The Body of God: An Ecological Theology*, Minneapolis, MN: Fortress Press.

Stewardship

Pope Francis (2015), *Laudato Si': On Care for Our Common Home*, London: Catholic Truth Society.

Animal theology

Clough, David L. (2012), *On Animals: Volume 1 Systematic Theology*, London and New York: T & T Clark.

Sabbath rest

Moltmann, Jurgen (2012), *Ethics of Hope*, London: SCM Press.

Glossary

Apophatic – (Gk. *apophasis*, meaning 'denial' or 'negation'). Theology that proceeds by way of negative statements (i.e. what God is not). Also known as 'negative theology'.

Atonement – expresses the 'at-one-ment' between God and humanity achieved through Christ's redemptive person and work.

Christology – doctrine of the person and work of Christ.

Complementarianism – gender theory whereby God has made male and female to be equal and to complement one another.

Dualism – absolute opposition between two elements, e.g. body/soul. May also be hierarchical (meaning that one element is given more value).

Ecclesiology – doctrine of the church.

Egalitarian – all human beings are equal. No roles are assigned on the basis of gender.

Enlightenment – European intellectual movement of the seventeenth and eighteenth centuries that focused on reason, God, humanity and nature. Immanuel Kant was a major figure.

Eschatology – (Gk. *ta eschata,* meaning 'the end things'). Doctrine of the 'end times'. Traditionally concerned with themes like heaven and hell, but also considers how the Second Creation shapes life in the here and now.

Expiation – sin is covered over by Christ's self-sacrifice on the cross.

Gnosticism – early and influential christological heresy (began in the first century) that disputed the full divinity of Christ, posited a dualism between God and the world and saw matter as evil.

Heresy – false teaching that compromises Christian orthodoxy.

Hermeneutics – study of the principles and methodology of interpretation.

Immanent – expresses how God is present in, and engages with, creation.

Incarnation – (Latin *incarnare*, meaning 'to make flesh'). Refers to the Son of God taking on human nature, such that Jesus Christ was and is fully divine and fully human.

Justification – atonement language, whereby God declares sinners to be righteous or of right standing with 'him' through their faith in the atonement of Jesus Christ.

Liturgy – most often thought to mean the repetition of words in a church service, but in a wider sense refers to the ways in which life is structured through rituals and practices.

Magisterial reformers – distinctions are drawn between reformation and radical reformation thinkers. Calvin, Luther and Zwingi are included, but not Anabaptists.

Mystical theology – the deepening of theological knowledge and personal union with God through mystical experiences such as contemplative prayer.

New Creation – otherwise known as Second Creation. Creation is destined for renewal and fulfilment through Christ and the Spirit.

Orthodoxy – beliefs that have been agreed by ecumenical councils.

Penal substitution – Christ on the cross is understood to 'take on' the punishment humans deserve as sinners.

Pneumatology – doctrine of the Holy Spirit.

Propitiation – atonement language whereby God's wrath is turned away by Christ's sacrifice on the cross.

Redemption – refers to God's act in redeeming Israel from slavery in Egypt and God's act in Christ to redeem humanity from sin.

Reformed – Reformed theology is associated with Calvin. Other than that, reformed theology (i.e. without the capital) may just refer to the theology coming from any other Protestant reformation or the Catholic counter-reformation.

Sacrament – sensory signs of God's grace. A form of material or type of action can become a site of encounter with God.

Salvation – process whereby believers are transformed into the likeness of Christ. Believers were saved through Christ's work of redemption, justification and reconciliation; are being saved through the Spirit's work of sanctification; will be saved for glorification in the Second Creation.

Soteriology – the area of theology that seeks to understand the means and nature of salvation through Jesus Christ.

Substitution – atonement language whereby Christ took the place of sinners on the cross. Not all substitution is penal.

Teleology – (Gk. *telos*, meaning 'end' or 'purpose'). Expresses the God-given directionality of creation. All things, processes and people are shaped by God for a purpose.

Theological anthropology – (Gk. *anthropos*, meaning 'man'). Theological account of human condition.

Transcendent – expresses how God is ontologically distinct from creation and cannot be grasped by what is not God.

Trinity – God's internal life of giving and receiving, known as Father, Son and Holy Spirit.

Bibliography

Ackerman, Diane. *A Natural History of the Senses*. New York: Vintage Books, 1991.

Aristotle. *De Generatione Animalium* (On the Generation of Animals). H. J. D. Lulofs edn. Oxford: Oxford University Press, 1963.

Asad, Talal *Formations of the Secular: Christianity, Islam, Modernity*. Stanford: Stanford University Press, 2003.

Ashbrook Harvey, Susan. *Scenting Salvation: Ancient Christianity and the Olfactory Imagination*. Berkley, Los Angeles and London: University of California Press, 2006.

Ashbrook Harvey, Susan. *Scenting Salvation: Ancient Christianity and the Olfactory Imagination*. Berkley, Los Angeles and London: University of California Press, 2015.

Ashwin-Siejkowski, Piotr. *Early Christian Doctrine and the Creeds*. London: SCM Press, 2010.

Augustine. 'De Trinitate (On the Trinity)'. In *Nicene and Post-Nicene Fathers First Series, Volume 3*, edited by Philip Schaff and Henry Wace, translated by Arthur W. Haddan, 3-228. Edinburgh: T&T Clark, 1887a.

Augustine. 'On the Morals of the Catholic Church'. In *Nicene and Post-Nicene Fathers First Series, Volume 4*, edited by Philip Schaff, 37–63. Edinburgh: T&T Clark, 1887b. Available online: www.ccel.org/ccel/schaff/npnf104.iv.iv.i.html (accessed 3 January 2020).

Augustine. *On Christian Teaching*. Translated by R. P. H. Green. Oxford: Oxford University Press, 1997.

Augustine. *The City of God against the Pagans*. Edited by Robert W. Dyson. Cambridge: Cambridge University Press, 1998.

Augustine. 'Letter 220 – Ad Bonifacem'. In *Political Writings*, edited by Margaret E. Atkins and Robert J. Dodaro, 218–25. Cambridge: Cambridge University Press, 2001.

Augustine. *On Genesis: A Refutation of the Manichees, Unfinished Literal Commentary on Genesis, the Literal Meaning of Genesis*. Introductions, translations and notes by Edmund Hill. Edited by John E. Rotelle. New York: New City Press, 2002.

Augustine. *Confessions*. Translated by Henry Chadwick. Oxford: Oxford University Press, 2009.

Balthasar, Hans U. v. *Truth Is Symphonic: Aspects of Christian Pluralism*. San Francisco, CA: Ignatio Press, 1987.

Barth, Karl. *Evangelical Theology: An Introduction*. Translated by Grover Foley. London: Weidenfeld & Nicolson, 1963.

Barth, Karl. *Church Dogmatics*. multiple volumes. Translated by Geoffrey. W. Bromiley and Thomas F. Torrance, Edinburgh: T&T Clark, 2004.

Bauckham, Richard. *God and the Crisis of Freedom: Biblical and Contemporary Perspectives*. Louisville, KY: Westminster John Knox Press, 2002.

Bauckham, Richard. 'Reading the Synoptic Gospels Ecologically'. In *Ecological Hermeneutics: Biblical, Historical and Theological Perspectives*, edited by David. G. Horrell, Cherryl Hunt, Christopher Southgate, and Francesca Stavrakopoulu, 70–82. Edinburgh: T&T Clark, 2010.

Beauvoir, Simone de. *The Second Sex*. Translated by Howard Madison Pashley. Harmondsworth: Penguin, 1984.

Beck, Alan, and Aaron Katcher. *Between Pets and People: The Importance of Animal Companionship*. West Lafayette, IN: Purdue University Press, 1996.

Beddington, Emma. 'A-Z of Climate Anxiety: How to Avoid Meltdown'. *The Guardian*, 8 December 2019. Available online: https://www.theguardian.com/environment/2019/dec/08/a-z-of-climate-anxiety-how-to-avoid-meltdown (accessed 3 January 2020).

Begbie, Jeremy. *Theology, Music and Time*. Cambridge: Cambridge University Press, 2000.

Begbie, Jeremy. 'Through Music: Sound Mix'. In *Beholding the Glory: Incarnation through the Arts*, edited by Jeremy Begbie, 138–54. Grand Rapids, MI: Baker Academic, 2001.

Begbie, Jeremy. *Resounding Truth: Christian Witness in the World of Music*. London: SPCK, 2008.

Begbie, Jeremy. *Music, Modernity and God: Essays in Listening*. Oxford: Oxford University Press, 2013.

Begbie, Jeremy S., and Steven R. Guthrie (eds). *Resonant Witness: Conversations between Music and Theology*. Grand Rapids, MI: Eerdmans, 2011.

Benedict XVI. (2005) 'Deus Caritas Est'. Available online: http://w2.vatican.va/content/benedict-xvi/en/encyclicals/documents/hf_ben-xvi_enc_20051225_deus-caritas-est.html (accessed 29 January 2015).

Bennett, Zoe. *Using the Bible in Practical Theology: Historical and Contemporary Perspectives*. Farnham: Ashgate, 2013.

Berry, Wendell. *What Are People For?* Berkeley, CA: Counterpoint, 2010.

Biggar, Nigel. *In Defence of War*. Oxford: Oxford University Press, 2013.

Bird, Michael F. *Bourgeois Babes, Bossy Wives, and Bobby Haircuts: A Case for Gender Equality in Ministry*. Grand Rapids, MI: Zondervan, 2014.

Bonaventure. *The Soul's Journey into God, the Tree of Life, the Life of St Francis*. Translated by E. Cousins. New Jersey: Paulist Press, 1978.

Bourne, Richard. *Seek the Peace of the City: Christian Political Criticism as Public, Realist and Transformative*. Eugene, OR: Cascade, 2009.

Bourne, Richard. 'Communication, Punishment and Virtue: The Theological Limitation of (Post)Secular Penance'. *Journal of Religious Ethics* 42, no. 1 (2014): 78–107.

Bradley, Mark (ed.). *Smell and the Ancient Senses*. New York and Abingdon: Routledge, 2015.

Brown, David. *Tradition and Imagination: Revelation and Change*. Oxford: Oxford University Press, 1999.

Brown, David, and Gavin Hopps. *The Extravagance of Music*. London: Palgrave Macmillan, 2018.

Brown, Peter. *The Body and Society Men, Women, and Sexual Renunciation in Early Christianity*. New York: Columbia University Press, 1988.

Bruggemann, Walter. *Theology of the Old Testament: Testimony, Dispute, Advocacy*. Philadelphia: Fortress Press, 1997.

Bruggemann, Walter. *Sabbath as Resistance: Saying No to the Culture of Now*. Louisville, KY: Westminster John Knox Press, 2014.

Butler, Judith. *Gender Trouble: Feminism and the Subversion of Identity*. London: Routledge, 1990.

Butler, Judith. (2013) 'Honorary Doctorate Address'. Available online: https://reporter.mcgill.ca/judith-butler (accessed 18 February 2019).

Calvin, John. *Commentary on Isaiah: Vol. 1*. Translated by William Pringle. Edinburgh: Calvin Translation Society, 1850.

Calvin, John. *Institutes of the Christian Religion*. 1559. Edited by John T. McNeil and translated by Ford L. Battles. Louisville, KY: Westminster John Knox Press, 1960.

Camosy, Charles. *For Love of Animals: Christian Ethics, Consistent Actions*. Cincinnati, OH: Franciscan Media, 2013.

Cavanaugh, William. 'Faith Fires Back: A Conversation with Stanley Hauerwas'. *Duke University Magazine*, January–February (2002) 8: 10–13.

Clague, Julie. 'Divine Transgressions: The Female Christ-Form in Art'. *Critical Quarterly* 47, no. 3 (2005): 47–63.

Classen, Constance. *The Colour of Angels: Cosmology, Gender and the Aesthetic Imagination*. 2nd edn. 1998. Reprint, London: Routledge, 2002.

Classen, Constance, David Howes and Anthony Synnott. *Aroma: The Cultural History of Smell*. London: Routledge, 1994.

Clavier, Mark. *Stewards of God's Delight: Becoming Priests of the New Creation*. Foreword by Barry Morgan. Eugene, OR: Cascade Books, 2015.

Clough, David. 'On the Relevance of Jesus Christ for Christian Judgements about the Legitimacy of Violence: A Modest Proposal'. *Studies in Christian Ethics* 22, no. 2 (2009): 199–210.

Clough, David. *On Animals. Vol. 1: Systematic Theology*. London: T&T Clark, 2012.

Clough, David. *On Animals. Vol. II: Theological Ethics*. Edinburgh: T&T Clark, 2018.

Coakley, Sarah. *Powers and Submissions: Spirituality, Philosophy and Gender*. Oxford: Wiley-Blackwell, 2002.

Coakley, Sarah. *God, Sexuality, and the Self: An Essay 'On the Trinity'*. Cambridge: Cambridge University Press, 2013.

Coakley, Sarah, and Paul L. Gavrilyuk. *The Spiritual Senses: Perceiving God in Western Christianity*, Cambridge: Cambridge University Press, 2012.

Coleridge, Samuel T. *The Statesman's Manual; or The Bible the Best Guide to Political Skill and Foresight: A Lay Sermon Addressed to the Higher Classes of Society*. Burlington, VA: Chauncey Goodrich, 1832.

Cook, Edward T., and Alexander Wedderburn (eds). *The Works of John Ruskin*. London: George Allen, 1903–1912.

Cornwall, Susannah. *Sex and Uncertainty in the Body of Christ*. London: Routledge, 2010.

Cornwall, Susannah. *SCM Core Text: Theology and Sexuality*. London: SCM Press, 2013.

Creamer, Deborah B. *Disability and Christian Theology: Embodied Limits and Constructive Possibilities*. Oxford: Oxford University Press, 2009.

Cunningham, David S. *These Three Are One: The Practice of Trinitarian Theology*. Oxford: Blackwell, 2002.

Cusack, Odean. *Pets and Mental Health*. 2nd edn. 1988. Reprint, New York and London: Routledge, 2013.

Davies, Oliver, and Denys Turner (eds). *Silence of the Word: Negative Theology and Incarnation*. Cambridge: Cambridge University Press, 2002.

Dahlhaus, Carl. *The Idea of Absolute Music*. Translated by Roger Lustig. Chicago, IL, and London: University of Chicago Press, 1991.

Debord, Guy. *The Society of the Spectacle*. Cambridge, MA: Zone Books, 1994.

Dickens, William T. 'Hans von Balthasar'. In *Christian Theologies of Scripture: A Comparative Introduction*, edited by Justin S. Holcomb, 202–19. New York: New York University Press, 2006.

Didion, Joan. 'Why I Write'. *New York Times Magazine*, 5 December 1976. Available online: https://www.nytimes.com/1976/12/05/archives/why-i-write-why-i-write.html (accessed 5 January 2020).

Edgar, Brian. *The God Who Plays*. Eugene, OR: Cascade Books, 2017.

Eisland, Nancy. *The Disabled God: Toward a Liberatory Theology of Disability*. Nashville, TN: Abingdon Press, 1994.

Eisland, Nancy. 'Encountering the Disabled God'. *Other Side* September/October (2002): 10–15.

Ellis, Robert. *The Games People Play: Theology, Religion, and Sport*. Eugene, OR: Wipf and Stock, 2014.

Epstein, Heidi. 'Immanence and Music Incarnate: Prelude to a Feminist Theology of Music'. In *The Annual Review of Women in World Religions Vol. 5*, edited by Arvind Sharma and Katharine K. Young, 90–116. Albany: State of New York Press, 1999.

Fiddes, Paul S. *Seeing the World and Knowing God: Hebrew Wisdom and Christian Doctrine in a Late Modern Context*. Oxford: Oxford University Press, 2013.

Ford, David. *Theology: A Very Short Introduction*. 2nd edn. 1999, reprint Oxford: Oxford University Press, 2013.

Ford, David, and Mike Higton (eds). *Jesus*. Oxford: Oxford University Press, 2002.

Fowler, David C., and John S. Hill. 'Harp'. In *A Dictionary of Biblical Tradition in English Literature*, edited by David Lyle Jeffrey, 330–2. Grand Rapids, MI: Eerdmans, 1992.

Gorringe, Timothy. *God's Just Vengeance: Crime Violence and the Rhetoric of Salvation*. Cambridge: Cambridge University Press, 1996.

Gregory of Nyssa. 'On Virginity'. In *Nicene and Post-Nicene Fathers Second Series, Volume 5*, edited by Philip Schaff and Henry Wace, 343–71. Translated by William Moore and Henry A. Wilson. Edinburgh: T&T Clark, 1895.

Gunton, Colin. *The Promise of Trinitarian Theology*. London: T&T Clark, 1997a.

Gunton, Colin. *Yesterday and Today: A Study of Continuities in Christology*. London: SPCK, 1997b.

Hampson, Daphne. *Theology and Feminism*. Oxford: Basil Blackwell, 1990.

Harribin, Roger. 'Bank of England Chief Mark Carney Issues Climate Change Warning'. BBC, 30 December 2019. Available online: https://www.bbc.co.uk/news/business-50868717 (accessed 3 January 2019).

Hart, Trevor. *Making Good: Creation, Creativity and Artistry*. Waco, TX: Baylor University Press, 2014.

Hays, Richard. *The Moral Vision of the New Testament: A Contemporary Introduction to New Testament Ethics*. New York: HarperCollins, 1996.

Higgins, Gareth. *How Movies Helped Save My Soul: Finding Spiritual Fingerprints in Culturally Significant Films*. Lake Mary, FL: Relevant Books, 2004.

Higton, Mike. *Christian Doctrine*. London: SCM Press, 2008.

Hollywood, Amy, and Patricia Z. Beckman (eds). *The Cambridge Companion to Christian Mysticism*. Cambridge: Cambridge University Press, 2012.

Holsinger, Bruce W. *Music, Body, and Desire in Medieval Culture: Hildegard of Bingen to Chaucer*. Stanford, CA: Stanford University Press, 2001.

Huntingdon, Samuel, P. *The Clash of Civilisations and the Remaking of World Order*. New York: Simon & Schuster, 1996.

Hurtado, Larry. *Destroyer of the Gods: Early Christian Distinctiveness in the Roman World*. Waco, TX: Baylor University Press, 2016.

The Independent. 'Payday Lenders? The Church Should Keep to Matters Spiritual'. 26 July 2013. Available online: http://www.independent.co.uk/voices/editorials/payday-lenders-the-church-should-keep-to-matters-spiritual-8733993.html (accessed 20 September 2013).

Irenaeus. *Against Heresies*. Edited by Anthony Uyl. 2nd edn. 1885. Reprint, Woodstock, ON: Devoted Publishing, 2018.

Isherwood, Lisa, and Elizabeth Stewart. *Introducing Body Theology*. Sheffield: Sheffield Academic Press, 1998.

Isherwood, Lisa, and Marcella Althaus-Reid (eds). *Trans/Formations*. London: SCM Press, 2009.

Jacobi, Martha S. 'Smelling Remembrance'. In *Sensing Sacred: Exploring the Human Senses in Practical Theology and Pastoral Care*, edited by Jennifer Baldwin, 27–40. London: Lexington Books, 2016.

Jerome. 'Against Helvidius, On the Perpetual Virginity of Mary'. In *Nicene and Post-Nicene Fathers Second Series, Volume 6*, edited by Philip Schaff and Henry Wace, 334–45. Translated by William H. Fremantle, G. Lewis and W. G. Martley. Edinburgh: T&T Clark, 1893a.

Jerome. 'To Eustochium'. In *Nicene and Post-Nicene Fathers Second Series, Volume 6*, edited by Philip Schaff and Henry Wace, 195–211. Translated by W. H. Freemantle, G. Lewis and W. G. Martley. Edinburgh: T&T Clark, 1893b.

Johnston, Robert K. *Reel Spirituality: Theology and Film in Dialogue – Part 1*. Grand Rapids, MI: Baker Academic, 2006.

Johnston, Robert K. 'The Film Viewer and Natural Theology: God's "Presence" at the Movies'. In *The Oxford Handbook of Natural Theology*, edited by Russell Re Manning, 595–609. Oxford: Oxford University Press, 2013.

Jüngel, Eberhard. *God as the Mystery of the World: On the Foundation of the Theology of the Crucified One in the Dispute between Theism and Atheism*. Translated by Darrell L. Guder. Grand Rapids, MI: Eerdmans, 1983.

Justin Martyr. *The First and Second Apologies*. Translated by Leslie W. Barnard. New York: Paulist Press, 1997.

Kimmelman, Michael. *Portraits: Talking with Artists at the Met, the Modern, the Louvre, and Elsewhere*. New York: Random House, 1998.

Knight, Rob. 'Average Person Takes 38 Seconds to Judge Someone's Home, Research Finds'. *The Independent*, 23 October 2019. Available online: https://www. independent.co.uk/news/uk/home-news/home-house-judge-clean-dirty-british-survey-a9167561.html (accessed 24 December 2019).

Korsmeyer, Carolyn. *Making Sense of Taste: Food and Philosophy*. New York: Cornell University Press, 1999.

Kozlovic, Anton K. 'The Structural Characteristics of the Cinematic Christ-figure'. *Journal of Religion and Popular Culture* VIII, no. 1 (2004): np.

Lamb, William. *Scripture: A Guide for the Perplexed*. London: T&T Clark, 2013.

Lampe, Geoffrey W. H., and Donald M. MacKinnon. *The Resurrection: A Dialogue Arising from Broadcasts by G.W.H. Lampe and D.M. MacKinnon*. London: A. R. Mowbray, 1966.

LaNave, Gregory F. 'Bonaventure'. In *The Spiritual Senses: Perceiving God in Western Christianity*, edited by Sarah Coakley and Paul L. Gavrilyuk, 159–73. Cambridge: Cambridge University Press, 2012.

Lilla, Mark. *The Stillborn God: Religion, Politics and the Modern West*. New York: Vintage, 2008.

Linzey, Andrew. *Creatures of the Same God: Explorations in Animal Theology*. 2nd edn. 2007. Reprint, Brooklyn, NY: Lantern Books, 2009.

MacIntyre, Alasdair. *After Virtue: A Study in Moral Theory*. 2nd edn. 1981. Reprint, London: Bloomsbury, 1985.

McCabe, Herbert. *God Matters*. 2nd edn. London and New York: Continuum, 2005.

McCarthy, Colman. '"I'm a Pacifist because I'm a Violent Son of a Bitch." A Profile of Stanley Hauerwas'. *The Progressive* 67, no. 4 (April 2003): np.

McFague, Sallie. *The Body of God: An Ecological Theology*. London: SCM Press, 1993.

McFague, Sallie. '*Human Dignity and the Integrity of Creation*'. In *Theology That Matters: Ecology, Economy, and God*, edited by Darby K. Ray, 199–212. Minneapolis, MN: Fortress Press, 2006.

McFarland, Ian. *From Nothing: A Theology of Creation*. Louisville, KY: Westminster John Knox Press, 2014.

McGrath, Alister E. *Christian Theology: An Introduction*. 4th edn. 1993. Reprint, Oxford: Blackwell Publishing, 2007.

McGrath, Alister E. *Heresy*. London: SPCK, 2009.

McIntosh, Mark. *Mystical Theology: The Integrity of Spirituality and Theology*. Oxford: Wiley-Blackwell, 1998.

McIntosh, Mark. *Divine Teaching: An Introduction to Christian Teaching*. Oxford: Blackwell Publishing, 2008.

McInroy, Mark. *Balthasar on the 'Spiritual Senses': Perceiving Splendour*. Oxford: Oxford University Press, 2014.

McKinnon, James (ed.). *Music in Early Christian Literature*. 2nd edn. 1987. Reprint, Cambridge: Cambridge University Press, 1993.

Merton, Thomas. *New Seeds of Contemplation*. New York: New Directions Publishing Corporation, 1961.

Milbank, John. *Theology and Social Theory: Beyond Secular Reason*. 2nd edn. 1990. Reprint, London: Wiley-Blackwell, 2006.

Miles, Margaret. *Bodies in Society: Essays on Christianity in Contemporary Culture*. Eugene, OR: Cascade Press, 2008.

Moltmann, Jurgen. *Creation in God: A New Theology of Creation and the Spirit of God*. Minneapolis, MN: Fortress Press, 1993.

Moltmann, Jurgen. *Theology of Hope*. London: SCM Press, 2002.

Moltmann, Jurgen. *The Coming of God: Christian Eschatology*. Translated by Margaret Kohl. 2nd edn. Minneapolis, MN: Fortress Press, 2004.

Moltmann, Jurgen. *Ethics of Hope*. London: SCM Press, 2012.

Moltmann, Jurgen. *Theology and Joy*. Translated by Reinhard Ulrich. Extended introduction by David Jenkins. 2nd edn. 1973. Reprint, London: SCM Press, 2013.

Nelson, James B. *Body Theology*. Louisville, KY: Westminster John Knox Press, 1992.

Niebuhr, Reinhold. *An Interpretation of Christian Ethics*. New York: Harper, 1935.

Niebuhr, Reinhold. *The Nature and Destiny of Man Vol. II*. London: Nisbet & Co, 1943.

Niebuhr, Reinhold. *Love and Justice*. Edited by D. B. Robertson. Gloucester, MA: Peter Smith, 1976.

Niebuhr, Reinhold. 'Why the Christian Church Is Not Pacifist'. In *The Essential Reinhold Niebuhr: Selected Essays and Addresses*, edited by Robert M. Brown, 102–22. New Haven, CT: Yale University Press, 1986.

Niebuhr, Reinhold. *Love and Justice: Selections from the Later Writings of Reinhold Niebuhr*. Louisville, KY: Westminster John Knox Press, 1992.

Niebuhr, Richard. *Theology, History and Culture*. New Haven, CT: Yale University Press, 1996.

Niebuhr, Reinhold. *Moral Man and Immoral Society: A Study in Ethics and Politics*. Louisville, KY: Westminster John Knox Press, 2013.

Nygren, Anders. *Agape and Eros*. Translated by Philip S. Watson. Philadelphia, PA: Westminster Press, 1953.

O'Donovan, Oliver. *Transsexualism and Christian Marriage*. Cambridge: Grove Books, 1982.

O'Meier, Harry. 'Green Millennialism: American Evangelicals, Environmentalism, and Ecclesial Perspective'. In *Ecological Hermeneutics: Biblical, Historical and Theological Perspectives*, edited by David. G. Horrell, Cherryl Hunt, Christopher Southgate and Francesca Stavrakopoulu, 246–65. Edinburgh: T&T Clark, 2010.

Pannenberg, Wolfhart. *Anthropology in Theological Perspective*. Translated by Matthew J. O'Connell. 2nd edn. 1985. Reprint, London and New York: T&T Clark, 2004.

Pelligrini, Anthony D. *The Role of Play in Human Development*. Oxford: Oxford University Press, 2009.

Peterson, Eugene H. *Working the Angles: The Shape of Pastoral Integrity*. Grand Rapids, MI: William B. Eerdmans, 1993.

Pickstock, Catherine. 'Music: Music, Soul and Cosmos after Augustine'. In *Radical Orthodoxy: A New Theology*, edited by John Milbank, Catherine Pickstock and Graham Ward, 243–77. London and New York: Routledge, 1999.

Pierce, Ronald W., Rebecca M. Groothuis and Gordon D. Fee (eds). *Discovering Biblical Equality: Complementarity without Hierarchy*. Downers Grove, IL: IVP Press, 2005.

Pilch, John J. *The Cultural Dictionary of the Bible*. Collegeville, MI: Liturgical Press, 1999.

Plantinga Pauw, Amy. *Proverbs and Ecclesiastes*. Louisville, KY: Westminster John Knox Press, 2015.

Pope Francis. *Laudato Si': On Care for our Common Home*. London: Catholic Truth Society, 2015.

Quash, Ben, and Michael Ward (eds). *Heresies and How to Avoid Them: Why It Matters What Christians Believe*. London: SPCK, 2007.

Roberts, Roberts. *Creation and Covenant: The Significance of Sexual Difference in the Moral Theology of Marriage*. London: T&T Clark, 2007.

Ruether, Rosemary R. *Sexism and God-Talk: Toward a Feminist Theology*. Boston, MA: Beacon Press, 1983.

Rylance, Mark. 'Research, Materials, Craft: Principles of Performance'. In *Shakespeare's Globe: A Theatrical Experiment*, edited by Christie Carson and Farah Karim-Cooper, 103–14. Cambridge: Cambridge University Press, 2008.

Schleiermacher, Friedrich. *On Religion: Speeches to Its Cultured Despisers*. Translated by Richard Crouter. Cambridge: Cambridge University Press, 1988.

Schmeeman, Alexander. *For the Life of the World: Sacraments and Orthodoxy*. New York: St Vladimir's Seminary Press, 1973.

Sherwood, Harriet. 'Being Parish Priest Was My Most Stressful Job, Says Justin Welby'. *The Guardian*, 10 July 2017. Available online: https://www.theguardian.com/uk-news/2017/jul/10/being-parish-priest-was-my-most-stressful-job-says-justin-welby (accessed 4 January 2020).

Shortt, Rupert. *God's Advocates: Christian Thinkers in Conversation*. London: DLT, 2005

Smith, Mark M. *Sensing the Past: Seeing, Hearing, Smelling, Tasting and Touching in History*. Berkeley, Los Angeles and London: University of California Press, 2007.

Southgate, Christopher. *The Groaning of Creation: God, Evolution and the Problem of Evil*. Louisville, KY: Westminster John Knox Press, 2008.

Stang, Charles M. '*Dionysius, Paul and the Significance of the Pseudonym*'. In *Re-thinking Dionysius the Aeropagite*, edited by Sarah Coakley and Charles M. Stang, 9–25. Oxford: Wiley-Blackwell, 2009.

Stang, Charles M. *Apophasis and Pseudonymity in Dionysius the Areopagite: 'No Longer I'*. Oxford: Oxford University Press, 2012.

Stoltzfus, Philip. E. *Theology as Performance: Music, Aesthetics and God in Western Thought*. London and New York: T&T Clark, 2006.

Storm, Sam. *Signs of the Spirit: An Interpretation of Jonathan Edward's 'Religious Affections'*. Wheaton, IL: Crossway Books, 2007.

Swinton, John. *Becoming Friends of Time: Disability, Timefullness and Gentle Discipleship*. Waco, TX: Baylor University Press, 2018.

Swoboda, Andrew J. *Subversive Sabbath: The Surprising Power of Rest in a Non-Stop World*. Foreword by Matthew Sleeth. Grand Rapids, MI: Baker Publishing Group, 2018.

Tanner, Kathryn. *Jesus, Humanity, and the Trinity*. Minneapolis, MN: Fortress Press, 2001.

Telford, William R. 'Jesus Christ Movie Star: The Depiction of Jesus in the Cinema'. In *Explorations in Theology and Film*, edited by Clive Marsh and Gaye Ortiz, 115–40. Oxford: Blackwell, 1997.

Tertullian. 'On Prescription of Heretics'. In The Ante-Nicene Fathers, Vol.4. Edited by Alexander Roberts, James Donaldson, Henry Wace and Philip Schaff. Peabody, MA.: Hendrickson, 1994.

Tertullian. 'On the Resurrection of the Flesh'. In *Ante-Nicene Fathers Vol. 3*, edited by Alexander Roberts, James Donaldson and Arthur C. Coxe, translated by Peter Holmes, 545–96. Edinburgh: T&T Clark, 1885.

Thatcher, Adrian. *God, Sex, and Gender: An Introduction*. Oxford: Wiley-Blackwell, 2011.

Torrance, Thomas F. *The Trinitarian Faith: The Evangelical Theology of the Ancient Catholic Faith*. 2nd edn. London and New York: Continuum, 1997.

Vanhoozer, Kevin, J. *Faith Speaking Understanding: Performing the Drama of Doctrine*. Louisville, KY: Westminster John Knox Press, 2014.

Wainright, Geoffrey, and Karen W. Tucker (eds). *The Oxford History of Christian Worship*. Oxford: Oxford University Press, 2006.

Walker, Matthew. '"Sleep Should Be Prescribed": What Those Late Nights Out Could Be Costing You'. *The Guardian*, 24 September 2017. Available online: https://www.theguardian.com/lifeandstyle/2017/sep/24/why-lack-of-sleep-health-worst-enemy-matthew-walker-why-we-sleep (accessed 2 January 2020).

Wells, Samuel. *Improvisation: The Drama of Christian Ethics*. Grand Rapids, MI: Brazos Press, 2004.

Wells, Samuel. *Be Not Afraid: Facing Fear with Faith*. Grand Rapids, MI: Brazos Press, 2011.

White, James F. *Introduction to Christian Worship*. 3rd edn. 1980. Reprint, Nashville, TN: Abingdon Press, 2000.

White, Lyn. 'The Historic Roots of Our Ecologic Crisis'. *Science* 155, no. 3767 (1967): 1203–7.

Williams, Rowan. *Resurrection: Interpreting the Easter Gospel*. London: Darton, Longman and Todd, 1982.

Williams, Rowan. 'The Body's Grace'. In *Theology and Sexuality: Classic and Contemporary Readings*, edited by Eugene F. Rogers, 309–21. Oxford: Blackwell, 2002.

Williams, Rowan. *Dwelling of the Light: Praying with Icons of Christ*. Norwich: Canterbury Books, 2003.

Williams, Rowan. *Tokens of Trust: An Introduction to Christian Belief*. Norwich: Canterbury Press, 2007.

Williams, Rowan. *Faith in the Public Square*. London: Bloomsbury, 2012.

Wink, Walter. *Engaging the Powers: Discernment and Resistance in a World of Domination*. Minneapolis, MN: Fortress Press, 1992.

Wirzba, Norman. *Food and Faith: A Theology of Eating*. Cambridge: Cambridge University Press, 2011.

Wittgenstein, Ludwig. *Philosophical Investigations*. Translated by G. E. M. Anscombe. 3rd edn. 1968. Reprint. Oxford: Blackwell, 2001.

Woollaston, Victoria. 'Forget Coffee and Fresh Bread – the Perfect Smell to Sell a House Is White Tea and Fig'. *The Daily Mail*, 18 March 2014. Available online: https://www.dailymail.co.uk/sciencetech/article-2583472/Forget-coffee-fresh-bread-perfect-smell-sell-house-WHITE-TEA-FIG.html (accessed 24 December 2019).

Wordsworth, William. *The Prelude: Growth of a Poet's Mind*. New York: Appleton, 1850.

Wright, Nicholas T. *What St Paul Really Said: Was Paul of Tarsus the Real Founder of Christianity*. Grand Rapids, MI: Eerdmans, 1997.

Wright, Nicholas T. 'God and Caesar, Then and Now'. In *The Character of Wisdom: Essays in Honour of Wesley Carr*, edited by Martyn Percy and Stephen Lowe, 157–72. Aldershot: Ashgate, 2004.

Wright, Tom. *Surprised by Hope*. New York: HarperCollins, 2008.

Yoder, John H. 'Armaments and Eschatology'. *Studies in Christian Ethics* 1, no. 1 (1988): 43–61.

Yoder, John H. *Body Politics: Five Practices before the Watching World*. Scottdale, PA: Herald Press, 1992.

Yoder, John H. *The Politics of Jesus: Vicit Agnus Noster*. 2nd edn. 1974. Reprint, Grand Rapids, MI: Eerdmans, 1994a.

Yoder, John H. *The Royal Priesthood: Essays Ecclesiological and Ecumenical*. Grand Rapids: Eerdmans, 1994b.

Yoder, John H. *The Original Revolution: Essays on Christian Pacifism*. Scottdale, PA: Herald Press, 1998.

Yong, Amos. *Theology and Down Syndrome: Reimagining Disability in Late Modernity*. Waco, TX: Baylor University Press, 2007.

Young, Frances. *The Making of the Creeds*. London: SCM Press, 2010.

Zuckerkandl, Victor. *Sound and Symbol: Music and the External World*. London: Routledge and Kegan Paul, 1956.

Index